The Ordnance Survey
OUTDOOR
HANDBOOK

The Ordnance Survey
OUTDOOR
HANDBOOK
Michael Allaby

MACMILLAN
LONDON

Quick Reference for Emergencies

Text copyright © Michael Allaby 1987
Maps copyright © Ordnance Survey 1987

First published 1987, in association with the Ordnance Survey, by
MACMILLAN LONDON LIMITED
4 Little Essex Street London WC2R 3LF
and Basingstoke

Associated companies in Auckland, Delhi, Dublin, Gaborone, Hamburg, Harare, Hong Kong, Johannesburg, Lagos, Manzini, Melbourne, Mexico City, Nairobi, New York, Petaling Jaya, Singapore and Tokyo

Designed by Robert Updegraff
Illustrations by Catherine Constable, Chris Evans and Robert Garrard

British Library Cataloguing in Publication Data

Allaby, Michael
    Ordnance Survey outdoor handbook.
    1. Natural history—Great Britain 2. Great
    Britain—Description and travel—1971–
    —Guide-books
    I. Title
    914.1'04858   DA667

ISBN 0–333–44816–2 (cased) 0–333–42505–7 (paperback)

Typeset by Wyvern Typesetting Ltd, Bristol
Printed in Italy by S R L Trento

Contents

Acknowledgements

Many people have given freely of their time, knowledge and experience to help in the preparation of this book, in particular Arthur Howcroft of the European Ramblers' Association and members of staff of the Ordnance Survey.

Picture Acknowledgements Ardea/photo David and Katie Urry, 184, 201; photo Bob Gibbons, 190. Biophoto Associates/photo D. K. Marden, 94. British Geological Survey, 47 above right. John Cleare/Mountain Camera, 47 above left, 49, 60, 62, 85, 136, 144. Bruce Coleman/photo Eric Crichton, 47 below left; photo G. Doré, 47 below right. English Heritage, 100. Peter Erskine, 164. John Glover, 155. Susan Griggs Agency/photo Adam Woolfitt, 2. A. F. Kersting, 104, 151, 196, 197, 208. John Mason, 177. National Trust, 141. Nature Conservancy Council/photo Peter Wakely, 149, 152, 156, 161, 169, 173, 192, 193, 204. Ordnance Survey, © Crown copyright reserved, 180. Royal Commission on the Historical Monuments of England, 77, 81, R. K. Pilsbury, 38–39. Scottish Tourist Board, 139. *Soldier* magazine, 64.

Using the Handbook

This book is designed to help you extract every last grain of information from a map. This is useful in two ways. It makes planning easier, because you can find out much more about a place before finally deciding whether or not it is worth a visit. When you do arrive, you will be able to relate the story told by the map to what you see around you, and find what you are looking for with the minimum of fuss.

The information in the book is arranged in three sections. The first deals with preparation, planning and safety. This includes details of how to predict the weather, how to use a map and compass to find your way, and what to do if things go wrong. It also includes simple guides to help you calculate the steepness of a hill before you try to climb it, and to help you work out how difficult a walk will be before you start.

Part II contains the 'clues'. Britain is much too diverse for any single book to attempt a comprehensive description, but that is not what you need when you are out in the countryside. You need to know how to understand and describe for yourself what you see. So in this part of the book you will find outlines of the way landscapes have been shaped by their underlying rocks, the way people have changed the countryside from earliest times to suit their needs, and the way the land is used now. There are simple guides to identifying the kinds of tree you will find in commercial forests, the crop plants you will see growing when you peer over hedges and gates, the most common breeds of farm livestock, and how to tell which are which among species of wild animals that look rather similar. All of us like being able to put names to things, and this section will help you name what you see.

Information in the final section is arranged a little differently. It deals with types of landscape – with mountains, heaths, upland moors, forests, farm land, wetland, rivers, coasts and offshore islands – the kinds of place you might visit, with lists of particular examples of each. In every case the list includes the 'map information' which will help you find the place that is named.

Finally, there are lists of telephone numbers for obtaining local weather forecasts, the addresses of organisations you may find useful, and the titles of books, including field guides, that may help you.

1

OUTDOORS IN BRITAIN

If you were to fly from the south-west coast of England to the north-east coast of the Scottish mainland you would travel 966 km (600 miles). You would start from somewhere near latitude 50°N, which passes through the Lizard Peninsula, and continuing past the Scottish coast you could travel all the way to 60°N, in Shetland: from the mild climate and palm trees of the 'Cornish Riviera' almost to the Arctic Circle. As you travelled, you would cross rocks from all the main geological periods: mountains and hills, high moorland plateaux, low-lying farm land, forests, acid heaths, rivers and lakes. At one time or another you would be close to as many types of landscape as it is possible to imagine crowded into so small an area in temperate latitudes.

The British countryside is diverse, and because the total area of the country is small, nearly all of it is within easy reach. We all visit the countryside, of course, at the very least for a picnic at a favourite beauty spot on a warm summer day, or on our way to the seaside. Many of us spend our holidays there, perhaps touring with caravan or tent, and whenever we stop we explore our new surroundings. This book aims to help you do just that. It is a book of clues, things to look for, things that reveal the history and wildlife that otherwise may remain hidden. Far from being a textbook, it aims to make visits to the countryside more enjoyable. That, after all, is what recreation should be.

The book also aims to make our visits safer. Small though our island is, diminutive though our mountain ranges may seem in comparison with the giants of the Alps or Rockies, they hold many dangers. The weather can change suddenly. Blizzards are common in winter on high ground, and blizzards can kill those who venture forth unprepared. Strong winds can be fun, but they can also sweep people from the tops of cliffs. In summer the sea seems friendly, but each year in Britain strong tides and currents claim a few lives.

Finding your way around, knowing where to look for features that interest you, and understanding what you see, all depend to a large extent on the ease with which you can use a map. We are particularly fortunate in Britain because, diverse though our countryside is, every last corner has been mapped, and mapped very thoroughly. Indeed, this may be the most intensively mapped country in the world. You can buy whatever maps you need in the sure knowledge that they are accurate, informative and, no less important, all prepared to the same standard. If you learn how to use one official British map you will be able to use any other.

The story of how Britain came to be so exhaustively mapped is fascinating in itself.

The mapping of Britain

The formation of the national mapping organisation owes much to the foresight of General William Roy, a renowned eighteenth-century surveyor, engineer and archaeologist. As a young man he was responsible for the production of a military map of Scotland following the 1745 Rebellion. Later he directed the first major scientific operation to be carried out in Britain: the precise measurement of a base line at Hounslow Heath (now Heathrow Airport) and the triangulation connection with France. He advocated the formation of a national survey organisation, but it was not until after his death in 1790 that the first steps in this direction were taken.

In 1791, under threat of invasion from France, there was a need for maps of the south coast of England for military purposes. The British Army required accurate mapping at one inch to one mile scale and the survey was carried out by the Board of Ordnance, a Crown organisation responsible for army engineering, artillery and other armaments at that time. The name Ordnance Survey comes from this period.

As the threat of invasion receded, the mapping application for civilian purposes was identified. With the Industrial Revolution underway – bringing with it the rapid development of towns and communications – politicians, administrators, civil engineers and others were quick to recognise the value of accurate maps. So the one-inch survey was gradually extended to cover the whole country, and the Ordnance Survey was given the task of carrying out the work. Along with one-inch maps, surveys were also carried out to produce maps at much larger scales providing even more detailed and accurate information. Maps at other scales ($\frac{1}{4}$ inch, $\frac{1}{2}$ inch and smaller) were later produced by the OS.

Today, Ordnance Survey is a civilian Government Department with a staff of 3000. Its present headquarters are at Southampton, with small local survey offices throughout the country.

Maps as history

The first series of OS maps was drawn to a scale of one inch to the mile (1:63,360). The first map at this scale was published in 1801; it covered part of Kent and was for military use. Today Ordnance Survey produces maps of major urban areas at 1:1250 scale (50 inches to the mile); rural areas at 1:2500 scale (25 inches to the mile) and the whole country at a scale of 1:10,000 (about 6 inches to the mile). On 1:1250 and 1:2500 maps every building and most other features are shown, even post boxes, but at these scales a single map

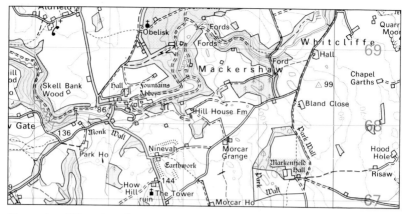

Fountains Abbey, North Yorkshire, at 1:50 000 scale. Map no. 99.

sheet covers only a small ground area. Information from these large scale plans, including 1:10 000, is used to produce a wide range of smaller scale maps each covering a larger ground area. At these smaller scales information to be shown has to be refined, names edited and detail generalised to avoid overcrowding the map and making it difficult to interpret.

A series of maps of a particular area published and revised over a period of years can tell you a great deal about changes that have taken place. The first map of the south coast, for example, drawn before the railway network was built, shows Bournemouth as a river mouth, 'Bourne Mouth', and some decoy ponds, but no town. Later maps record the arrival of the railway and the development of Bournemouth as a seaside resort accessible from London. Maps of the London dockland also begin before the arrival of the railways, show the expansion of rail tracks and sidings with more and more warehouses beside them, and then show the removal of the railway lines and the closure and demolition of many of the warehouses. The maps record an important part of the Industrial Revolution and its passing.

How maps are made

When those early OS surveyors went out into the towns and countryside, their first task was to establish a framework of survey control points throughout the country. These points (there are now about 20,000 of them) are known as triangulation stations. They are located on prominent buildings such as church spires, towers and factory chimneys, and in open country the points are marked by concrete or stone pillars. Their exact position on the earth's surface has been determined by taking precise angular and distance measurements. Today electronic measuring instruments are used, replacing the traditional measuring chains and tapes. Working from this framework of fixed points, surveyors are able

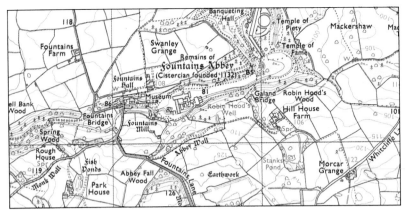

Fountains Abbey at 1:25 000 scale. Map no. SE 26/36.

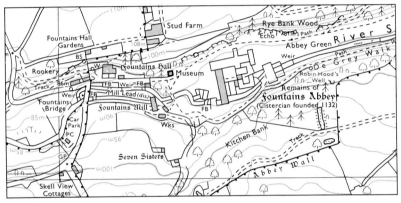

Fountains Abbey at 1:10 000 scale. Map no. SE 26 NE.

accurately to position and record all features that are to appear on OS maps.

In addition to the control points that record horizontal position, OS surveyors have set up a framework of reference points for height information above sea-level, so that a three-dimensional picture of the landscape can be established. There are some 500,000 of these points in existence, placed at frequent intervals along most main roads in Britain. From these reference points, known as 'bench marks', surveyors are able accurately to record the height of the surrounding land and to build up a graphic picture of the terrain to be recorded on Ordnance Survey maps as spot heights and contours.

Aerial photography has provided the surveyor with an additional tool with which to gather information about the landscape. A camera mounted in an aircraft takes strips of overlapping photographs. Adjacent pairs of photos, placed side by side and seen through a pair of stereoscopic lenses, merge to give a three-dimensional image. This image can be converted into a map using precise

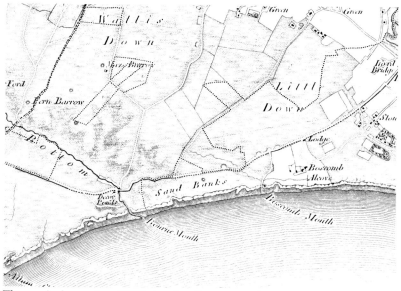

The one-inch map (no. XVI) showing Bournemouth, dated 1811. Compare this with the map on p. 199.

stereoscopic plotting instruments. The survey control points already described are used to obtain correct scale and map position of the features plotted from the photographs. Aerial photographs do not provide all the information, however; some detail may be hidden by trees or clouds and photographs do not provide names of roads or features. A surveyor therefore always visits the area to record this information and complete the map in all other respects.

Computer maps

To bring the story right up to date: an increasing number of OS 1:1250, 1:2500 and other maps are being produced using automated cartographic technology. Information collected and recorded by the surveyor in graphic form is converted by electronic means into digital form and stored in a computer databank. The graphic information is recorded as a series of numerical co-ordinates which identify the precise location of the feature on the ground. The process of converting graphics to digits which the computer can accept is known as digitising. Once the information is digitised it can be recalled to produce an exact-scale map copy, or a larger or smaller scale copy as required. Furthermore, selected detail can be recalled, rather than recalling the whole map. All in all it is a far cry from the original surveys of the early nineteenth century. The customers for accurate detailed mapping are basically the same, however, with digital information being much in demand from local authorities and from the coal, gas, electricity and water industries, etc., all of whom like the flexibility that computerised map data provide.

PART I
PREPARATION

2

PLANNING

Careful planning does not guarantee the success of any enterprise, but lack of planning may come close to guaranteeing its failure. A trip to the countryside is no exception to this general rule. Of course you do a certain amount of planning. You decide where it is you will go, you make sure the car has enough petrol, you check the weather, and you take food or money to buy food if you know you will be away from home for more than an hour or two.

Unless you are very familiar with the area you plan to visit, you may also look through the family collection of maps. You will probably restrict your visits to places covered by the maps you have or buy the additional maps you need. This, too, is part of the planning. It may be fun to pretend to lose yourself, but it can be exasperating to be really lost, and if you are on foot in open country it can be dangerous. Stiles and gates are not shown on OS maps, and hedges are not distinguished from walls, fences or banks. It is important to note the scale and date of a map, which are printed on all OS maps. Apart from alterations in roads and paths, the Magnetic North Pole moves constantly, affecting the relationship between north as indicated on a magnetic compass and true north. (This is explained on p. 54.)

The amount of information you require from a map depends on the way you intend to use it. If you are driving several hundred miles on main roads you will need to find your way quickly and easily. Roads and towns are important, but too much detail may simply confuse you. If you are walking in the hills, on the other hand, you will need every landmark to help you navigate. The amount of information a map can provide is determined by its scale. A map of the room in which I work could show every item of furniture, but not the title of every book on the shelves. A map of the small town in which I live could show my home, but not the location of particular rooms in it. A map of the county could show the town, but not my house. A map of the world might not show the town. There is a hierarchy of maps, at different scales to satisfy different needs. There are also specialised maps, to be used in conjunction with other maps, for people with particular interests. Some maps show features of historical interest; others show geological structures and formations. There are maps showing the distribution of soil types, and maps showing drainage basins.

The Ordnance Survey National Grid

The National Grid is a reference system of squares which have been overprinted on all OS maps since the 1940s. This system of breaking the country down into squares allows you to pinpoint any place in the country with varying levels of precision depending on which scale of map you are using. For example, on a 1:50 000 (2 cm to 1 km or 1¼ inches to 1 mile) Landranger map you can give a reference for a place or feature to an accuracy of 100 metres (333.3 feet); at the largest map scale of 1:1250 (50 inches to 1 mile) you can pinpoint the place to within 10 metres (33.3 feet).

The squares of the basic grid cover an area 100 × 100 km and are identified by letters, e.g. SU, TQ, NJ, etc. These squares are subdivided into smaller squares, map scale by map scale, covering areas ranging from 10,000 × 10,000 metres (33333.3 × 33333.3 feet) on the smaller scale maps to 100 × 100 metres (333.3 × 333.3 feet) on the largest scale.

The National Grid reference for a place or feature is unique and will always be the same, no matter which map or scale you are using – although, as we will see, the more figures we use in our reference the more precisely we can pinpoint the place. But it must be stressed that to ensure the 'uniqueness' of the reference, the National Grid letters as well as the numbers must always be included.

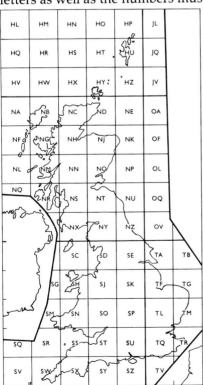

Diagram showing the division of Britain into 100 km squares and the letters used to designate them.

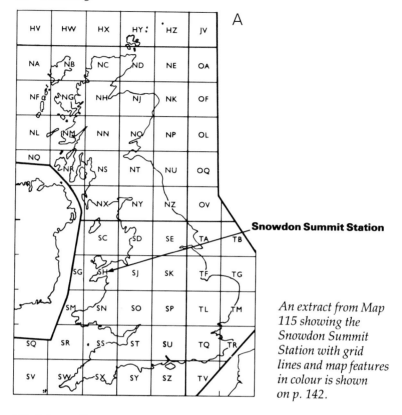

An extract from Map 115 showing the Snowdon Summit Station with grid lines and map features in colour is shown on p. 142.

Grid references

For example, the summit station of the Snowdon Mountain Railway has a grid reference SH 609543. It is constructed as follows:

SH   These letters identify the 100 km grid square in which the named feature falls. The diagram (diagram A) shows the arrangement of squares across the country. Information on the relevant 100 km grid squares covered by specific OS maps is always given in the map legend. The 100 km squares are subdivided into smaller squares. In the case of 1:50 000 scale Landranger and 1:25 000 Pathfinder and Outdoor Leisure maps, these smaller grid squares cover an area of 1 × 1 km. They are defined on the map by grid lines, each line being identified by a two-figure number.

609 543   This six-figure reference locates the summit station within the 100 km square.

60   This part of the reference is the number for one of the grid lines running north–south on the 100 km grid square (see diagram B). This number can be found in the top and bottom margins of the relevant OS map (Landranger 115, in this case).

54   This part of the reference is the number for one of the grid lines running east–west across the 100 km grid square (diagram B).

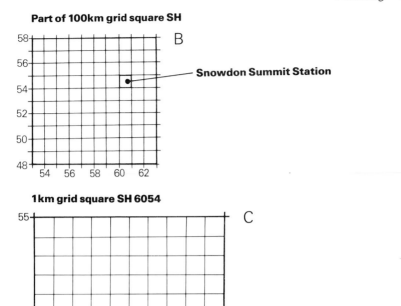

Part of 100km grid square SH

Snowdon Summit Station

B

1km grid square SH 6054

C

Snowdon Summit Station

The lines within the square and their associated numbers do not appear on the face of the map

These two numbers together located the bottom left-hand (southwest) corner of the 1 km grid square in which the Snowdon Summit Station appears. The remaining figures in the reference (60<u>9</u> 54<u>3</u>) pinpoint the feature within the grid square to the nearest 100 metres, as shown on diagram C.

Grid lines, magnetic north and true north

The grid lines on a map are there purely for reference purposes, to help the map user locate a given point easily and accurately. The vertical grid lines, while they may run parallel to the edge of the map, do not run true north.

In fact, there are three 'norths': grid north, which, as we have seen, refers to the direction of the vertical grid lines on the map; magnetic north, which is the direction pointed out by the compass; and true north, which is the North Pole, the northern point of the axis upon which the earth rotates. (See also p. 54.)

In the case of our example, the Snowdon Summit Station, the nearest grid line on the map (61 on the Landranger) is 1° 26' west of true north and 6° east of magnetic north.

Map scales

Without knowing it, we have no real idea of the distances represented on the map. A short distance on a small-scale map, for example, will represent a much longer distance on the ground than the same distance on a larger scale map.

Map scale is normally given as a ratio such as 1:50 000, but may sometimes appear as a 'representational fraction' and be written thus: 1/50 000. This indicates that 1 unit on the map is equivalent to 50 000 units on the ground. The smaller the ground-unit number the larger the scale:

> 1:1250 maps, where 1 unit on the map represents 1250 units on the ground,
> are at a larger scale than
> 1:50 000 maps, where 1 unit on the map represents 50 000 units on the ground.

The ratio values can be expressed in either metric or imperial measurements provided that they are applied uniformly to both map and ground elements. Thus, for 1:1250 maps:

> 1 inch on the map is equivalent to 1250 inches on the ground
> 1 mm on the map is equivalent to 1250 mm on the ground
> 1 cm on the map is equivalent to 1250 cm on the ground

Equally for 1:50 000 maps:

> 1 inch on the map is equivalent to 50,000 inches on the ground
> 1 mm on the map is equivalent to 50,000 mm on the ground

For ease of understanding, however, and to help to relate map and ground detail, scales of maps are normally given as so many inches to 1 mile (or centimetres to 1 kilometre). Thus the scale description for 1:1250 maps is normally 50 inches to 1 mile on the basis that:

> if 63,360 inches = 1 mile
>
> and 1 inch on the map = 1250 inches on the ground
>
> then 50(.68) inches on the map = 1 mile on the ground.

For 1:50 000 maps the scale description is 2 cm to 1 km on the basis that:

> if 100,000 cm = 1 kilometre
>
> and 1 cm on the map = 50,000 cm on the ground
>
> then 2 cm on the map = 1 kilometre on the ground.

Suggested applications	Series Title	Scale	Coverage	No. of Maps	Area of coverage of each map
Detailed touring map for the motorist	Routemaster	1:250 000 1 inch to 4 miles 2 cm to 5 km	Great Britain	9	Orkney, Shetland & Western Isles Northern Scotland Western & Central Scotland Central Scotland & Northumberland Northern England East Midlands & Yorkshire Wales & West Midlands SW England & South Wales SE England
All-purpose map for the walker, cyclist & motorist	Landranger	1:50 000 1¼ inches to 1 mile 2 cm to 1 km	Great Britain	204	40 km × 40 km 25 miles × 25 miles
To explore a particular holiday area on foot or by road	Tourist	1:63 360 1 inch to 1 mile 1 cm to 0.63 km	Selected holiday areas	11	Dartmoor · Ben Nevis & Glen Coe North York Moors · Cotswold Lake District · Loch Lomond Peak District · Snowdonia Exmoor · Anglesey New Forest · The Broads
Detailed map for the walker	Pathfinder	1:25 000 2½ inches to 1 mile 4 cm to 1 km	Great Britain	1373	Normally 20 km × 10 km 12½ miles × 6¼ miles Also some 10 km × 10 km 6¼ miles × 6¼ miles
Detailed map for walker & visitor to leisure areas	Outdoor Leisure map	1:25 000 2½ inches to 1 mile 4 cm to 1 km	Selected leisure areas	31	Peak District (2) · Purbeck Yorkshire Dales (4) · Snowdonia (4) Aviemore & Cairngorms · South Devon English Lakes (4) · South Pennines Cuillen & Torridon Hills · New Forest Brighton & Sussex Vale · Isles of Scilly Brecon Beacons (3) · North York Moors (2) Wye Valley & Forest of Dean · Dartmoor · Isle of Wight

Feature chart — detail available on each map series:

Feature	Routemaster	Landranger	Tourist	Pathfinder	Outdoor Leisure map
Field Boundaries				•	•
Railways	•	•		•	•
Tourist Information	•	•	•		•
Vegetation				•	•
Forest	•	•	•	•	•
Selected Named Buildings		•		•	
Contours	*	•	*	•	•
Rivers	•	•	•	•	•
Bridleways		•		•	•
Footpaths		•		•	•

The above chart shows the detail available on each map series

All map series show towns, villages, major and minor roads.

Features specified here are selected items of interest.

* plus relief shading

Clothing and equipment

With the maps in your pocket, petrol in the car, sandwiches in the hamper and tea in the Thermos you may think your plans are complete. If you intend to stay in the car, or at any rate close to it, they are, but if you intend to explore on foot you need more equipment yet.

Out in the open the map will be of much more value if you use it in conjunction with a compass. (How to find your way with map and compass is explained on p. 53.) When making your preparations remember to pack the compass, and make sure it is a good one, accurate and reliable.

Pack one whistle for each member of the party and make sure that everybody carries one. Pack an emergency kit with:

- a needle and enough thread to sew on a button or mend a tear;
- antiseptic and a packet of dressings for cuts;
- a bandage and dry dressing in case of a larger wound;
- aspirin.

If you are walking in remote country, and especially in the hills, you should take a survival bag for each person. This is a bag, often brightly coloured to make it easily visible from a distance, made from heavy-duty polythene and large enough to cover the body completely. It is totally waterproof and prevents heat loss from the body. You can buy a survival bag from any good camping or outdoor sports shop; it costs very little, is light and folds into a small package, and could save a life.

In addition to the sandwiches or whatever you plan to eat during the day, you should take emergency rations. These should consist of 'energy' foods, rich in sugar, such as Kendal mint cake, chocolate, barley sugar or other boiled sweets. They are for use in an emergency, so resist the temptation to eat them in the car before you even arrive.

You will need clothing suitable for the conditions. This means you must always take waterproof garments. Leggings will keep the lower part of your legs dry while you are walking through wet bracken or long grass, and the kind that fasten with a zip are easy to put on and remove. Overtrousers will serve the same purpose and keep your knees dry as well. An anorak or other lightweight coat, with a hood and a big pocket for maps, is also essential. Trousers give better leg protection than skirts. Jeans give little protection against wind and are uncomfortable when they get wet, and corduroys take a long time to dry. Wool is best, provided it is strong. Take gloves, for the weather could turn cold. In winter mitts are more comfortable than gloves with fingers. You should also carry a spare sweater and spare socks, in case you need to change into something dry.

Walking as a group

If you organise or lead a group on a walk in the countryside you must make special preparations and take reasonable precautions to ensure the safety and comfort of the participants.

- Choose a route that avoids metalled roads as far as possible. Paths are easier on the feet and safer.
- Be sure the route sticks to paths where the public has right of way. If you must enter private land, obtain permission in advance.
- Do not make the walk too long. Over gentle terrain experienced adult walkers can sustain a pace of about 4–6 km/h (2.5–4 mph), covering 15–25 km (10–15 miles) in a full day. Inexperienced walkers and children may manage half this. Shorten the walk if there are many stiles to cross, remembering that people can cross only one at a time, or if the ground is muddy. Shorten the walk by up to 3 km per 300 m (2 miles per 1000 feet) climb or descent.
- Walk the route yourself some weeks before the planned excursion to check for difficulties and obstacles. Report to the county council any hazards or obstructions on public footpaths, bridleways or by-ways. Travel the route again a few days before the excursion to make sure that it is safe and passable.
- If necessary, arrange transport to the start and finish of the route. Unless the route ends where it began, people may need transport back to their vehicles.
- If the excursion is to last all day, pick a place to stop for lunch. It should offer shelter in case of bad weather. If you plan to stop at a pub or café, give the proprietors advance warning.
- Tell all members of the party in advance whether dogs are allowed. If they are, make sure that they remain under close control at all times, and on leads when crossing farmland.
- Keep the party small. The maximum practical number is 15.
- Check that all members of the party are adequately equipped for the conditions you anticipate. Those who are not properly equipped may be sent home if in your opinion they could endanger themselves or others.
- When you meet make sure that everyone knows you. If you are leading the party yourself pick someone to bring up the rear, and make sure everyone also knows him or her.
- The person bringing up the rear should be responsible for closing all gates and for seeing that no one strays from the party and that the walkers do not form too straggly a line.
- Walk at the speed of the slowest member and keep an eye on the party to make sure people are keeping up with you.
- If you stop to rest or to allow stragglers to catch up, do not start again until the last arrivals have had time to rest.
- Make sure that everyone walks in single file across ploughed fields or fields with a growing crop, and no more than two abreast on the right-hand side of roads. Do not allow anyone on land to which you have no right of access.

Finally, think of your feet. Good walking boots, kept well greased to make them supple and really waterproof, are best for general use. They support the ankles, cushion the foot on rough or stony ground, and have a deep tread to provide a good grip on slippery surfaces. Plimsolls, training shoes and ordinary shoes are less satisfactory, although they may be comfortable enough for short walks on roads or smooth paths. Wear two pairs of socks if you plan to walk far – this helps to prevent blisters.

How do you intend to carry all your equipment and spare clothing? The general rule is that you should carry it on your back so that the strongest muscles bear the weight and your hands remain free. It is a good idea to place everything inside a plastic dustbin liner before loading it into the pack. This adds nothing to the weight but provides additional protection against water. If you are rock climbing or mountaineering the pack should not swing about on your back because this can throw you off balance. You should therefore use a rucksack with a waist-strap. If you are carrying a heavy load, a well-designed rucksack is a sound investment. It will distribute the weight efficiently and keep the centre of gravity high, near your shoulders. It is much less tiring to carry a weight there than lower down, where it can pull savagely on your shoulders.

Trespass

Now, at last, your plans are complete and you are ready to go anywhere; anywhere, that is, to which you have a right of access. If you enter land you do not own, against the wishes of the owner, you are trespassing. If you are allowed to enter, but only between certain hours (some parks close at dusk, for example) and are present outside those hours, you are trespassing. If you misbehave and refuse to leave when asked to do so, you are trespassing. Ignorance of the fact that you are trespassing is not a defence.

Sponsored walks

If you organise a sponsored walk you should observe all the rules for group walks, and take certain additional steps.

- Give advance notice to the police and landowners.
- Make sure that some members of the group are competent to administer first aid, and have the necessary equipment.
- Appoint marshals. Give them armbands or badges that are clearly visible, and station them in advance at intervals along the route. They must see that everyone sticks to the planned route and must arrange help or treatment for anyone who is injured or too tired to continue.
- If you put up signs to waymark the route, make sure they are removed when the walk has ended.

What constitutes misbehaviour? A journalist was once seen standing on a public footpath, where he had every right to be, watching racehorses training near by and making notes, which he was not entitled to do. A court held that he was trespassing. If you carry a metal detector on a public footpath you may be trespassing, and quite apart from any other offences you may be committing you may be trespassing if you fire a gun or light a fire even on land you are entitled to enter.

Misbehaviour may constitute an offence in its own right. On certain land belonging to the Ministry of Defence and British Rail simple trespass (that is, just being in the wrong place) is a criminal offence for which you can be prosecuted. On all other land it is a civil offence.

Access to open country

All land in Britain, including land inside National Parks, belongs to someone, but there are areas of open land to which you have a right of access, such as most local authority town and country parks. Town parks, country parks, official picnic sites and similar places are designated legally as 'public open spaces', and are obviously intended for public use. In other places, there may be an access agreement or order between the landowner and local authority or National Park authority. This allows public access, but usually only on foot, and dogs may have to be kept on leads. Camping may be forbidden. Areas of open country where there are access agreements are marked on some OS Outdoor Leisure maps (1:25 000 scale), and on the ground usually by signs where paths enter them.

There are other open spaces to which the public has a right of access by long-established custom. In some places, especially on mountains and upland moors, this may apply to everyone, but elsewhere such access may apply only to local residents. You may also enter private land with the permission of the landowner. National Trust land is owned by the Trust, but the public is invited to enter it at times and on conditions laid down by the Trust. Most Forestry Commission land is also open under similar conditions.

You have no automatic right to enter land belonging to the Crown, nor to enter common land. Common land is owned privately, but certain people, the 'commoners', are entitled to take or use some part of the produce of its soil. They may graze livestock, for example, or cut peat for fuel. Some common land in London and in most urban areas, but also other popular sites such as Epping Forest, the Clent Hills and Bexhill Downs, is owned by local authorities and dedicated to public use. Anyone may enter such common land, and it cannot be closed even at night.

Most beaches are open to the public, and subject to maritime law and regulations issued by harbour or navigation authorities you have an absolute legal right to sail a boat on salt water. However,

Countryside Access Charter

The Countryside Commission has summarised your rights in the English and Welsh countryside in the form of an Access Charter. The Charter is explained in detail in a booklet *Out in the Country – Where you can go and what you can do* (CCP 186) obtainable, free, from the Countryside Commission. Because the law relating to land ownership, tenure and public access is somewhat different in Scotland the Charter applies only to England and Wales.

Your rights of way are:
Public footpaths – on foot only. *Sometimes waymarked in yellow.*
Bridleways – on foot, horseback and pedal cycle. *Sometimes way-marked in blue.*
Byways (usually old roads), most 'Roads Used as Public Footpaths' and, of course, all public roads – all traffic.
Use maps, signs and waymarks. OS Pathfinder and Landranger maps show most public rights of way.

On rights of way you can:
Take a pram, pushchair or wheelchair if practicable.
Take a dog (on a lead or under close control).
Take a short route round an illegal obstruction or remove it sufficiently to get past.

You have a right to go for recreation to:
Public parks and open spaces – on foot.
Most commons near older towns and cities – on foot and sometimes on horseback.
Private land where the owner has a formal agreement with the local authority.

this does not give you the right to cross private land to reach salt water. There is a right of way along most canal towpaths, but access to river banks and the shores of lakes depends on whether the public has access to the surrounding land. Access is allowed to land surrounding most reservoirs. Landowners may permit the public to sail boats on canals, rivers, lakes or reservoirs but without such permission it is illegal to do so, and where it is allowed there may be conditions attached – you may need a licence, for example.

Rights of way

You can travel through the countryside by highways over which the public has a right of way. There is a right of way over all public roads in Great Britain.

In England and Wales there is also a network of footpaths, bridleways and byways designated as Public Rights of Way. Public footpaths are open only to people on foot. Bridleways are open to people on foot, horseback and pedal cycle. Byways are open to all

In addition, you can use by local or established custom or consent (ask for advice if you're unsure):
Many areas of open country such as moorland, fell and coastal areas, especially those of the National Trust, and some commons.
Some woods and forests, especially those owned by the Forestry Commission.
Country parks and picnic sites.
Most beaches.
Canal towpaths.
Some private paths and tracks.
Consent sometimes extends to riding horses and pedal cycles.

For your information:
County councils and London boroughs maintain and record rights of way, and register commons.
Obstructions, dangerous animals, harassment and misleading signs on rights of way are illegal and you should report them to the county council.
Paths across fields can be ploughed, but must normally be reinstated within two weeks.
Landowners can require you to leave land to which you have no right of access.
Motor vehicles are normally permitted only on roads, by-ways and some 'Roads Used as Public Paths'.
Follow any local by-laws.

traffic but are usually mainly for walking and horseriding. If you find a designated Public Right of Way obstructed, you can remove the obstruction if this is possible or take a short route around it. However, if you do find yourself confronted with an obstacle, your best course of action is to report it to the local authority who will take appropriate steps to have the route cleared.

In Scotland no designated Rights of Way as such exist. Neither is there any law of trespass. That being said, while you may traverse moorland and mountain paths taking due care to avoid damage to property and the natural environment, landowners can and do impose restrictions on access, such as during the grouse shooting season. They also have a legal remedy against any person causing damage on or to their land and may use reasonable force to remove such a person.

The following simple guidelines should therefore be followed: obey restricted access notices and if asked to leave, do so; always take care to avoid damaging property and the natural environment;

if you are not clear about access rights, seek permission of the landowner first.

Cars, caravans, tents

You may not pitch a tent or park a caravan anywhere without the permission of the landowner. It is illegal to drive, camp or park a caravan on any town or village common, or to park a caravan overnight in a layby.

If there is no car park you may park a car beside the road provided parking is permitted and it causes no obstruction, but you may not drive off the road into a field or other private land to park unless you have permission. It is part of motoring folklore that you may park a car anywhere within 15 yards of a road. This is not true.

Wildlife

It is an offence to destroy or damage any wild plants or animals. Unless you are a landowner or the occupier of land, or have written permission, you may not kill or injure even animals counted as 'vermin', or such common species as rooks. You must not uproot wild plants.

The Country Code

While you are in the countryside you should observe the general code of behaviour drawn up by the Countryside Commission.

- Enjoy the countryside and respect its life and work.
- Guard against all risk of fire.
- Fasten all gates.
- Keep your dogs under close control.
- Keep to public footpaths across farmland.
- Use gates and stiles to cross fences, hedges and walls.
- Leave livestock, crops and machinery alone.
- Take your litter home.
- Help to keep all water clean.
- Protect wildlife, plants and trees.
- Take special care on country roads.
- Make no unnecessary noise.

·3·
WEATHER

British weather is notoriously variable. At times it is possible to experience weather typical of all four seasons within a single day. That is why you should prepare for the worst if you intend to spend several hours in the open air. Always take warm and waterproof clothing.

More preparation than this is called for, however. If the weather deteriorates you could be marooned, unable to move on or to return to your starting point. Every spell of harsh winter weather brings stories of motorists trapped by drifting snow, but it is not only in deepest winter that people are trapped in the open. Driving rain or fog, as well as blizzards, can reduce visibility and make it dangerous to continue walking unless you are on a road or clear, well-marked path. When navigation becomes impossible you may simply walk in circles, and where there are cliffs or bogs you may come across them unexpectedly. In remote country there is the possibility that you may be out all night.

The wind is always stronger on high ground, and a fierce head-wind will tire walkers. Strong winds are a danger near cliff tops: they can change direction suddenly and the wind that was pushing you back from the edge can push you forward hard and without warning. Every summer the coastal cliffs claim a few victims this way.

The mountains of Britain are small compared with those of the great mountain ranges of the world, but this fact has lulled many a mountain walker into a false sense of security. They are smaller partly because their bases are closer to sea-level than mountains which rise from high ground. The Rockies, for example, rise from the gently rolling plains of the prairies that in Alberta and Montana are already 1000–1200 m (3000–4000 feet) above sea-level. Because the British climate is maritime, and most large mountain ranges lie deep inside continents, conditions in the British mountains are more changeable than those in other mountains, and in winter they can be much worse than conditions even in the Alps, though usually only for short periods.

Before setting out you should obtain the most recent weather forecast for the local area. This will provide useful but fairly general information. In most cases the forecast will be reliable, but there may be small yet important variations, especially near the coast or

Average change of temperature with height

As you climb the temperature will fall. As you descend it will increase. To estimate, very approximately, the temperature you should expect at a different altitude, measure the change in altitude and if the weather is clear and dry subtract the figures below if you are climbing and add them if you are descending. If the weather is very cloudy, halve the values before adding or subtracting.

metres	°C	feet	°F
100	1	300	1.6
200	2	600	3.2
300	3	900	4.8
400	4	1200	6.4
500	5	1500	8.0
600	6	1800	9.6
700	7	2100	11.2
800	8	2400	12.8
900	9	2700	14.4
1000	10	3000	16.0

on high ground. While out of doors you should keep a look out for changes, especially visible changes in the sky. The forecast and the signs you can read for yourself will be of much more value if you understand a little of the way in which our weather is formed and behaves.

Where do we get our air?

During the day the Sun warms the surface of the Earth, in our high latitude, much more strongly in summer than in winter. At night the surface cools again. Water warms and cools much more slowly than land. Air may be warmed or cooled as it passes over land and water warmer or cooler than itself.

When air is warmed it expands, and warm air can hold more moisture than cool air. When air is cooled it holds less water vapour and becomes denser. Just how much water vapour the air actually collects depends on the amount available to it. It will collect more over the sea than it will over very dry land.

The difference between the actual amount of water vapour in the air and the total amount which air at that temperature could hold is called the *relative humidity* of the air. Usually it is expressed as a percentage, so that if the relative humidity is 100 per cent the air is saturated and you may expect cloud to start forming.

Because the density of the air is reduced when it expands, the warmed, usually moist air rises. Air that rises because it is being warmed from below is said to be *unstable*. As air rises it cools, which

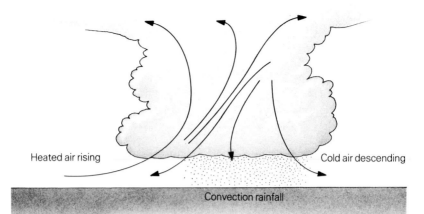

Heated air rising   Cold air descending

Convection rainfall

Convection rainfall.

reduces its capacity to retain water vapour, and unless the air is very dry the vapour will start to condense on to particles of dust, to form clouds. Air that is cooled by passing over relatively cooler land or water will tend to settle: it will become *stable*.

The atmospheric pressure is the force exerted by the weight of the column of air above any particular point. If the air is less dense it obviously weighs less, and so in warm air the pressure is reduced. Air pressure decreases with increasing altitude because the higher you go the less air there is above you to exert pressure.

Air pressure is usually measured in *millibars* (abbreviated to mb), one millibar being one-thousandth of a bar, or one *atmosphere*. The world-wide average sea-level pressure is 1013.2 mb. Weather reports and forecasts always give the pressure corrected to mean sea-level, and the variation from 1013.2 mb will tell you whether the pressure is higher or lower than average. Correcting to sea-level is a fairly complex operation because many factors are involved, and on high ground the reported pressure may be only approximate. This is less important than it may seem because changes in the weather are indicated by changes in pressure, caused by the movement of masses of air at different pressures, and by the rate at which this movement occurs. The pressure of a mass of air is shown on weather maps as *high* or *low* in relation to the pressure of the air to either side, so it is quite common for there to be a low area in which the pressure is more than 1013.2 mb.

This process of warming and cooling may occur locally, but it also occurs on a vast scale, affecting the air over thousands of square kilometres to produce great masses of air within which the surface pressure and humidity are fairly constant. Air masses formed in high latitudes where there is less solar heating are more dense, and so have a higher atmospheric pressure, than air masses formed in low latitudes, closer to the equator, and the humidity of the air

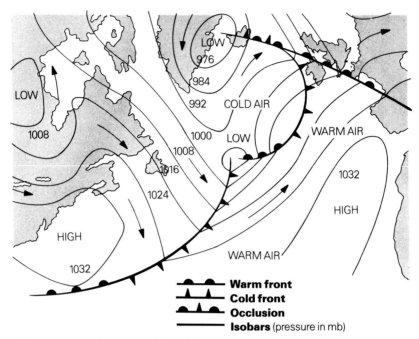

The type of weather map published in newspapers.

depends on whether the air mass formed over land or sea. Air masses are known as 'polar', 'arctic' or 'tropical' according to the latitude in which they originated, and 'continental' or 'maritime' according to whether they formed over land or sea. Air masses move across the Earth and are modified as they do so, but certain general characteristics are associated with them.

Where two air masses meet and one is less dense than the other, air should pass from the denser to the less dense until they are both at the same pressure. This, however, is not quite what happens, for two reasons. The first is the rotation of the Earth, which sets moving air swirling (much as water going down a plughole swirls), spiralling inward towards an area of low pressure, which gradually fills, or outward from an area of high pressure, which gradually weakens. In the northern hemisphere the air moves in an anti-clockwise direction (seen from above) around an area of low pressure and in a clockwise direction around an area of high pressure. The second reason that the two meeting air masses do not merge into one of the same pressure is that when they collide the less dense air rides up over the denser air with only a small amount of mixing.

The point on the ground where two air masses meet is called a *front*. Fronts move and are called 'warm' or 'cold' depending on the relative density of the air behind them. Eventually the gradual mixing of the two air masses causes the front between them to disappear, but air masses are constantly forming.

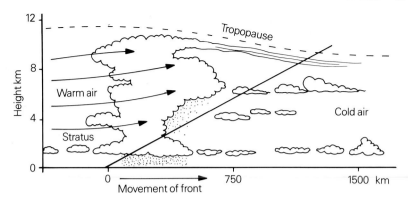

A warm front, where warm air is riding over colder, denser air.

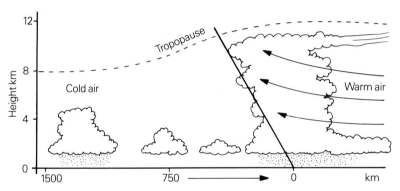

A cold front, with cold air undercutting warmer, less dense air.

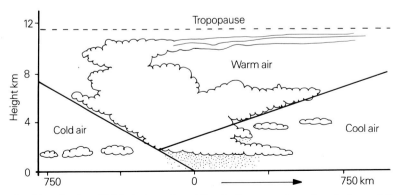

A cold occlusion. Cold air is undercutting both warm air and cool air, and the cold and warm fronts are merging.

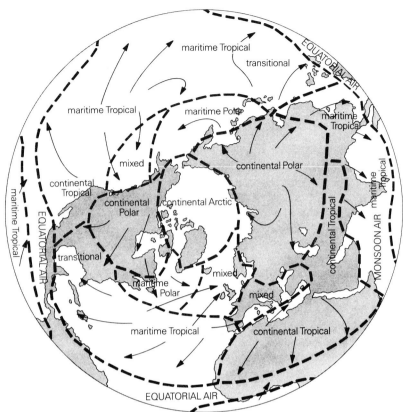

Northern hemisphere air masses in winter.

A front appears on a weather map as a straight or wavy line. A cold front is indicated by a series of triangles along the line of the front; a warm front is drawn with a series of semicircles. If the map is printed in colour, the warm front will be red and the cold front blue. The front is a boundary, and is labelled warm or cold depending on its direction of movement. If it were to change direction, obviously a warm front would become a cold front, and vice versa. A sharp wave may develop along a front, due to warm air riding over cold air, while near-by cold air is undercutting warm air. When this happens one front becomes two because a wedge of warm air is surrounded by cold air. This is called a *depression*. Because cold air undercuts more vigorously than warm air overrides, the cold front begins to overtake the warm front. This is an *occlusion*, marked on a map as alternate triangles and semicircles.

In winter, continental arctic and continental polar air masses develop over the Arctic itself, over North America and over Siberia, and a maritime polar air mass develops over the Atlantic. Continental polar and arctic air is cold and dry. Maritime polar air is a little warmer because in winter the sea is warmer than the land and air passing over the Gulf Stream is warmed by it, and it therefore carries

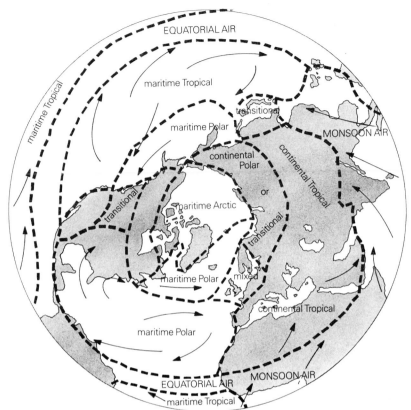

Northern hemisphere air masses in summer.

some moisture. So the maritime polar air to the west of Britain forms an area of low pressure, centred approximately over Iceland and sometimes called the 'Icelandic low'. To the east of Britain pressure builds steadily towards the 'Siberian high'. Britain is more or less where these two areas of pressure meet. To complicate matters further, Britain lies just to the north of the boundary between polar and tropical air masses, the 'Atlantic polar front', which often runs along the English Channel.

In summer, when the northern hemisphere receives more solar heating, the Icelandic low retreats northward and Britain comes under the influence of an area of high pressure to its south, the 'Azores high'. The continental polar air mass over Siberia also contracts northward, giving way to continental tropical air with a lower pressure. Again, Britain lies just about where the contrasting air masses meet. The Atlantic polar front also moves very slightly northward, but in summer the boundary between continental tropical and maritime tropical air masses moves from Spain to about the Bay of Biscay, so that southern England may sometimes be covered by continental tropical air and sometimes by continental maritime air.

Effects of the weather

For much of the time we experience the weather associated with the air mass covering us. Since fronts are a common feature on British weather maps, clearly we change air masses rather frequently; and since fronts sometimes move quickly, the change can take place in just a few hours.

Britain is often windy because of these changes from one air mass to another. As air tries to move from an area of high pressure to one of low pressure and is deflected, the speed at which it moves – the wind speed – is proportional to the difference in pressure between the two areas. Lines drawn on a map to join places with the same atmospheric pressure are called *isobars*. The bigger the contrast between low and high pressure, the closer together the isobars.

Fronts may also bring weather in their own right. A front, as explained, is a place where relatively less dense air is riding over denser air. As air rises it cools, the water vapour it carries condenses to form clouds, and there may be rain or snow caused directly by the front itself. Once the front has passed the weather is determined by the air mass. Fronts tend to develop depressions, however, and depressions often bring cloud and rain.

Maritime tropical air is warm and moist. As it moves northward it is cooled gradually by contact with the Earth's surface, so the air nearest the ground is cooler and more dense than air above it. This makes it very stable. The cooling causes clouds to form, and the stability makes them form as featureless, flat, layered sheets. We rarely experience maritime tropical air in winter, but occasionally in summer it will bring prolonged periods of warm, heavy rain.

Flat, layered cloud whose base is at a height of less than 2 km (about 6500 feet) is called *stratus*. If rain or snow is falling the cloud is *nimbostratus*. If the base is at a height of 2–6 km (about 6500–20,000 feet) it is *altostratus*; if higher than that it is called *cirrostratus*.

Continental tropical air originates over the deserts of North Africa and the Near and Middle East and is warm and dry. It is also unstable. Because it is dry there are few clouds and the ground is exposed to strong sunshine. Some surface materials absorb and retain heat better than others, so although the amount of solar heat striking the ground may be the same everywhere, some places will be warmer. This causes local differences in the amount of heating of the air from below, so that small *parcels* of strongly heated air rise through the main air mass. Sometimes they rise rapidly, as *thermals*, much sought after by glider pilots. These parcels carry with them such moisture as may have evaporated into them. The air cools, the water vapour condenses, and clouds form in heaps, causing showers.

Heaped cloud is called *cumulus*; if it spreads out at the base it is called *stratocumulus*. Cumulus clouds can build to great heights.

Average rainfall

	England and Wales		Scotland	
	mm	*inches*	*mm*	*inches*
January	92	3.6	154	6.1
February	66	2.6	106	4.2
March	57	2.2	89	3.5
April	60	2.4	88	3.5
May	63	2.5	87	3.4
June	55	2.2	87	3.4
July	79	3.1	114	4.5
August	81	3.2	122	4.8
September	76	3.0	128	5.0
October	92	3.6	158	6.2
November	95	3.7	143	5.6
December	88	3.5	143	5.6

When the rising air reaches the height at which its density is the same as that of the air above, it can rise no further, but it may still be 'fed' by vigorously rising air from below. This will make the top of the cloud fan out, often into a shape reminiscent of an anvil. A cloud of that shape, called *cumulonimbus*, produces violent storms, with rain, thunder and lightning. Where the cloud base is at middle altitudes the cloud is called *altocumulus*, and at very high altitude it is *cirrocumulus*.

Fine, wispy cloud that forms at very high altitude is called *cirrus*. Most cloud is composed of water droplets, but cirrus, cirrocumulus and cirrostratus are made from ice crystals. Obviously, moist air must have been carried to a great height for cirrus to form, and this lofting of air is most likely to occur ahead of an approaching warm front. If you see large amounts of cirrus you are probably still in the cold air mass, but the air high above you belongs to a warm air mass. You are in the 'wedge', and as the front draws nearer the clouds associated with it will form at lower heights.

Maritime polar air starts cold but is warmed somewhat by its passage across the sea. It usually brings clear weather which feels cold in winter because there is little cloud to prevent heat radiating from the ground at night. It also feels cold in summer, by comparison with tropical air. The ground surface is often heated unevenly during the day, causing instability, cumulus clouds, and showers of rain or snow. This is because skies are clear and the sunshine is bright, so there are shadows on the ground, and some substances absorb heat more strongly than others.

Maritime arctic air is always cold and moist and also tends to be somewhat unstable, bringing showers which are of snow in winter.

Continental polar air is dry. In winter it is very cold, bringing clear, bitter weather. In summer it is much warmer because the region from which it comes is being warmed strongly during the long hours of daylight in very high latitudes. As it crosses the sea it collects moisture, and local variations in surface heating can make it unstable, producing cumulus clouds and showers.

Local variations

In Britain, July and August are the warmest months, January and February the coldest. Rainfall is distributed fairly evenly throughout the year. Remember, though, that temperature decreases as you climb from sea-level. Anywhere above 500 metres (about 1500 feet) you must expect freezing temperatures during daytime in December, January and February throughout Britain.

As air rises and cools its capacity to hold water vapour decreases and its relative humidity increases. The encounter between air masses with different densities is only one of the causes of air rising. High coastal cliffs will make it rise, and so will hills and mountains. As air masses move over such major obstacles they lose some of their moisture, so it is more likely to rain or snow on the exposed side of an obstacle than on the sheltered side, in the 'rain shadow'.

Wind speeds increase near coastal cliffs and on high ground. Close to the ground, trees and buildings provide shelter from the wind, which is deflected and eddies so that its force is reduced and its direction cannot be measured with any certainty. The ground surface itself exerts friction on the moving air, also slowing it. In open country, away from the shelter of trees and buildings, the wind speed increases. On hillsides facing the wind it will increase still more, because a greater proportion of the moving air will be travelling high above the valley floors, clear of surface friction.

Wind speed is given in miles or kilometres per hour, but you may often hear it described as 'force' with a number between 0 and 12. This is the Beaufort Scale, devised for the sailing ships of the Royal Navy in 1806 by Admiral Sir Francis Beaufort (1774–1857), and now

As moist air crosses mountains it is forced to rise, cools, cloud forms and rain falls. The far side of the mountains is sheltered, in a 'rain shadow'.

WIND

No rain here

The Beaufort Wind Scale

	force	mph	km/h	
Calm: smoke rises vertically	0	0	0	
Light:, smoke moves in the wind, but wind vane is not affected	1	1–3	1.5–5	
Light breeze: can be felt on the face, leaves rustle, wind vane moves	2	4–7	2.5–11	
Gentle breeze: small twigs and leaves move constantly, a light flag will wave	3	8–12	13–19	
Moderate breeze: small branches move, dust and loose paper blow about	4	13–18	21–29	
Fresh breeze: small trees begin to sway	5	19–24	30–39	
Strong breeze: large branches move	6	25–31	40–50	
Moderate gale: becoming hard to walk against it, whole trees move	7	32–38	51–61	
Fresh gale: twigs break from trees, walking difficult	8	39–46	62–74	
Strong gale: loose roof tiles and chimney pots removed	9	47–54	75–87	
Fierce gale: trees uprooted, serious structural damage	10	55–63	88–101	
Storm: may cause widespread damage, rare inland	11	64–75	102–121	
Hurricane: causes devastation	12	76+	122+	

an internationally recognised standard. Admiral Beaufort defined force 0 as calm, and force 12 as 'that which no canvas could withstand'.

Haze, mist and fog

Cool air descends. Especially at night, it will descend into valleys, making them cold. Valleys are sheltered and because water drains into them they are often relatively wet. Grass may grow longer there than on the exposed hillsides. At night heat is lost more rapidly from long grass than from short grass, because the total surface area of the leaves, and in effect, therefore, the total surface area of the ground warmed during the day, is greater. Cool air descending into a valley may be cooled still more by the cold valley floor. Cooling increases its relative humidity, and cloud is likely to form at ground level. Cloud at ground level is mist or fog.

Visibility is the distance you can see in a horizontal direction. *Haze* is a reduction in visibility caused by solid particles, usually of dust, in dry air. *Mist* is a reduction in visibility due to the condensation of water droplets, when the visibility remains more than 1 km (1094 yards). *Fog* is a reduction of visibility due to condensed water droplets when visibility is less than 1 km.

Cirrus advancing across the sky, indicating approach of a warm front.

Cirrostratus with a halo: a sure sign of bad weather approaching.

Altostratus, bringing rain.

Altocumulus, a sign of instability aloft with the approach of thundery weather.

Fair weather' cumulus, with lots of blue sky and little vertical development.

Cumulonimbus, with distinctive anvil shape, a sign of heavy rain or hail.

Reading the signs

Without resorting to old wives' tales, it is possible to make reasonable predictions about the weather from the signs you can see around you. The clouds or lack of them, the temperature and the wind can all be induced to impart useful information.

Provided that you know the average sea-level temperature for the time of year you can guesstimate the highest or lowest temperature you are likely to experience during the day, based on what type of air mass is producing the weather. A weather report may tell you this; if not, you will have to judge it for yourself. If the air feels warm for the time of year it is tropical, if it feels cold it is polar or arctic, if it is moist or 'close' it is maritime, if dry it is continental. Now look to see whether the sky is clear or cloudy, and feel the wind to see whether it is calm or light, or windy.

Tropical air, with clear skies and light winds, can add up to 10°C (18°F) to the average temperature. If it is cloudy or windy it can add 5°C (9°F). Polar or arctic air can reduce the temperature by as much as 10°C (18°F) if it is cloudy or windy, and by 5°C (9°F) if it is clear and fairly calm. Having adjusted the sea-level temperature to the value you expect, remember to adjust the new temperature for altitude if you are above sea-level.

The temperature falls at night at a fairly constant rate from about an hour after sunset until about an hour before dawn, after which it begins to rise again. If you take the temperature an hour after sunset and again an hour later you will be able to predict the lowest temperature for the night with reasonable accuracy.

A sustained accumulation of cirrus is a sign of an approaching warm front, with cloud and precipitation.

Average temperatures at sea-level

	England and Wales		Scotland	
	°C	°F	°C	°F
January	4.0	39.2	3.5	38.3
February	4.2	39.7	3.7	38.7
March	6.2	43.2	5.4	41.7
April	8.8	47.8	7.5	45.5
May	11.6	52.9	9.9	49.8
June	14.7	58.5	12.7	54.9
July	16.3	61.3	14.1	57.4
August	16.1	61.0	14.0	57.2
September	14.3	57.7	12.5	54.5
October	11.2	52.2	9.9	49.8
November	7.2	44.5	6.3	43.3
December	5.1	41.2	4.6	40.3

When fairly high clouds have a red tint to their bases at dawn, the air to the east of them is fairly dry and the weather there fine. If you know which way the air masses are moving (most often they move from west to east) you may know what to expect. 'Red sky in the morning' does not necessarily mean that the air to the west is moist, but if the clouds are drifting eastward expect rain.

If the undersides of the clouds are red around sunset it means the air to the west is dry, and if the air is moving westward fine weather is on its way (but could pass through during the night). The colour must be red, however. An orange sky at sunset indicates that the weather is about to deteriorate.

The clouds can tell you whether or not it is likely to rain or snow within the next few hours. Only clouds whose base is at a fairly low level will produce precipitation. You can forget high clouds.

If the clouds are of the stratus type, but bright, it will not rain. When they are dull, but the air pressure is rising or steady, it will not rain. If they are dull and pressure is falling it will rain unless the temperature is close to freezing, in which case it will snow.

When the clouds are of the cumulus type, but with clear skies among them so you can see the tops and they are not growing larger, it will not rain. If they are growing larger, but the pressure is steady, it will not rain. If they are growing larger and the pressure is falling and the bottoms of the clouds are darkening, it will rain, or snow if the temperature is close to freezing. Cumulonimbus clouds that are dark at the bottom will bring thunderstorms.

If the cumulus clouds are merging into one another and the sky is darkening and pressure falling, there may be a very heavy shower. Whenever the pressure is steady you may expect more prolonged rain or snow.

4

NAVIGATION

When you read this page of text you are converting groups of symbols into words and groups of words into intelligible messages. Like a page of printed text, a map is composed of symbols printed on a flat piece of paper. You can read a map in much the same way as you read anything else, once you have mastered the symbols and the way they are used.

There are differences, however. A map uses more than the 26 symbols of our alphabet, and it mixes different kinds of symbol. It uses words, letters, numbers, lines and pictures, and most maps also use colour. The symbols and colours are used in a very precise way, so it is possible to translate the information on a map into a description in words.

When you do so, remember that the map views the landscape from above, so the literal picture you build up from it will give you a bird's-eye view. You will need to interpret this if you are to translate it into the picture you will see from ground level. You will see large features from only one aspect, for example, and features lying behind them will be hidden from you.

Planning the route

It is important to acquire the skill of translating from the map to a verbal description of a landscape, because the first lesson in navigation is to plan the journey before you start. Find on a map the place from which you will start, and trace the route to the end of the journey. If you want to be really thorough you can prepare a written guide to the route, and if the journey takes you across open country you should at least prepare a few notes. When you are arranging a walk for a group of people a written guide will help them, not least because it will tell them about interesting features they will pass and where to look for them.

Note the National Grid reference for the starting and finishing points. Look for interesting features along the route, or close to it, and note where they are, perhaps by noting their grid references. If you are planning to walk in hilly country, see whether there are places along the route from which you may have good views of the surrounding countryside, and note them too. Quite apart from their scenic interest they may be helpful in navigating on the ground. Many good viewpoints are marked on OS maps with a fan-like symbol. The 'fan' may be fully or partly open and shows the direction in which the view lies.

1:50 000 Second Series Map
CONVENTIONAL SIGNS

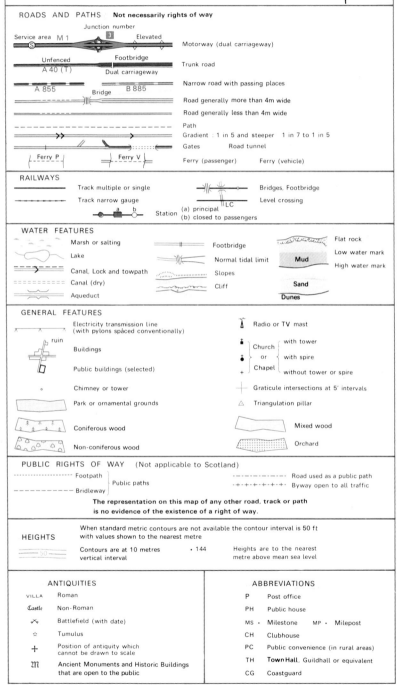

Some of the standard symbols used on 1:50 000 scale maps.

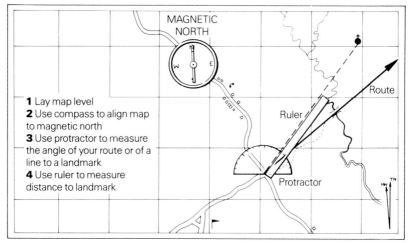

1 Lay map level
2 Use compass to align map to magnetic north
3 Use protractor to measure the angle of your route or of a line to a landmark
4 Use ruler to measure distance to landmark

Plotting a heading and a route using protractor, compass, ruler and map.

Measure the direction in which you will start travelling. You can do this with an ordinary protractor. Lay the map on a level surface and place the protractor on it, with the centre of the flat edge over the starting point and the 90 degree mark pointing to the top of the map, parallel to the grid lines, then move it to one side or the other so that instead of pointing to grid north it points to true north. This will mean turning the 90 on the protractor about two degrees to the right. The legend in the margin of the map will give you the precise amount of correction. The protractor now points to true north. Count the number of degrees between true north and the line of your route. If the route lies to the right of the 90 mark, the degrees you count will be the heading you need. If it lies to the left of the 90, subtract the number of degrees from 360 to find the heading. If the route is generally to the south, so it is not beneath the protractor, draw a pencil line lightly (so that you can erase it afterwards) along the straight edge, then turn the protractor around until the centre of the straight edge is over the starting point and the straight edge lies along the line. Now the 90 mark will be pointing south, 180°. Count the number of degrees from the 90. If the route is to the right add the degrees to 180; if it is to the left, subtract them from 180. Make a note of this heading.

The task is easier if you use a compass that incorporates a ruler and protractor. Lay the long straight edge of the compass baseplate along the direction of the route, so that the 'direction of travel' arrow on the baseplate points along a path parallel to your route. Turn the compass housing until the orienting arrow ('North' on the dial) points towards north on the map, remembering to correct for grid north. Then read the number on the dial where the dial meets the base of the arrow. That is the direction in which you will travel. (The design and use of a compass is explained more fully on p. 53.)

Follow the route and note where and how the direction changes. You need not measure each change by starting again from north. It is sufficient to measure the number of degrees and direction through which you turn. If the turn is to the right, add this number to your last heading. Subtract it if you turn left.

Measure the distance you will walk. Remember that at the 1:50,000 scale two centimetres on the map represent one kilometre on the ground (or 1.25 inches represent one mile), and that the sides of the small grid squares are two centimetres long. At the 1:25 000 scale 4 cm = 1 km (2.5 inches = one mile), and the sides of the small grid square are 4 cm long. It is very important to measure distance carefully. Unless you intend to walk in an absolutely straight line, using a ruler to measure your route will cause you to underestimate the distance, and unless you use an extremely large number of pins to guide it, and perforate your map badly, a piece of string, cotton or wool will wander and give a result that may be greater or smaller than the true one (wool will stretch, and cotton will bunch, just to add another source of inaccuracy). The instrument to use is called an 'opisometer', a small wheel linked to a counter which measures centimetres as you wheel it across the map.

Now look along the route for climbs and descents by seeing whether the route lies more or less parallel to the contour lines, or whether it crosses them, and if it crosses them the angle at which it does so. The contour lines join places at the same height above sea-level, so if you walk parallel to them you will remain at the same height. If you cross them at an angle you will be walking more or less diagonally up or down a slope, and if you cross them at right angles you will be going directly up or down. The closer together the lines are the greater the change of altitude with distance, and therefore the steeper the gradient. In Sutherland, for example, a walk planned as a straight line on the map that includes the section from NC 308462 to 303462 would take you up about 300 m in a horizontal distance of about 400 m. That is a gradient of about 1:1.3, a very steep climb up what is almost a cliff! It may be possible to ascend it, but to do so you might need proper climbing equipment. In the uplands, rivers often cut deep, steep-sided valleys, so if you plan to follow a river make sure before you get there that no part of the valley is impassable because of its sides descending sheer to the water.

Every time your route crosses contour lines make a note of the number of metres it climbs or descends and add these together, so that by the end you have a total. This will tell you how hilly your route is. It is quite possible to walk long distances through hilly country without ever climbing or descending, so the general type of landscape is not in itself an adequate guide to how easy or difficult a walk will be. You should not assume that it is invariably much easier to walk downhill than it is to walk uphill.

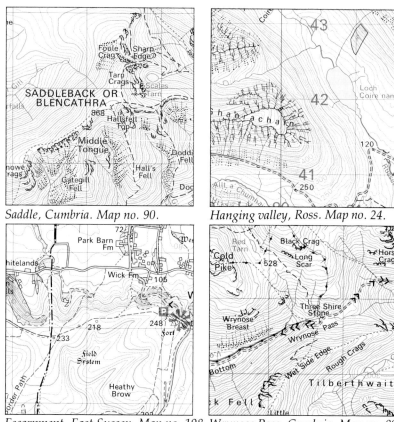

Saddle, Cumbria. Map no. 90.   Hanging valley, Ross. Map no. 24.

Escarpment, East Sussex. Map no. 198. Wrynose Pass, Cumbria. Map no. 89.

Identifying important features

Use place names and the contour lines to identify features that may be useful in navigation. Hills are easy to recognise. A small, round hill is often called a *knoll*. In Britain a hill usually has to be more than 600 m to be classed as a mountain. Mountains often have clearly defined summits. Knolls, hills and mountains usually have names, and since they can be seen easily from a distance they are helpful landmarks.

Passes may also have names. A *pass* is a depression between hills or mountains, at a high or low level, and earns its name because it provides a way through a line of hills or a mountain range. A *col* is also a depression, but closed on all sides. If it is at high altitude and has sides that slope gently, a col is known as a *saddle*, which is what it resembles in shape.

Where the ground rises sharply to a crest then slopes more gently to a lower level behind, this is known as an *escarpment, scarp* or *cuesta*. A projection of high ground, like an arm extending from a hill into the lowland, is a *spur*, and a long, narrow region of high ground that links two hills or mountains is a *ridge*. If you think you have

Saddle, Cumbria.

Hanging valley, Ross.

Escarpment, East Sussex.

Pass, Cumbria.

identified a spur, check the numbers on the contour lines carefully, because the contours of a spur are identical to those of a particular kind of valley. If it is a spur the ground rises towards the centre; in a valley the lowest ground is at the centre.

A fairly large expanse of more or less level ground at a high altitude is a *plateau*. In good weather you should be able to see a long distance from a plateau. Walking conditions across it should not be difficult, but it may be windy, subject to sudden changes in the weather, and the ground may be wet and even marshy.

All these landforms can be recognised easily from an OS map, so that from studying the map you should have a good idea of the kind of country through which you will walk. With practice you will be able to spot other features and so learn much of the history of the landscape just by studying the map. Some of these features will be visually interesting and possibly worth a short diversion. You will be able to spot hanging valleys with waterfalls, for example, in a landscape formed by glaciers, and tell at a glance whether a river is fast-flowing, possibly with rapids, or slow, and that information will give you a good idea of the plants and animals living in the water.

How to calculate a gradient

A compass that is modified to measure inclines (a clinometer) can be used to measure the angle of a slope. Gradients are not usually given as angles, however, but as the ratio of vertical to horizontal distance, either directly as the ratio (one in ten, for example, written as 1:10), or as the ratio expressed as a percentage (1:10 is the same as 10%). The table below allows you to convert the angle of a slope into a more familiar expression of the gradient. The gradients down to 1:1 have all been rounded to the nearest whole number, which is why the steeper slopes have one gradient value for a range of angles. At 45 degrees the gradient is 1:1, so at steeper angles you are moving further vertically than you are horizontally.

Angle (degrees)	Gradient	Gradient (as percentage)
1–2	1:33	3
3	1:20	5
4	1:14	7
5	1:11	9
6	1:10	10
7	1:8	12.5
8–9	1:7	14.3
10	1:6	16.7
11–12	1:5	20
13–15	1:4	25
16–22	1:3	33.3
23–33	1:2	50
34–49	1:1	100
50–53	1:0.8	125
54–56	1:0.7	143
57–60	1:0.6	167

Assessing difficulty

You should turn your attention next to the terrain over which you will be walking. You can be certain about the surface of metalled roads. They are marked clearly on OS maps, although on the small-scale maps their widths are not drawn to scale, for if they were they would be very difficult to see. Footpaths and bridleways are also marked, but conditions on them can change. If it has rained heavily, or snow has melted, they are often muddy. On the 1:25 000-scale map there are symbols indicating rough grassland or bracken, heathland, marsh, reeds, saltmarsh, scrub, woodland and whether it is mainly coniferous, broadleaved, mixed, coppiced or orchard. You will also find symbols for scree, loose rocks, boulders, outcropping rock, sand or shingle, and mud. The 1:50 000-series maps give rather less detail than this.

Once you know how far you will walk, the amount of climbing and descending you will do, and the kind of surface over which you will be walking, you are in a position to assess the overall difficulty of the walk. There is no standard way to do this. Guidebooks published on behalf of the organisations that arrange walking holidays give walks graded according to one of four possible schemes, but unless you know how the grading system works you will be little wiser. There is an international standard scheme for grading the difficulty of climbs and mountain walks, and efforts are being made to devise and agree a similar standard system for all walkers that will apply throughout Europe. Until such a system appears you will have to improvise as best you can, and the scheme offered here may provide a basis for you. (See the box on pp. 50–1.) If you try it and find it tends to classify walks as too easy, or too strenuous, alter the values you assign when scoring the answers to its questions. After all, what is an easy walk for one person may be strenuous for another, and if the scheme is to be of use it must be adapted to you personally.

Do not set out in advance to overtire yourself or anyone accompanying you. Your close examination of the map may suggest that the route you have chosen is too difficult. If so, change it. No one awards marks for foolhardiness. By being too ambitious you run the risk at least that you, or someone in your party, could be made extremely uncomfortable, which would obviously detract from the enjoyment of what is meant to be a form of relaxation and regeneration. You might even have to cope with an emergency, possibly requiring the help of the rescue services – and while they are always reliable, they are also very outspoken in their criticism of bad planners and bad leaders.

A 45° angle, or 1:1 (100%) gradient. The walkers climb 1 metre for every metre they advance horizontally.

Scale of difficulty

It is important to estimate the difficulty of a walk before you start, especially if you are planning an excursion for a group of people. There is no standard method for assessing difficulty, although efforts are being made to produce a European standard scheme. Until that appears you will have to improvise. The scheme set out below may help. It has been devised for this book.

Three factors combine to make a walk easy or difficult: distance, terrain and gradient. You should begin by assessing each of these separately.

1 Distance

Measure the route on the map. Is it:

  a less than 6 km
  b 6–10 km
  c 11–15 km
  d 16–25 km
  e more than 25 km?

2 Terrain

What is the ground like? Here you will have to use your judgement. The map shows metalled roads, unmetalled paths and bridleways. If it has rained heavily in the last few days you should assume that open ground will be wet and possibly muddy, and paths may also be muddy. Unless you know the route you may not be able to tell whether the ground is stony, or whether you will have to negotiate heaps of large boulders, so you may have to guess. Then you must estimate approximately how much of the route takes you over each type of terrain. Choose from the selection and allot a proportion to each (make sure the fractions add up to 1).

Will you be walking over:

		Proportion of the route			
		25%	*50%*	*75%*	*100%*
f	metalled road				
g	well-made path				
h	firm beach				
i	open ground				
j	muddy ground				
k	stony ground				
l	loose sand				
m	large boulders				
n	heather or tussocky ground with no path				
o	ice or snow?				

3 Amount of climbing and descending

Study the contours on the map, following your proposed route. Every time you climb or descend note the difference between the height at the bottom and at the top. Add all the numbers together to produce a total for the number of metres of climb and descent.

Will you climb or descend:

p less than 50 m
q 51–100 m
r 101–300 m
s 301–500 m
t 501–700 m
u 701–1000 m
v more than 1000 m?

Calculating the score

When you have made your choices allot marks to them as follows:

1		**2**		
a=1		f=1	k=4	
b=2		g=2	l=4	
c=3		h=2	m=5	
d=4		i=3	n=5	
e=5		j=4	o=6	

Then take the percentage of each score in section 2, according to the proportion of the route allotted to it, and add together all the terrain scores.

3			
p=1	s=4	v=7	
q=2	t=5		
r=3	u=6		

Calculate a single score by multiplying the three scores: $1 \times 2 \times 3$. Remember this number.

Return to section 1 (distance) and score it again in reverse order: a = 4; b = 3; c = 2; d = 1. Multiply this score by the score for 3 (gradient): 1×3. Note this number.

Now you have two scores. Add them together and divide the total by 5. This is the final score, which will tell you the relative ease or difficulty of the route you have chosen.

> 1–5: easy
> 6–10: moderate
> 11–15: fairly strenuous
> 16–20: strenuous
> 21–25: very strenuous
> more than 25: very strenuous and difficult

The procedure seems complicated, but if you have access to a computer the following simple BASIC program may simplify it.

BASIC program

```
10 REM Program to calculate the difficulty of a walk
50 PRINT TAB(14) "CALCULATING THE DIFFICULTY OF A WALK"
60 PRINT "How long is the walk? Is it:"
70 PRINT "less than 6 km? Type 1;"
80 PRINT "6-10 km? Type 2;"
90 PRINT "11-15 km? Type 3;"
100 PRINT "16-25 km? Type 4;"
105 PRINT "more than 25 km? Type 5."
110 INPUT A
112 PRINT: PRINT
120 PRINT "What is the terrain like? Select from the list"
130 PRINT "below. After each selection, type on the next"
140 PRINT "line .25, .5, .75, or 1, to show the proportion"
150 PRINT "of the walk accounted for by each type. You may"
160 PRINT "choose up to 4. Type a zero (0) and on the"
170 PRINT "following line a 1 for any choices you do not"
180 PRINT "use. Is the terrain:"
190 PRINT "metalled road? Type 1;"
200 PRINT "well-made path? Type 2;"
210 PRINT "firm beach? Type 2;"
220 PRINT "open ground? Type 3;"
230 PRINT "muddy ground? Type 4;"
240 PRINT "stony ground? Type 4;"
250 PRINT "loose sand? Type 4;"
260 PRINT "large boulders? Type 5;"
261 PRINT "heather or tussocky ground with no path? Type 5;"
265 PRINT "ice or snow? Type 6."
270 INPUT B
280 INPUT C
290 INPUT D
300 INPUT E
310 INPUT F
320 INPUT G
330 INPUT H
340 INPUT I
350 PRINT: PRINT
360 PRINT "How much climbing and
descending will you do?"
370 PRINT "less than 50 m? Type 1;"
380 PRINT "51-100 m? Type 2;"
390 PRINT "101-300 m? Type 3;"
400 PRINT "301-500 m? Type 4;"
410 PRINT "501-700 m? Type 5;"
420 PRINT "701-1000 m? Type 6;"
425 PRINT "more than 1000 m? Type 7."
430 INPUT J
440 PRINT: PRINT
450 B=B*C
460 D=D*E
470 F=F*G
480 H=H*I
490 K=B+D+F+H
500 L=A*K*J
510 IF A=1 THEN 550
520 IF A=2 THEN 560
530 IF A=3 THEN 570
540 IF A=4 THEN 580
545 IF A=5 THEN 585
550 A=5
560 A=4
570 A=3
580 A=2
585 A=1
590 M=A*J
600 N=(L+M)/5
610 IF N<6 THEN 660
620 IF N>6 AND N<11 THEN 680
630 IF N>11 AND N<16 THEN 700
640 IF N>16 AND N<21 THEN 720
650 IF N>21 AND N<26 THEN 740
655 IF N>26 THEN 745
660 PRINT "The walk will be easy."
670 GOTO 750
680 PRINT "The walk will be moderate."
690 GOTO 750
700 PRINT "The walk will be fairly
strenuous."
710 GOTO 750
720 PRINT "The walk will be strenuous."
730 GOTO 750
740 PRINT "The walk will be very
strenuous."
741 GOTO 750
745 PRINT "The walk will be very
strenuous and difficult."
750 END
```

Navigating with map, compass and signposts

Navigation begins with good planning, but its purpose is to enable people to travel from one place to another by a predetermined route. It is not necessary to make difficulties for yourself. When you walk along a road or well-marked path, use the signposts or waymarks. A *waymark* is a small mark, usually an arrow, placed on a gate, stile, wall, tree or other fixed object, indicating the direction of the path. Waymarking is often done by the local authority, but landowners may also do it. The Countryside Commission recommends that yellow waymarks be used to indicate footpaths, blue for bridleways and red for byways, but you may well find other colours and symbols. Countryside Commission long-distance paths are way-marked with a white acorn symbol.

Where there are no signs you will need to use your map and a compass. Ideally, you should have a protractor and ruler as well. These are combined in one instrument if you buy the most popular type of compass for use in the countryside, one of the Silva range. This range includes a clinometer, a compass that can also measure the angle of dip of rock strata. This is useful for measuring the angle of slope of a hill.

Navigation – method for plotting a heading and planning a route using a Silva compass and a map.

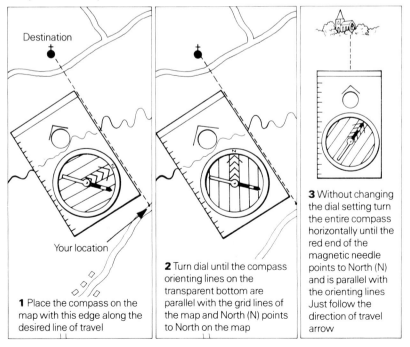

Destination

Your location

1 Place the compass on the map with this edge along the desired line of travel

2 Turn dial until the compass orienting lines on the transparent bottom are parallel with the grid lines of the map and North (N) points to North on the map

3 Without changing the dial setting turn the entire compass horizontally until the red end of the magnetic needle points to North (N) and is parallel with the orienting lines Just follow the direction of travel arrow

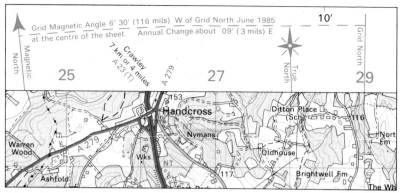

Magnetic North, True North, Grid North, as they are shown for Map no. 198.

Grid north, magnetic north, true north

A compass needle points to the magnetic north pole. This is located in northern Canada, but it wanders. It is not the same as the geographical North Pole. When you use a magnetic compass you must make a correction by adding or subtracting so many degrees. The amount of correction varies from place to place, because obviously the angle between you and the magnetic and geographical poles depends on where you are. All OS sheets include the amount of correction you should make for different parts of the sheet, and tell you the year in which the correction was calculated and the rate at which it is changing. Before you start you should check this figure. With some compasses the orienting arrow can be moved by itself by means of a small screw, so you can set it in advance to one side of the N mark on the housing.

Which way to go?

When you arrive at your starting point you will want to know in which direction to walk. Lie the map on a flat surface. Place the compass on the map so that one edge of the baseplate is along the route you wish to follow. Turn the dial housing until the orienting lines are parallel to the grid lines and N on the compass points to the top of the map. Turn the whole compass until the needle points to N. Now correct the compass so that it reads true north rather than grid north. Using the figures and instructions printed in one of the margins of the map, turn the compass until the needle points to the correct number of degrees west or east of N. The direction-of-travel arrow now points in the direction you should follow.

To walk in a particular direction, set the direction by turning the compass housing until the direction is touching the base of the direction-of-travel arrow. Holding the compass steady, turn until the needle points to N. The direction-of-travel arrow indicates the direction you should walk.

Bearings and fixes

If as you walk you see a landmark you can recognise on the map and wish to know the direction that will take you towards it, you must take a bearing. Point the direction-of-travel arrow at the landmark. Turn the compass housing until the needle points at N. Where the housing meets the end of the direction-of-travel arrow you will find the number which is your bearing, and if you are following the compass you need not correct for grid or magnetic north.

You may need to calculate your position. Provided you can see at least two landmarks which you can identify on the map (and three will give you a more accurate fix), this is simple. Take a bearing on each landmark in turn, and correct the compass for grid and magnetic north. Place the compass on the map with one edge of the baseplate touching the landmark on the map. Turn the whole compass until the orienting lines and arrow point to grid north, parallel to the grid lines. Draw a pencil line using the edge of the baseplate as a ruler. You are somewhere along this line. Repeat the process for your second and third bearings. You are where the lines intersect. This method is extremely accurate.

You must remember that any bearing relating to your map must be a grid bearing, with the compass corrected. A bearing to take you towards a landmark, without reference to the map, however, does not need correction. This is known as a compass bearing or field bearing.

Providing you can identify at least two landmarks around you (A and B in the diagram above), you can calculate your position (C above) using a map and a Silva compass.

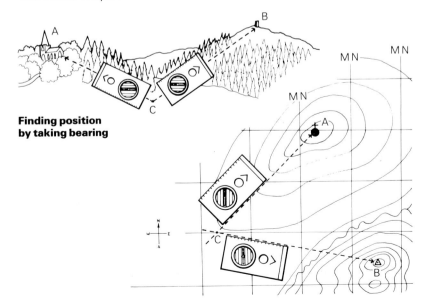

**Finding position
by taking bearing**

Care of the compass, and what to do if you lose it

A magnetic compass needle is very sensitive to the smallest disturbances in the magnetic field. It will be deflected if there is a metal object nearby, and by electrical apparatus. A photographic light meter will also affect it. You must make sure the compass is working without interference before you trust it.

Treat the compass with respect. In particular you should never leave it close to a radiator or heater. The damping fluid will expand if it is heated and may distort or even burst the housing.

If you lose your compass, you can navigate by the Sun, at least approximately, provided you have a watch with hands (not a digital watch). The watch must be accurate, and set to Greenwich Mean Time (one hour is added for British Summer Time). Turn the watch so that the hour hand points at the Sun. Halfway between the hour hand and the 12 is due south.

With your watch set to Greenwich Mean Time, point the hour hand at the sun. Halfway between the hour hand and '12' is south. If you use a digital watch, draw a clock face on a scrap of paper or on your hand.

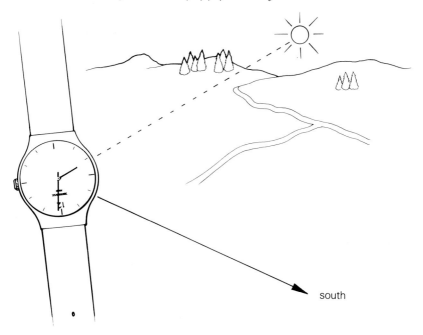

south

5

WHEN THINGS GO WRONG

Planning what should happen is not the same thing as predicting what will happen, and sometimes the best of plans must be abandoned. Someone may be taken ill, be injured, or lost. The weather may deteriorate suddenly, drastically reducing visibility despite what the forecast promised. When the unexpected happens your very survival could depend on taking appropriate action, and that may involve seeking outside help. While making your preparations you should bear in mind that you may have to depart from your planned route to take a short cut to safety, and you must do what you can to make it as easy as possible to reach help, or for helpers to reach you.

Safety in open country

- Plan your trip carefully
- Make sure you have enough warm clothing
- Take a survival bag
- Pack a first-aid kit and manual
- Take enough food and emergency rations
- Check the weather before you start
- Be sure you know how to use a map and compass
- Trust your compass
- Do not attempt a walk that is beyond you
- Unless you are very experienced, do not walk alone in the mountains or in very remote country
- Never go alone into caves or potholes
- Never climb alone
- Never throw or deliberately dislodge stones
- Leave details of your party, your route, your destination and your estimated time of arrival with a responsible person or authority
- Report your safe arrival
- Know at all times the direction and approximate distance of the nearest road, farm or village
- Know what you will do in an emergency
- If someone is ill or injured give first aid, then head for safety
- Except on a road or clearly marked path do not continue after dark
- If the weather deteriorates do not hesitate to turn back
- Observe the Country Code

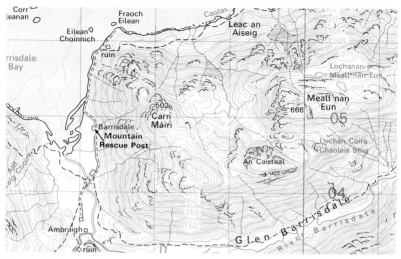

Mountain rescue post, Barrisdale, Highlands. Map no. 33.

If you plan to walk along roads, or along paths that are never far from roads, you have little to fear. Problems are most likely to arise when you are walking across remote open country. As you plan the route, before you set out, make a note of places from which you could obtain help if it were needed. Remember where the nearest road is, where there is a village or farm. In the mountains note the location of mountain rescue posts or kits, which are marked on OS maps. If you have done this, as you walk there will always be one corner of your mind that remembers where you can turn if things go badly wrong.

Unless you are very experienced and know that conditions are safe, or that you will be able to reach safety should they deteriorate, never walk alone in remote areas, especially in the uplands. Never go alone if you are climbing, caving or potholing, no matter how experienced you may think you are.

While walking, always keep away from the edges of cliffs. Note the location of disused mines and avoid them. They are marked on OS maps, but their entrances may be concealed by vegetation. The entrance may open immediately to a deep shaft.

Before walking along a beach check the times and heights of the tides. Many beaches disappear altogether at high tide and it is easier than you may think to be drowned, or find yourself marooned on a narrow ledge that is very difficult for rescuers to reach. Tide tables are available in coastal towns: you can buy them from most news-agents for a few pence.

As you walk, eat energy foods at frequent intervals, especially on high ground or in cold weather. You need much more food to keep you going than you would eat normally. Allow for this when calculating the rations.

When all your plans are made, write out a brief description of the party and of your route. Give your name, the number in the group, and note any people under 15 or over 60 in the party, or people with any physical disability. Estimate how long the walk will take you and write down the time you expect to arrive at your destination. Give this list to someone you trust. If you are setting out from home, leave it with someone there – a neighbour perhaps. If you plan to stay at a hotel, guest house or hostel when the walk is over, tell someone there, if necessary by telephoning ahead. If you are walking in a National Park, tell someone at the office or visitor centre. If there is no one else, tell the police.

When you arrive safely, remember to notify the person with whom you left your plans. Should you fail to arrive on time the emergency services will be notified. They will allow more time, in case you are simply late, how long depending on conditions and the distance you planned to cover. If you fail to arrive they will start looking for you along the route you have given. Should you be trapped, therefore, you will know it is only a matter of time, and probably only a few hours, before help reaches you. Failure to give proper notice of your route, destination and estimated time of arrival could waste a great deal of time, and it could cost lives – yours and possibly those of rescuers.

Cliffs on the Lleyn Peninsula, Gwynned. Map. no. 123.

Rescues are expensive and often hazardous for the rescuers.

Distress signals

There is an internationally recognised system of signalling for help. Give six blasts on a whistle, wait for one minute, and then repeat the signal. Continue until it is answered. If you have no whistle, make the same signal with waves of a piece of cloth. At night you can make the signal by flashing a torch.

If you in turn see this signal, acknowledge it by whistle, waving or flashing a light three times, waiting for one minute, and then repeating the signal. Take a bearing on the source of the distress signal and start moving towards it. The bearing is necessary, especially if the signal is made with a torch or cloth, because visual contact may be broken, for example if you have to move to lower ground.

Once contact has been made between the person needing assistance and the rescuer, the signals should be continued until they are within sight of one another, to make sure that contact is not lost.

If you get lost

You may find, perhaps because of reduced visibility, that suddenly you fear you may have wandered from your route. Call a halt at once and try to work out what may have happened. Above all, do not panic. Get everyone to sit down and relax.

Find on the map the last place where you were certain of your position. Work out how much time has elapsed since you were there. Trace on the map what you believe to be the direction you have walked. Reckon that you will have taken about 15 minutes to walk a kilometre, plus an additional 10 to 15 minutes for every 100 metres you have climbed. That should bring you to an approximate position.

Now look around you, examine as much of your surroundings as you can see, and try to recognise nearby landmarks. If you cannot see more than a few metres to either side, and you are not on a clearly marked path, stay where you are until conditions improve, even if this means spending the night in the open. See 'When you cannot go on or back', p. 66. Even if the visibility is good enough for you to examine your surroundings, identifying landscape features may take a little time because one hill or mountain may look much like another. Study your surroundings carefully. Examine the shape of the land, the ridges, spurs, escarpments or peaks you can see, and look for rivers. Try to relate what you see to what is on the map. As soon as you are sure that you have identified one feature both on the ground and on the map, take a bearing from it. Once that is done it should not be too difficult to find a second feature to give you another bearing, and you will have fixed your position. (For how to take a bearing and fix your position, see p. 55.)

Know how to use your compass, use it correctly, and believe it at all times. If visibility is poor it is especially important to trust the compass because your impressions can be very misleading. Trust your instincts and you can walk in circles. Trust the compass and you will walk in straight lines.

If a member of the party is lost

If a member of the party disappears, call an immediate halt. Listen for whistle signals. If you hear no whistle or shout, organise a search. Agree a signalling system for members of the search party. Do not use either the distress call or the acknowledging call, but agree:

- a call to be given at certain intervals to maintain contact among the searchers;
- a call to abandon the search and return to the place where the party halted;
- a call to indicate that the missing person has been found.

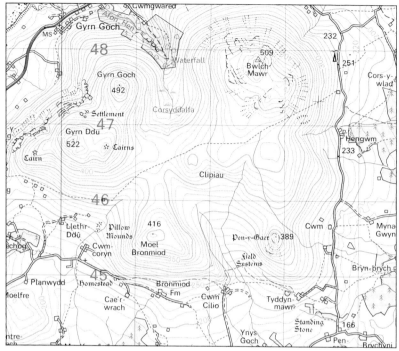

Mountains on the Lleyn Peninsula, Gwynned. Map no. 123.

The same area seen from the ground. Can you plot the position of the photographer on the map above?

If a searcher needs help the distress signal can be used. Help may be required if the missing person is found injured.

Leave at least one person at the place where the party halts in case the missing person is simply trailing behind, or manages to find his or her own way back to the route.

Have the searchers spread out to either side of the route to cover as broad a sweep as possible, then work back the way you have come. The searchers must keep in contact with one another to make sure they remain approximately abreast, and to make sure their tracks remain parallel and do not converge, leaving an area unsearched.

Examine muddy ground for footprints, especially on the banks of rivers and pools, but do not enter water. Beware of approaching the edges of cliffs. At the base of cliffs listen and look out for falling rock.

If you fail to find the missing person within about an hour, or what seems to you a reasonable time, recall the search party and send for help. Note the grid reference at the resting place as accurately as you can (see p. 16): this will be needed by the rescue party. Decide where you will go for help, and when you arrive make this your base. People you leave behind will need to know where they can find you.

This time, if possible, leave at least two people behind at the resting place. If the missing person is found before anyone else returns they will be able to give immediate assistance. If the person is injured one of them will be able to give continued support, either staying put or, if the injured person is able to continue, walking slowly towards the agreed meeting place while the other goes ahead to report.

Carrying or helping an injured person. If you cannot leave someone behind, make a cairn and place a note in it explaining where you have gone.

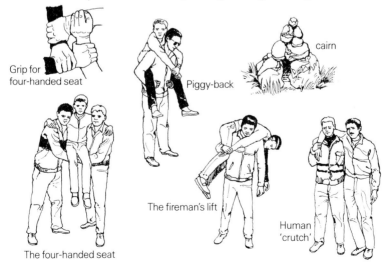

Grip for four-handed seat

Piggy-back

cairn

The four-handed seat

The fireman's lift

Human 'crutch'

Entering lakes or rivers

Except in the case of an emergency you should not go into a river or lake unless you can see the bed and can tell that the water is no more than knee-deep. Otherwise enter water only if it is absolutely unavoidable, and then only if you have rope that is long enough and strong enough to keep you secured to the bank. This is especially important after heavy rain, when rivers may be in spate, flowing very rapidly with muddy water of uncertain depth.

If you have to cross a river, try to find a place where it divides into two or more channels. That is where the crossing can be made most safely. If there is no such place, cross where the river is flowing straight, well away from bends where the water is often deep, the currents strong, and banks may be undercut.

If the water is more than knee-deep, remove your trousers (which cause drag) and socks, but replace your boots. If you are crossing, rather than going in to rescue someone, seal any plastic bags you are carrying and place them at the top of your rucksack for buoyancy: the river may be only waist-deep but you could fall or step into a depression. Loosen the straps of your rucksack: you may need to abandon it quickly. Find a strong stick to use as a walking stick. Break a branch from a tree if necessary.

Attach one end of a rope to a tree or boulder. Attach the other end to yourself by passing it around your body so that you can pay it out as you move but it will hold you if you fall or are swept off your feet. On no account should you try to cross unless you have found a secure anchor for your rope. If there is no suitable object to which you can fasten the rope, follow the course of the river until you find

Never cross a river if you can avoid it – and if you must cross, make sure you always use a rope.

one. Enter the river and move in small steps, checking the bed with your foot before trusting your weight to it. Cross diagonally, moving a little way downstream as you go. Do not try jumping from stone to stone.

If you are rescuing someone, fasten him or her to your rope before starting to return, so that you are both secured. If there is someone on the bank, have them haul in the rope as you return; otherwise haul yourself back, winding the spare rope around your body.

If a group is to cross and you are the first, when you reach the other side attach your end of the rope to a tree or boulder. Each following person should be tied to the main rope by a loop. If you are the last to cross, unfasten the rope and wind it around your body as you advance.

Taking shelter

Do not continue walking if you encounter heavy rain or snow. Hints on how to recognise the approach of bad weather are given on pp. 40–1. If you realise that a storm is imminent it is usually better to take shelter and wait for conditions to improve. Find a spot sheltered from the prevailing wind by high ground or a cliff, but not directly under a tree or inside a cave. Use your equipment to make a seat rather than sitting on the bare ground, sit with your feet together and knees drawn up beneath your chin, and wait.

If the sky is dark and you feel a 'prickling' sensation in your scalp, or hear a buzzing noise from nearby rocks or any metal objects you are carrying, it may be that a violent thunderstorm is about to begin. Lightning is attracted to high projections, so bear this in mind when you seek shelter.

If the wind speed increases and it begins to snow, there may be a full blizzard on the way, with freezing temperatures, a gale-force wind, and snow so intense as to reduce visibility virtually to zero in a 'white-out'. At the first hint of a blizzard start at once to make for lower ground and safety. If the blizzard begins and you are caught, seek shelter nearby. Do not try to continue in any direction.

You can walk in fog if you are careful. Trust your compass. Walk on a planned heading. Measure the distance you cover in each stride, count your steps, and use this to estimate your progress. The method of navigating by plotting your heading and the distance covered from your last known position is called 'dead reckoning'. Before the days of radar and radio beacons, ships and aircraft used it regularly, and it is fairly reliable. When you do see objects you can identify, note their position and use this to plot your own. You may find it helpful in keeping to a compass heading if two people do the navigating. Have one 'navigator' walk ahead of the other, just in sight, and following the heading. Stop from time to time to allow the second navigator to take a bearing on the first. This should make doubly sure that you walk in a straight line.

When you cannot go on or back

It may be that weather conditions deteriorate to such an extent that you cannot go on. Nor should you try to continue after dusk, unless you are on a road or very clear path; you are benighted and must look for somewhere to spend the night. Always stop if it could be dangerous to continue. Even in winter you should be able to survive in the open for one night provided you are properly equipped.

Look for a place that is sheltered from the wind. If there are loose rocks use them to build a windbreak. If the ground is covered with thick snow you can use that for shelter. Where there are deep drifts, hollow out a cave with a small entrance. If there are no drifts, clear the snow to make a hollow down to the ground surface, and use the snow you have removed to make walls around your hollow.

If you have a tent, pitch it inside the stone or snow walls you have made, or in the sheltered place you have chosen. Use rocks to secure the guy-ropes if the ground is too hard for pegs, but be sure the guys are held firmly or the tent may blow away in the night.

Spending the night in the open without a tent is called bivouacking, and if you have no tent that is what you must do. Use a groundsheet or plastic raincoat to make some kind of roof over your head. Unfasten your belt and loosen your boot laces. Put on all your warm clothing, with a layer of dry clothes next to your skin. Any additional garments that you cannot get on should be wrapped around yourself. Use coiled rope or your rucksack as a cushion: with some insulation below you, less heat will be lost from your body. If you have a survival or 'bivvy' (slang for bivouac) bag, climb into it. Survival bags are made from heavy-duty polythene and are completely windproof and waterproof.

Plan to eat your emergency rations at intervals through the night, then stick to the plan.

If it is very cold, try not to fall asleep. Get up every so often and exercise by walking around, stamping your feet, and swinging your arms. When you sleep your body temperature, heartbeat and respiration rate all fall. You may not be able to afford this drop.

Provided you do not panic, have adequate clothing and a survival bag, and are reasonably healthy, you will come to no harm.

Illness and Injury

Take a first-aid manual with you. The one issued jointly by the St John Ambulance Association, the St Andrew's Ambulance Association and the British Red Cross Society is excellent, inexpensive, and will fit easily into a pocket. Follow its instructions. The basic requirements for a first-aid kit are listed on the facing page.

When you plan to lead a party of walkers, try to include in the group someone trained in first aid. If you intend to walk in the open country often, go to first-aid classes yourself and become qualified.

First aid

Basic first-aid equipment

adhesive sterile wound dressings, in small, medium and large sizes
non-adhesive absorbent dressings
Steri-strip dressings
sticking plaster
ordinary bandages
crêpe bandage
triangular bandage (unbleached)

sterilised eye-pad
cotton wool
safety pins
aspirin or paracetamol
mild disinfectant (e.g. TCP)
insect repellent cream
cream for treating insect bites

The person in charge of the first-aid equipment must find out whether any member of the party is taking medication or has special medical needs.

Exposure

People can suffer from exposure in Britain at any time of year. In some areas they are more liable to do so in summer than in winter, because in summer they are likely to be less prepared. The condition is dangerous and must be treated at once. Look out for it in yourself and members of your party if the temperature is below about 3°C (37°F), especially if there is a cold wind. Exposure may occur if you remain in one place for any length of time, as you might if you were studying some feature of the environment. Expect it if you become wet.

The early symptoms are:
• a slowing down of physical and mental responses;
• irritability;
• signs of unreasonable speech or behaviour;
• difficulty in speaking or seeing;
• repeated stumbling;
• cramp or shivering.

Stop at once, find shelter from the wind, and rest. Lie the patient down and use warm clothing, a sleeping bag, and a survival bag to prevent any further loss of body heat. Give the patient energy foods and a warm drink. Do not proceed until he or she has rested and is warm again.

Someone suffering from prolonged exposure, after having waited a long time in the open to be rescued, for example, must be treated in this way, but urgent medical help is also necessary and the patient may have to be carried to it. The patient will feel extremely cold to the touch, breathing will be slow and shallow, and the pulse will be slow and weak, perhaps very weak indeed.

Frostbite

Frostbite to exposed parts of the body may occur without symptoms of exposure. The affected part will be white and feel numb. It may be stiff and painful. Warm it quickly but gently, without rubbing or the use of a hot-water bottle or fire, and restore the circulation to it. Unless it is treated, frostbite can lead to gangrene.

Heat exhaustion

In hot weather, if a member of your party is pale and feels exhausted, is sweating, is breathing rapidly and has a rapid pulse, he or she may be suffering from heat exhaustion. The patient may also have cramp and feel faint, or actually faint, after standing or sitting up quickly.

Take him or her to the shade – the cooler the better – and administer water. You may add a little sugar (one teaspoon of sugar to the litre). If the sufferer sweats only a little, complains of headache or dizziness, is restless and has a high pulse and respiratory rate, the problem is lack of water.

Take him or her into the shade and administer cool drinks.

Heatstroke

Heatstroke is more extreme. The patient passes urine frequently, is very restless, complains of the heat, of headache and of dizziness, and has hot, dry skin. This condition may lead very quickly to a deep coma.

Strip the patient, wrap him or her in wet, cold cloth and keep the cloth wet until the body temperature falls and the patient appears to recover. Then remove the wet cloth and cover the patient loosely with dry garments.

A person who has suffered from heat exhaustion or heatstroke must have professional medical attention as soon as possible.

Cramp

Cramp is an involuntary shortening of a muscle. The remedy is to stretch the muscle and gently massage it.

If the cramp is in the thigh, straighten the leg so that it is rigid, and push the thigh forward.

If it is in the calf, straighten the leg and stand on the ball of the foot or twist the foot up towards the shin.

If it is in a hand or foot forcibly straighten the fingers or toes.

Snake bites

Adders are fairly common on the heaths and mountainsides of Britain. They are not aggressive, never look for trouble, and will not stalk you, leap at you from ambush, or drop on you from an overhanging branch or ledge. If one bites it is because you have violated its civil liberties, by trying to pick it up or by treading on it – in which case it may strike you in the ankle, lower leg, or through your boot.

Very few people ever die from the bite of an adder, but it is painful, the affected part swells, and patients are often terrified. It is not unknown for someone to die from fright.

Reassure the patient.

Administer a mild painkiller, such as aspirin, but nothing stronger.

Use soap and water to wash away any venom from the skin around the two small puncture marks that comprise the wound.

Cover the wound with a sterile dressing.

Immobilise the limb as best you can, keep it lower than heart level, and if it is a leg do not allow the patient to walk on it.

Seek medical help. If this means you have to travel, the patient must be carried if the bite is in a leg or foot.

A stretcher improvised from poles, coats and jackets and belts.

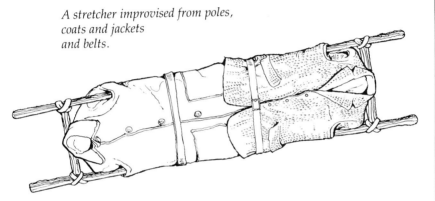

Shock

Anyone who has been injured or badly frightened may suffer from shock and this must be treated. If the shock is emotional the patient may faint and the pulse will be slow. If the shock is due to injury the patient may exhibit some or all of the following symptoms:

- feeling of giddiness or blurring of vision;
- collapse;
- paleness, possibly extreme;
- sweating;
- cold, clammy skin;
- shallow, rapid breathing;
- fast, weak pulse, perhaps becoming weaker;
- anxiety;
- yawning and restlessness, which may indicate serious loss of blood.

Reassure the patient and treat any injury. Do not move him or her unnecessarily while treating injuries. Seek professional help as quickly as possible. Protect the patient with a blanket or similar covering but on no account allow the body temperature to rise above normal. Insulate the patient with something between him or her and the ground.

Broken bones

If a bone breaks the patient or someone else may hear the snap as it fractures. There may be obvious deformity, for example with a limb that bends between joints. The affected part of the body will be painful, movement will increase the pain, and in the case of a limb control of movement will be lost. If in doubt, assume that the limb is broken.

Immobilise the limb by tying it to the body or to a splint. Never place a bandage or fastening over the site of a fracture, but tie the limb above and below the injury and, if appropriate, above and below the two joints on either side so that they are immobilised too. Make sure knots are always over the sound part of the body or the splint. If you use a splint, wrap it in padding. Place padding between exposed skin surfaces that will be held together.

If the injury is to the face or jaw make sure the patient can breathe. If the jaw is broken tie a scarf or strip of cloth around the jaw and head to hold the mouth closed. Do not leave the patient alone as he or she may vomit and the cloth will need to be removed.

If the spine is broken keep the patient warm and seek help. Do not attempt to move the patient except under the supervision of someone fully qualified in first aid.

Applying splints to immobilise a fracture.

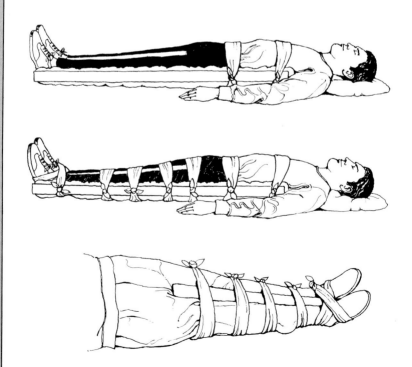

Bruises, strains, sprains, dislocation

Rest the affected part of the body. Massage it gently. Encourage the patient to move it. Support it if necessary by bandaging it.

Swelling may be reduced by applying a cold compress, made by wetting a cloth, squeezing out surplus water, applying it gently, and keeping it wet.

If the injury seems severe and you are in doubt, assume that there is a fracture and treat accordingly. A sprain may cause acute pain, sudden swelling, and loss of limb movement, and an apparent sprain may mask a fracture.

Support a sprained joint, control the swelling with a cold compress, and seek professional help. If in doubt, treat the injury as a fracture.

Do not attempt to correct a dislocated joint. Immobilise the limb and make the patient as comfortable as possible and seek professional help.

Bandages.

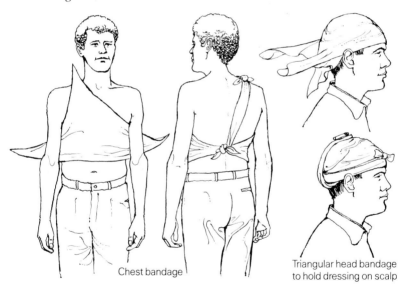

Chest bandage

Triangular head bandage
to hold dressing on scalp

Burns, scalds

Reduce the heat, if possible by immersing the affected part in cold water, preferably running, for at least ten minutes or until the pain has been relieved. After that keep it dry and clean.

Remove or loosen any rings, belt, boot, or other article of clothing that might cause constriction of the affected part.

Do not apply any ointment or lotion, and if the injury should be covered to prevent infection, cover it with a clean, dry dressing only.

Never prick a blister.

Reassure the patient, who may have been badly frightened. Give small sips of a cold drink.

Unconsciousness

Make sure the patient can breathe freely. Check frequently to make sure the airway is not blocked. Allow plenty of fresh air. Do not let people crowd around.

Loosen all clothing. Lie the patient on his or her stomach with the head turned to the right, the left leg straight, the right leg flexed so the knee approximately makes a right angle, and both arms flexed so the hands are level with the head and pointing forward.

If breathing stops, resuscitate at once.

Do not heat the patient. If consciousness returns, moisten the lips with fluid, but otherwise allow no drinks. Ask the patient questions to determine the level of consciousness: can she or he answer you coherently?

Check for injuries and, if necessary and possible, treat them.

Get help.

Artificial respiration

Mouth-to-mouth ventilation and external chest compression are specialised skills which must be taught in practice. Learn how to do them from your local St John Ambulance or Red Cross.

Cardiopulmonary resuscitation.

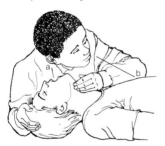

1. Tilt the head back and lift the chin to keep the airway open. Feel for breathing (a) and for pulse (b).

2. Seal your mouth over patient's mouth, pinch his nose to close it, and exhale into his lungs. Let air escape and repeat.

3. After two breaths check for pulse.

4. If no pulse, interlock fingers of both hands, place hands on patient's chest 5cm (2 inches) above the notch where the ribs divide, hold your elbows locked, and rock back and forth. Depress patient's chest about 5cm, about 80–100 times per minute. After 15 compressions inflate lungs twice.

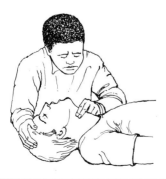

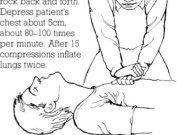

PART II

CLUES IN THE COUNTRYSIDE

6

THE BUILDING OF BRITAIN

Many of us would like the British countryside to be unchanging. It should provide us with a sense of permanence, we feel, a firm foundation on which we can rely amid the constant turmoil of our ordinary lives. It must be there when we need it for reassurance, and always the same. When woods are cleared, roads built, hedgerows removed, many people object, and in most cases that is the reason. The rural landscape we knew when we were children, and that our parents and grandparents knew, is part of us, part of our personal history. Its alteration robs us of that history, leaving us with only memories of a past we are almost bound to consider better than the changed present. It is like rewriting history, and because we are not consulted when changes are made we feel that our privacy has been violated. There is some sense in which the countryside belongs to us all, and no individual or institution is entitled to damage it without our permission.

The feeling is not wrong. The countryside supplies us with food, timber, minerals and other raw materials, but it also provides habitats for our wildlife, places where we ourselves can be refreshed, and inspiration for painters and poets. There is a real sense in which it does belong to us all. We cannot prevent change. The landscape of Britain is not eternal. Paradoxically, it is its own history, and some of ours, written in it for those able to read the language it uses, that makes it one of the most interesting and valuable landscapes in the world.

Fields and woods

Almost all our worries about change in the landscape can be centred around fields and woods. We resent the removal of hedges to make larger fields, the clearance of broadleaved woodland and the planting of commercial stands of conifers. Large conifer plantations are a new invention. Indeed, the growing of trees of any kind in plantations to supply timber is a comparatively modern practice. A few small plantations were grown in the seventeenth century, but their total area did not exceed that of native woodland until the eighteenth century in Scotland and later than that in England. The big increase began in about the 1920s, following the establishment of the Forestry Commission, the statutory body charged with developing forests to provide a national stock of timber. Fields, on the other

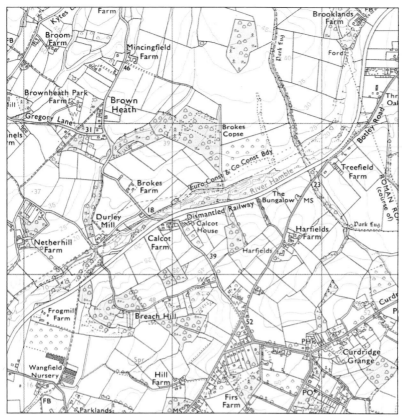

Market gardening, nr Botley, Hampshire, Pathfinder Map no. SU 41/51.

hand, have been altered repeatedly ever since people began farming in Britain, and that was about 5,000 years ago. That, too, was when our ancestors began clearing woodland.

The OS 1:25 000-scale Pathfinder series of maps shows field boundaries, and your reading of British landscape history should begin with them. You can even use them to see history being made now.

People who live in cities expect to be able to buy fresh vegetables. These have to be sold within hours of being harvested, and so many of the market gardens supplying them are close to the edge of the urban area. You can recognise them because their fields are very small. When the railway network was built, in the last century, many formerly remote places found themselves with good, fast links to the cities. Market gardens began to develop further from the cities and you can see them, too, if you follow railway lines away from the urban areas. Where the railway has closed, the market gardens may nevertheless still survive because today they can move their produce by road, but their position marks what used to be a railway line.

Many airfields were built during the Second World War, and abandoned when the war ended. Farmers began to graze animals on them, then to plough them. Runways and perimeter tracks deteriorated and eventually were removed, until nothing of the airfield remained – except its shape. Runways and old taxi-tracks are often visible from the air, and the shape of an airfield is usually recognisable on a map as a single large field, or pattern of fields, that very obviously does not fit into the surrounding field pattern. The countryside remembers the war long after all trace of it has been obliterated in the cities.

The history of fields

Look at the general size and shape of fields. They will tell you something of the age of the farming pattern, and of the kind of farming being practised today. Modern farm machines, especially combine harvesters, are large and need plenty of room in which to work, so they require large fields. They are used in the production of arable crops, crops that are grown in fields, such as cereals, peas, beans used to feed livestock, and these days oilseed rape. These machines cannot work on land that slopes too steeply. The machinery used to cut and process grass, however, is smaller and can work on rather steeper slopes. For part of the year most fields bearing grass have livestock grazing them, and if the grass is not to be cut, the animals can graze on very steep slopes. It is also more convenient to keep livestock in smaller fields. So large fields on more or less level ground are likely to be growing arable crops; small fields on sloping ground are likely to be growing grass.

If the fields are very regular in shape, and more or less square or rectangular, they are likely to be modern. If they are very large indeed, with approximately straight sides 1.5 km (one mile) or more long, they are very modern and part of the open 'prairie' landscape that has been formed since about 1960. Such fields grow arable crops, in many cases wheat for humans or barley to feed livestock. If the fields are smaller than this, but still very regular in shape, they were probably made during the eighteenth or nineteenth centuries, when changes in farming led to the enclosure of open land to make arable fields. The enclosures were authorised by Acts of Parliament and this, combined with the people's love of geometry at the time, accounts for their shape. In Northamptonshire more than half the open land was enclosed, but in Somerset the figure was only 3.5 per cent, in Essex just over 2 per cent, and in Shropshire less than 1 per cent. Some counties were not affected at all.

The fields were made by planting hedges, often of hawthorn, or in some parts of the country by building walls, but before those enclosures the land was open, much like a modern arable farming landscape. Enclosing the open landscape led to protests just as strong as those that oppose the removal of hedgerows today.

The plough patterns show how these enclosure fields ignore the boundaries of older medieval fields.

Fields more than about two hundred years old are usually small and often, but not always, of irregular shape. A pattern of irregular, small fields usually suggests that the land was once forested. The fields were made a few at a time as trees were removed, and have retained their shape ever since. Such fields may date back to the sixteenth or seventeenth century.

Medieval fields

Small, narrow rectangular fields may have been made on an even older landscape, especially if you find them in central England, where that older farming system was established most strongly. When the Normans arrived in Britain they inherited the Saxon system of land ownership and tenure, and probably the field pattern associated with it. There were many local variations, but in general three kinds of farmland prevailed. Near to a village fields were laid out in long, narrow strips. Each strip grew a crop in some years and in others was left fallow, according to definite rules. Some were permanent pasture. Each strip was owned by one of the village farmers, but they were worked collectively. After they had been harvested, and while they lay fallow, they were grazed by livestock. Beyond the strips were larger fields used only for grazing, and beyond them again was the 'waste'. This was uncultivated land

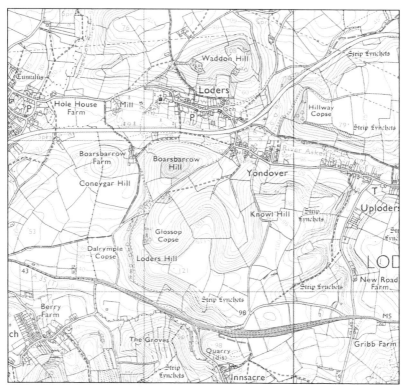

Strip fields, nr Bridport, Dorset. Pathfinder Map no. SY 49/59.

belonging to the landlord, where village farmers were allowed to graze their animals or collect fuel. They held the right to do so in common, a right formalised by Norman law. They were declared 'commoners' and the land was 'common land'. It was a kind of reserve, a resource that could be used as it was needed to augment what the commoners produced from their own land.

Later, after the medieval farming system had disappeared, many of these old fields were subdivided by hedges or walls. More recent changes may have removed those subdivisions, yet in places the old medieval pattern can still be seen. This is because of the way the strips were cultivated, and the long period during which the farming system endured without change. You can see it today at Laxton (NG reference SK 725670) in Nottinghamshire, south of Tuxford.

Because crops were rotated on the strips, year after year and century after century, each strip had to be ploughed separately. This was done by making a furrow first down the centre, throwing the earth to one side. The plough would be turned and would make a second furrow parallel to the first, so the earth was heaped against the earth from the first furrow. After that the plough worked parallel to the existing furrows, up one side, across the top – the 'headland' –

and down the other, always throwing earth towards the centre of the strip. This created a ridge at the centre and a furrow along either side of the strip, because when the ploughman reached the edges of the strip he moved to the centre of the next strip to start again. There was always a furrow at either side of each strip, and always a ridge at the centre, and over many ploughings these became permanent features. Where you see long, straight ridges, running parallel to one another, with depressions evenly spaced between them, you may be looking at what was once a medieval farm.

Roman fields

The medieval system may have been constructed on an even earlier pattern, dating back to Roman or even prehistoric times, traces of which can still be found. Look on the map for a very regular grid pattern of fields and see whether parish boundaries follow field edges rather than crossing fields. Parish boundaries were established a very long time ago, and where a field lies across one the field is more recent than the boundary. Check the dimensions of the fields, because anything designed to a grid must conform to some sensible unit of measurement. If you find that the pattern looks old because boundaries respect it, yet it seems not to be based

These fields, in East Sussex, may have been laid out in Roman times. Pathfinder Map no. TQ 41/51.

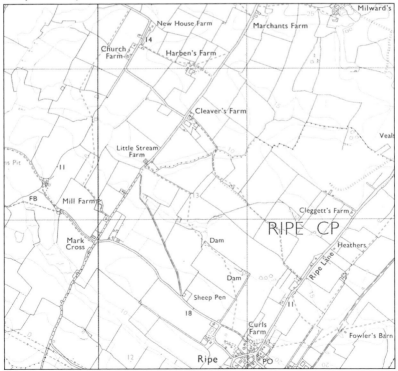

on any very obvious unit of yards (1 yard = 0.914 m), chains (22 yards or 20 m), or acres (1 acre = 4840 square yards, or about 4050 square metres), then the layout could have been designed by the Romans. The field layout near the village of Ripe in East Sussex is a possible example of Roman fields.

Pre-Roman fields

You are most likely to see evidence of ancient farming systems where that evidence is most difficult to erase. A thorn hedge can be removed, the land ploughed, and in time all trace of it may disappear. A stone wall is more difficult to remove, and the 'hedges' of Cornwall are the most difficult of all. They are made as substantial stone walls topped with earth or turf so in time they are covered with vegetation. Old evidence also survives in Cornwall, Devon, Kent and Lancashire because no land was enclosed in these counties by Act of Parliament in the eighteenth or nineteenth century. Even after it has been removed a Cornish hedge often remains visible as a ridge.

The older system also divided land into three kinds. A farm settlement lay at the centre, so the first thing to find is a farm or small village that has some claim to being pre-Roman. Look for a holy well, a standing stone or some other pre-Christian relic. Around the settlement there were small, irregular fields, used to grow crops and to keep animals. They were farmed all the time and were often very fertile because they received most of the animal manure. The Cornish name for them is *gew*, and it may survive in a place name. Beyond these small 'in-fields' were the larger 'out-fields', called *gweal* in Cornish, or sometimes *parc*. They were farmed in rotation. Beyond them again was the 'waste', the unfarmed land, which was often moor. Everyone worked out from the buildings at the centre, and so they tended to surround themselves with concentric circles. If you find what might be an ancient centre, surrounded by an irregular patchwork of small fields and beyond them a circle of larger fields, you could be looking at a pre-Roman farm. Even if you can no longer find the whole pattern, a group of fields lying side by side whose outer edge forms the arc of a circle may have been made 2000 years ago.

The wasteland may be called a forest. This does not mean necessarily that trees grow on it because the word 'forest' comes originally from the Latin *foris*, which means 'outside'. The 'forest' was the land outside the walls or hedges of the enclosed land, and it was reserved for hunting. Dartmoor Forest is not wooded today, and it was not wooded when it earned its name. It was an area set aside for the royal hunt. Most of Sherwood Forest is not wooded, either, and even in the days of Robin Hood (supposing he was a real person) it was not densely wooded: it was heathland with some woods on it.

Pre-Roman fields, still in use in West Cornwall, with the site of a Roman-British courtyard and house settlement.

Land hunger

Where the good farm land of the valleys gives way to open hillside or moor you may find traces of fortunes won and lost in the past. Naturally enough, farmers prefer to cultivate the best land, but in times of hardship when other trades disappear, anyone may have to turn a hand to farming in a desperate attempt to earn a crust. When farming is very prosperous and incomes high, the farmers themselves may wish to expand. They have been expanding during the last twenty years and that is why we worry so much today about their hunger for more and more land to plough. In the past non-farmers forced into trying to grow food, or farmers seeking expansion, usually moved to the marginal land on the edges of moors or on hillsides. They cleared the bracken, carried stone to build walls, encouraged grass to grow, and kept livestock. Then, when times improved and the old, better-paid employment returned, or when farm prices fell and farmers contracted, the marginal fields were abandoned and the bracken returned. The recurring episodes of this hunger for land have left their mark, as broken walls or just ridges where walls used to be.

The human shaping of the British landscape has been going on for much longer than many people suppose, and on a much larger scale. At one time, it is true, most of lowland Britain was blanketed by forest, in the usual sense of extensive woodland, but that forest was cleared long ago, and it was cleared to provide land for farming. When William I commissioned Domesday, his great survey of land ownership and use, the *legati* who travelled the country in 1086 collecting the data recorded surprisingly little forest. There were few places where you could travel through forest in a straight line for more than about six miles without emerging on to farm land, and many villages had no woodland at all within easy reach. This was important to them because the forests were the main source of fuel and of many raw materials. Most of the original forest had gone, and England was a place of villages and farms with some woodland, rather than a forest with clearings. The main clearance probably took place in Roman and Saxon times.

Beneath the soil

Trees grow and farmers work on the uppermost surface of the land. They shape it, but in a purely cosmetic way. The real flesh is provided by the soil, or in some places its absence. The soil is mainly the product of the reaction between the climate and the underlying rock. Farming has been practised in Britain for about 5,000 years. The more ancient reaction has been going on for about 4600 million years, and it continues to this day.

Part of the Geological Survey Map no. 318/333, South Downs, East Sussex, showing the escarpment in the map on p. 46.

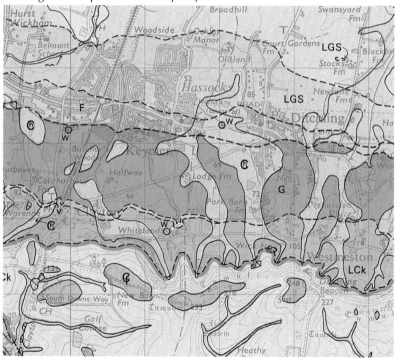

The British landscape is interesting, and valuable, not only because of the human history written on the face of it, but also because of the pre-human history of our planet which it records. It is here that much of the geological story of the Earth was unravelled, and it is an exciting story. Dinosaurs once walked this land. Hippos wallowed in the tropical swamps where later tenants built Trafalgar Square Mammoths roamed the Surrey tundra.

You can buy maps that show the geology of the whole of Britain. They are produced by the Geological Survey, based on 1:63,360, now being replaced by 1:50,000 Ordnance Survey maps, and they are published by the Ordnance Survey. There are also maps, produced by the Soil Survey, showing types of soil throughout the whole country, and still other maps that show various aspects of the geology of the seabed around Britain. If you decide to study the geological structure of the countryside in more detail, sooner or later you are likely to make use of them, but you need some knowledge of geology or pedology (the science of soils) to understand them.

Drifting continents

Changes in climate, producing tropical swamps at one time and glaciers at another, can be explained partly by the fact that Britain has wandered around the world in the course of its history. It was not always where it is now. The Earth consists of a hot, metallic, very dense core, surrounded by a thick *mantle* of hot, dense rock. Although it is so dense, its temperature and the pressure under which it is held make it plastic, so currents flow through it. At the surface, where heat can escape, it forms the solid rock of the crust. The crust 'floats' on the denser material beneath it as a number of pieces, or *plates*. There are seven major plates and several smaller ones. Where plates meet their edges may slide against one another, or one plate may ram the other, or one may ride over the top of the other. Or they may drift apart, or join permanently to form a new, larger plate. Where a plate moves in relation to its neighbour earthquakes are common, and *magma*, hot material from the upper mantle, may erupt at the surface as volcanoes. Where one plate rams another rocks are folded, twisted, and sometimes pushed upward to form mountains.

Where the crust is thinnest, and low-lying, it is covered by water and forms the bed of the oceans. Where it is thicker, but less dense, parts of it may protrude above the surface of the water, as continents. The constant movement of crustal plates means that continents wander, or 'drift'. At the present time the Atlantic Ocean, which did not exist at all 150 million years ago, is growing wider, and the Pacific Ocean is growing smaller. It is the collision of the North American and Nazca Plates with the Pacific Plate, in which one is disappearing beneath another, that causes the earthquakes along the west of North and South America.

Code of behaviour for geologists

If you are a geologist, a student of any of the geological sciences, or simply interested in rocks or minerals, you should observe the code of behaviour prepared by the Geologists' Association, on which the following guidelines are based. You can obtain copies of the full code from the Librarian, c/o Geology Department, University College London, Gower Street, London WC1E 6BT. The code is free, but please enclose a stamped addressed envelope.

- Observe the Country Code
- Always seek permission in advance before entering private land
- Leave machinery alone
- Do not leave rock fragments littering fields or roads; they could injure livestock or people, or damage vehicles
- Do not disturb wildlife more than you can help
- If you are visiting the coast, consult the coastguard service to learn of unstable cliffs or dangerous tides
- If you are visiting mountains, or going underground, make sure you have the proper equipment and experience; inform someone of your intended route and time of arrival; never go alone
- Do not disturb rock if it might fall on someone below
- Do not leave a site untidy or dangerous
- Do not hammer rocks indiscriminately
- Keep collecting to a minimum
- Do not remove fossils, rocks, or minerals that are *in situ* unless you really need them for serious study
- Collect samples only from places where they are abundant, or from scree, fallen rocks or waste tips
- Never collect samples from walls or buildings
- Always wear a safety helmet when visiting quarries
- If you are visiting a working quarry obtain permission in advance, ask the manager where you may go and what local dangers you must avoid, and make sure you understand signals used to warn of blasting
- Contact your local trust for nature conservation, field study centre, natural history society, or the nearest office of the Nature Conservancy Council to find out whether you can help in cleaning overgrown sites and assisting generally in the conservation of geological sites

About 400 million years ago, the land which is now England, Wales and Ireland probably lay in the tropics of the southern hemisphere, with Scotland separated from it by an ocean. They had joined together by about 300 million years ago, and lay on the Equator. Since then we have been drifting more or less due north. As we have done so we have experienced a humid tropical climate, we have been hot, dry desert, parts of what is now land have lain beneath the sea and, very recently indeed, most of Britain has been

Part of the Whin Sill – Hadrian's Wall and remains of a Roman frontier post.

covered by ice. How can we know this? How else are we to explain the large amounts of limestone, for example in Derbyshire, containing fossils of shellfish, fossils of tropical plants and animals found in coal – itself made from tropical vegetation – or sandstones reminiscent of deserts? How are we to explain the ripple marks, made by the sea just as it makes ripples on sandy beaches today, on rocks far inland?

The story of continents is mainly one of the rise and fall of mountains. Volcanoes erupt, collisions between plates crumple the crustal rocks as though they were cloth, and mountains are formed. At once the frost, wind and rain begin eroding them, wearing them away, and little by little they disappear as small particles. The particles settle, accumulating to great thickness, and where pressures and temperatures are sufficient they form new, sedimentary rocks. Eventually these are crumpled again by movements of great violence, and become mountains once more. Yet sometimes rocks remain from an earlier time, tough, little changed, surviving all the turmoil. In parts of the far north-west of Scotland, but mainly on Lewis, there are rocks more than 2500 million years old.

We live today on the Eurasian Plate, and well clear of its edges, but it was not always so. Hadrian's Wall was built along the top of the Whin Sill, a major escarpment running for miles across northern England. That sill may have marked the ancient edge of a plate long before Hadrian sought to keep out the unruly northerners. And long before the Atlantic Ocean appeared there was an earlier ocean,

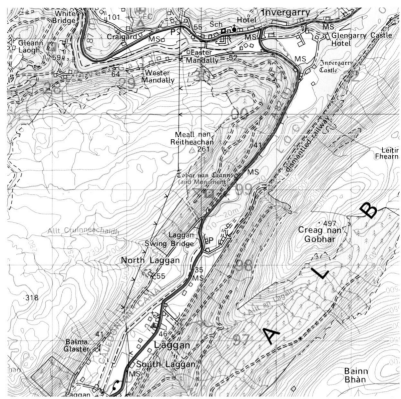

Glen Mor, Highlands, on the Great Glen Fault. Map no. 34.

called Iapetus, which may have had the Whin Sill as part of its coastline. (The Atlantic is named after Atlas, and Iapetus was his father.) The opening of the Atlantic produced a small continent between what are now Norway and Greenland. It disappeared at last, some 50 million years ago, and today all that remains of it is Rockall.

The Whin Sill is not the only ancient plate margin you can find in Britain. The Moine Thrust, in Sutherland, and the Great Glen (Glen More) Fault south-east of it, which runs right across Scotland from Loch Linnhe and Fort William to Inverness, may also mark old boundaries. The plates have merged and there is no more move-ment at their margins, but they have left weaknesses in the crust that now and then give one of the little shudders we feel as minor earthquakes. Our volcanoes no longer erupt, which is as well because the most famous of them is Arthur's Seat, dominating Edinburgh.

It was a collision between plates associated with the closing of the Iapetus Ocean, some 400 million years ago, that raised the moun-tains of the Scottish Highlands, an event known as the Caledonian orogeny. An 'orogeny' is the raising of a new mountain range. The smaller hills of Wales and the Lake District of England were formed at the same time. This collision occurred on a roughly north-east–south-west line. In south-west England the effect was to allow magma to intrude beneath the overlying rocks to form great masses of granites, harder than the surrounding rocks. As the rocks above and around them were weathered away the more resistant granites remained. Today these are the granite moors: Dartmoor, Bodmin Moor, and the smaller moors to the west that provide Cornwall with its china clay and other minerals.

Later southern England was affected by thrusting from the south, along an east–west line, and more recently still, a mere 10 or 20 million years ago, the Downs, running across much of southern England, and the Chiltern Hills were formed as ripples on the edge of the orogeny that raised the Alps.

Changing sea-levels

Land rises and falls, and so does the sea. At present the north of Britain is rising, the south-east is sinking, and the sea-level may be rising. The rise in sea-level is most probably due to the fact that for several years the climate has been growing warmer in the northern hemisphere, so the sea has warmed and, being warmer, has expanded to occupy a greater volume. The rise and fall of the land is the after-effect of the last ice age, which ended about 12,000 years ago. The ice sheets were 1.5 km or more thick, and very heavy. The weight of the ice depressed the crust beneath it and the more plastic mantle material was displaced. When the ice melted the weight was removed and gradually the rocks are returning to their former level. Land is also subsiding in the south-east of England as soft rock is eroded by the sea.

Large ice sheets are made from water, a great deal of it. The water falls as snow, is trapped as ice, and so is prevented from returning to the sea and the sea-level falls. As it does so more land is exposed. At one time the sea-level around Britain was more than 130 m lower than it is today. The Shetlands and Orkneys were hills rising above dry land extending all the way northward from Scotland. The Irish Sea, Western Approaches, English Channel and North Sea were all dry land. Beyond the edges of the ice, where water can exist as a liquid, rivers flow, and in their lower reaches, where the gradient is shallow, large rivers become slow and meandering. Where the river bends the flow of water cuts away the bank on the outside of the bend, and silt is deposited on the inside of the bend, so that the bend itself is advancing the whole time as the river creates a swathe of silt deposit across a plain. If it carries enough water the river may divide into several streams near to its mouth, and form a delta. If the sea level then rises, the huge valley made by the estuary will be flooded, or 'drowned'. A drowned valley is called a *ria*, and there are many of them around the coasts of southern England.

Records of the ice

Moving glaciers carve valleys of their own, and there are many glacial valleys in the uplands of northern England and Scotland. A mountain river cuts a V-shaped valley; a glacier cuts a broad, U-shaped one. Where a river flows through a valley that is smoothly rounded and much too wide for the amount of water being carried, the valley was probably made by a glacier and the river is merely following the easiest route.

In hollows among the hills ice may be trapped by accumulating below the level of the surrounding terrain, so that it cannot flow away and escape. Through repeated freezing and thawing at its edges the ice in such a hollow may crack pieces of rock away from its base and banks. This enlarges and deepens the hollow, to form a *cirque*. When the ice melts it may remain as a mountain lake or tarn.

Like rivers, glaciers are fed by tributaries. Where a tributary joins the main stream, provided the bed of the tributary is lower than the surface of the main stream, ice will flow. The bed of the main stream is often very much deeper. When the glaciers all disappear they leave behind a pattern of deep, main valleys with smaller valleys feeding into them but joining high up on their sides, sometimes ending in a sheer drop. These are called *hanging valleys*, and where rivers flow through them they often join their main streams as waterfalls.

The lochs of Highland Scotland and the lakes of the Lake District were all formed by glaciers. As a glacier moves, its great weight scours the underlying rock. It ends where the ice descends to an altitude where summer temperatures are high enough to melt it, and because water flows much more rapidly than ice, the glacier loses material. It becomes lighter, and no longer has the power to carve its valley ever deeper. The ice behind it still has that power, and continues to advance, and so the end of the glacier moves the only way it can. It starts to ride up over the rocks, and actually goes uphill. The end of a glacier is called the 'snout' for this reason. The valley at the snout is deepened, but closed at the end, and when the ice melts it remains as a long, narrow lake. In fact it is a flooded glacial valley.

The material scoured out by a glacier, much of it consisting of large boulders, is carried as far as the snout, but obviously it can be carried no further, so it is deposited there as a *moraine*. As the glacier retreats, what actually happens is that the ice melts at a higher and higher level. That is where the moraine occurs, following the retreating glacier back towards its source, but the amount of moraine decreases because the shorter the glacier the less material it can collect. You can find moraine material from the edge of the last ice sheet along a line from Essex to Bristol, but wherever you find loose rocks of a different type from the solid bedrock beneath them you can be fairly certain they have been transported by a glacier.

The coastline of NW Europe when ice-age sea-levels were at their lowest.
(Right) *Britain as it would appear were the sea to rise 80m.*

The tundra

Beyond the edge of the ice there lies the *tundra*, a region of sparse, stunted vegetation growing above a layer of permafrost – permanently frozen ground. Each summer the uppermost layer of ground thaws, the water in it flows, and it may carry soil with it, as mud moving quite slowly downhill. Any large boulders left on the surface in earlier times by a glacier will also slide a little further downhill each summer, their movement lubricated by the soft, slippery mud below them. If the ground warms more, however, the permafrost itself will melt, the surplus water will drain away more quickly, and the process will be halted, as though time itself had been stopped, waiting until the cold weather returns. You can see landscapes like this on upland moors, most clearly on Dartmoor.

Will the ice return? Most scientists believe that it will, that today we are living through a brief period of warm weather between two ice ages. Other scientists begin to fear that the future may be even more alarming. If the climate continues to grow warmer, as it seems to be growing warmer now, in time the polar icecaps may melt. Were they to do so, sea-levels would rise further, perhaps by as much as 80 m, and the sea would cover all land lower than that. England would become a group of islands, the most northerly of them including southern Scotland, Wales would be one island, and the remainder of Scotland would be two islands, or perhaps three. Many of our major cities would disappear. Is it likely? No one can tell, but it is possible.

History is not only recorded in documents and in the pages of books. It is written into the land itself, and as you travel the countryside you can read its fascinating story.

· 7 ·
PLANTS AND PEOPLE

For two million years the ice sheets have advanced across Britain and then retreated again several times. With each advance the soil beneath the ice has been scoured away and such communities of plants and animals as may have lived there have been utterly destroyed. Each retreat has left a bare, barren landscape. Yet even during the deepest part of each long glacial episode a few areas have been missed. The ice did not always reach everywhere, and vegetation from an earlier time occasionally survived.

On the Lizard Peninsula, in southern Cornwall, you may find an unusual kind of heather, Cornish heath (*Erica vagans*). It grows about 80 cm (30 in) tall and in summer it bears white or pale pink or lilac flowers with protruding dark purple or brown anthers. Or you may see the small pink or lilac flowers of the pale butterwort (*Pinguicula lusitanica*). If you are a keen botanist and search hard you could find seventeen different species of clover and, indeed, you might notice the great profusion of flowering plants, some of which are rare elsewhere, even in the rest of Cornwall. The plants of the Lizard are like those you might find in parts of south-west Ireland, or in Spain and Portugal. They are classed as a 'Lusitanian' flora, typical of a warm, oceanic climate. Probably they were much more widely distributed during the Hoxnian Interglacial, a period of warm weather that lasted for some 40,000 years and ended perhaps 250,000 years ago. There have been two full-scale ice ages since then, but the Lusitanian plants of the Lizard survived both of them. They are reminders of a time long ago, even earlier than the Ipswichian (or Trafalgar Square) Interglacial, at its warmest about 100,000 years ago, when elephants, rhinoceroses and hippopotami lived in what is now London. They have gone, and the plants associated with them, but the Lusitanian flora of the Hoxnian survives.

Tundra landscapes

During the glaciations nothing grew on the ice itself, but around its edges the landscape must have looked very much as parts of Greenland look today. Below the surface the ground was frozen permanently, but in summer the topmost layer would thaw and for a short time plants could grow, flower and set seed. There were grasses, sedges and many herbs, plants such as alpine meadow-rue

☐ Approximate limit of the Weichsel glaciation

▨ Approximate limit of the Wolstonian glaciation

▩ Approximate limit of the Anglian glaciation

▨ Areas of the country untouched by glaciation

Limits reached by the ice sheets during the last three glaciations. The Anglian was the earliest, followed by the Hoxnian Interglacial. Then came the Wolstonian, followed by the Ipswichian (or Trafalgar Square) Interglacial. The most recent, Devensian (or Weichsel) glaciation ended about 10,000 years ago. We are now in the Flandrian Interglacial.

Where to see the past vegetation of Britain

Tundra landscape	Upper Teesdale, Co. Durham
Caledonian Forest	Rothiemurchus Forest, in the Cairngorms National Nature Reserve; the Glen Affric Forestry Commission nature reserve; the slopes above Loch Maree, in the Benn Eighe National Nature Reserve
Holly woods	New Forest; Epping Forest; Staverton Park, Suffolk; Stiperstones Forest, Shropshire
Natural broadleaved woodland	Coltswood Beechwoods, Gloucestershire; Coed Llyn Mair woods, near Ffestiniog in Gwynedd; Kingley Vale National Nature Reserve, Sussex; The Men's woods, Sussex
Stone Age industrial site	Grimes Graves, Norfolk; Breckland around nearby Hockham Mere
Early farm land	The chalk downs
Medieval royal forest	New Forest, Epping Forest, Forest of Dean, Wyre Forest

(*Thalictrum alpinum*), but few shrubs and even fewer trees. Here and there you might have seen some juniper shrubs, or small willows, or the dwarf birch (*Betula nana*), all of which are plants of the tundra. Some of the herbs produced bright flowers; they included mountain avens (*Dryas octopetala*) and purple saxifrage (*Saxifraga oppositifolia*).

As the weather grew warmer these tundra plants were replaced, but they did not disappear entirely. Temperatures decrease the higher the latitude, but they also decrease the higher the altitude, and while glacial conditions vanished from the lowlands, in the mountains something very like them survived, and survives still. If you want to see what a British periglacial tundra landscape may have been like you can find it in the highlands, in the mountains of Scotland or North Wales, above the tree line. There is one place, however, that escaped the ice and where 3500 hectares (more than 8500 acres) of land remain much as they were during the last glaciation, complete with their tundra vegetation. Upper Teesdale National Nature Reserve, County Durham, is 26 km (16 miles) north-east of Barnard Castle, and the grid reference of the visitor centre (Bowlees Visitor Centre) is NY 907283. You can obtain explanatory leaflets at the Centre, and the nature reserve is open to the public provided you keep to the paths.

The first trees

Draw a line from the River Thames to the Severn and 11,000 years ago most of the land to the north of the line was covered by ice, and the land to the south was tundra. Britain was still joined to continental Europe, of course. The last – or, more correctly, most recent – of the glaciations is called the Devensian, and by 10,000 years ago it was coming to an end. The glaciers were retreating, new land was being revealed, and the meltwaters flowed as rivers, sparkling, pure and cold. The ground itself was thawing so deeper roots could penetrate it, and seeds from the south, blown by the wind or dropped by birds, could germinate to produce plants that might live. Trees began to return.

The first to establish itself was the birch: not the dwarf birch of the tundra, which is no more than a shrub, but the true tree birches, downy birch (*Betula pubescens*) and silver birch (*B. pendula*). Birch is a vigorous coloniser of open ground. Its seeds are tiny enough to be carried by the wind and the tree produces vast quantities of them. When they germinate the trees can tolerate cold and all but the wettest or most acid soils. If you had visited Britain about 9000 years ago you would have seen extensive birch woodlands. It was not long, however, before the birches were joined by Scots pine (*Pinus sylvestris*), and the birch woods became great birch and pine forests.

The glaciers were retreating northward and warmer conditions were advancing from the south, so the whole vegetational pattern was slowly migrating northward. This is less obvious than it may sound. If a plant can grow once conditions improve, a further improvement in conditions is unlikely to harm it. You can grow birch and pine perfectly well today in southern England, so why did the forests disappear? There are two answers. Some plants, including juniper and birch, can tolerate many things, but they must have plenty of sunlight. Juniper grows in periglacial and mountain environments as a shrub. If the temperature rises it grows larger, eventually into a small tree, but if other plants arrive, and neighbours grow faster and taller, the juniper is shaded out, and in time it vanishes. Birch, too, cannot tolerate being shaded.

Pine fell victim to wetter weather, which led to its poisoning. Its needles decompose only very slowly, and so tend to accumulate on the forest floor, where they are joined by fallen dead trees and other vegetation. This accumulation, on poorly drained land with a high rainfall, created perfect conditions for the development of acid bogs, and waterlogged soil together with high acidity killed the trees.

The forests were also being cleared by humans, almost from the start, and pine, with its long, straight stems found many uses. If shading by new arrivals and changing soil conditions are one reason for the replacement of one kind of vegetation by another, human interference is the other, and in the long run the more influential.

Remnant of the Caledonian Forest.

Eventually the birch and pine forests disappeared from southern England, but they survived in parts of Scotland, and remnants of them are there still. When the Roman historian Cornelius Tacitus (about AD 56–120) described Britain he gave that forest the name it has borne ever since: the Caledonian Forest. Today Scots pine is grown in many forestry plantations, and in places the modern conifer plantations merge with the original forest, but you can see what the Caledonian Forest may have been like if you visit Rothiemurchus Forest, in the Cairngorms National Nature Reserve, the Glen Affric Forestry Commission nature reserve, or the slopes above Loch Maree, in the Benn Eighe National Nature Reserve.

Arrival of broadleaved trees

Hazel (*Corylus avellana*) arrived about 9500 years ago, followed by aspen (*Populus tremula*) and rowan (*Sorbus aucuparia*) about 9000 years ago, and by about 8000 years ago the British forests included wych-elm (*Ulmus glabra*) and oak (*Quercus*, but it is impossible to tell which species). By 7500 years ago holly (*Ilex aquifolium*) was growing in Scotland. Holly woods were once common, but today you will find only small patches, for example in the New Forest. Holly is an important indicator of climate. It is a broadleaved evergreen tree, and such species occur mainly in low latitudes, where the ground does not freeze for long in winter and so deprive the plants of moisture. Holly conserves water by having thick, waxy leaves that do not lose their moisture readily, but even so it thrives only in an oceanic climate and cannot tolerate drought, so its spread across Britain suggests that the climate was becoming milder and wetter.

The Atlantic Forest

In fact the climate was moving towards a long warm period, called the Atlantic Period. This lasted for about 2500 years and as it developed more broadleaved trees arrived. Small-leaved lime, or winter linden (*Tilia cordata*), one of the early arrivals, began to spread about 7500 years ago. This lime is another tree that prefers warm weather, and at about the time it began to spread the broadleaved lime (*T. platyphyllos*) arrived. Britain was still linked to continental Europe, remember, and the forest that was spreading here was arriving from the south. The British forest was part of a truly immense forest that covered most of western Europe called, because of the climatic period that produced it, the Atlantic Forest.

The British part of the Forest is known to scientists as the 'wildwood', a name used to describe the original, primeval forest that developed without help or interference from humans. What was it like, that primeval forest? We do not really know, at least not with any certainty, and although today you can find areas of very ancient woodland that may be something like the wildwood, too much time has elapsed, there have been too many changes (not least

Regional variation in the composition of the British primeval forest. Blank areas were also forested, but the trees that grew there have not been identified.

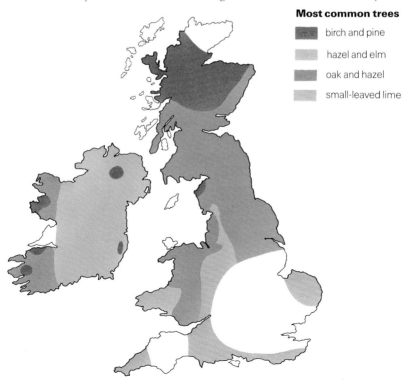

Most common trees

- birch and pine
- hazel and elm
- oak and hazel
- small-leaved lime

in the climate) for anyone to be certain. We do know some things, though. We know, for example, that the old idea of a Britain blanketed with forests dominated everywhere by oak is quite wrong. Oaks were common over much of the country, but only in some places were they the most common tree. The wildwood contained many tree species and its composition varied from place to place. We cannot see it today, but there are places where forest has grown undisturbed for many centuries which may give a flavour of what Britain was like so long ago. Coltswood Beechwoods in Gloucestershire, Coed Llyn Mair woods near Ffestiniog in Gwynedd, Kingley Vale National Nature Reserve in Sussex, which contains the finest yew-woods in Britain, and The Men's woods, also in Sussex, are just a few places that are worth visiting, but there are many more patches of ancient broadleaved woodland dotted throughout the country.

The forest covered most of Britain, but there were open spaces and clearings, as there are in all forests. These are made when old trees die and fall, often bringing down some of their neighbours with them. All at once the sunlight shines directly on the ground and an area that was formerly shaded by the trees is exposed. This allows smaller plants to flourish. Grasses and herbs can grow, and will continue to grow until young seedlings grow tall, replace the fallen trees, and restore the shade. Many herbivorous animals graze the grasses and herbs, and they also trample or eat tree seedlings, so that once formed a forest clearing may last for a long time.

Flowers of the wildwood

If we cannot see the wildwood as it was in its prime, we can see many of the herbs associated with it because these, or their domesticated descendants, flourish in hedgerows and in our gardens. All the spring-flowering herbs, the snowdrops, primroses, daffodils, crocuses, tulips and many more, are woodland plants. In the wild they take advantage of the fact that broadleaved trees shed their leaves in the autumn, an evolutionary strategy for conserving moisture. New leaves appear in the spring, but there is a delay, a gap between the first appearance of the spring sunshine and the thawing of the winter snow and ice, and the full burst of leaves on the trees. During this short time the sun shines directly through the bare branches of the trees on to the floor of the forest, and flowering plants can flower, fruit, release seed to germinate during the summer, and then die back and become insignificant again. It must all happen quickly, during that limited period before the trees produce their leaves, and so many woodland plants flower together in early spring. From time immemorial we have associated them with the end of winter, and we have taken them into our gardens, from where they have escaped into hedgerows, roadside verges, and any small corners that we leave undisturbed.

The rise of the sea, and the cooling of the climate

All the time the forest was spreading, water was being released from the retreating glaciers and sea-levels were rising. By the time this process ended, the sea around Britain had risen some 60 to 90 m (200 to 300 ft). It flooded the low-lying land to the east and the west, producing the North Sea and the Irish Sea. Ireland became an island. Then, by about 5000 years ago, it invaded a strip of land joining the North Sea to the Atlantic, forming the English Channel. Britain became an island and natural immigration was reduced dramatically.

The Atlantic Period came to an end, which is another way of saying the climate began to cool, at about the time Britain was separated from the rest of Europe. The trees that had invaded from the south prefer a rather warmer climate, and although most of them survived, today they are close to the climatic limit of their geographical range. This affects the reproductive behaviour of some of them. They can produce seed, but either the seeds germinate poorly or the survival of seedlings is low. Therefore they tend to reproduce vegetatively, by producing suckers, rather than from seed. Survivors from the Atlantic Period may still be declining. It is possible that oak and hazel, two of the commonest of our trees, will become rare in time, and without human aid perhaps they will become extinct in Britain. At present they are reproducing errati- cally and more slowly than old trees are dying.

Botanists classify species as *native, naturalised* or *exotic*. The system is somewhat arbitrary, but it does provide us with useful informa- tion. A native species is one which was present in the wildwood. Oak, elm, hazel, holly and aspen are native to Britain. Scots pine is our only native conifer. Sweet chestnut (*Castanea sativa*) was intro- duced to Britain during the Iron Age, perhaps by the Romans although this is far from certain, and sycamore (*Acer pseudoplatanus*) was introduced most probably in the fifteenth or sixteenth century. Both these species now thrive in Britain without any help from humans, and you can find them in woodland. They are fully naturalised. Where you see the horse chestnut (*Aesculus hippo- castanum*), on the other hand, you can be sure someone planted it, for its nearest natural habitat is in the Balkans, it cannot survive in Britain without human help, and it is not a natural or even a common constituent of woodland. It is exotic. It is not related to the sweet chestnut, although their seeds look much alike.

Pollen grains are very tough and can survive for thousands of years. Scientists can tell what plants grew here in the past by examining the pollen found in soil at sites that can be dated, and some plants indicate change in climate. Holly and ivy prefer mild, wet conditions, for example, and mountain avens thrives in tundra.

Principal British native and naturalised trees

Alder	*Alnus glutinosa*
Ash	*Fraxinus excelsior*
Aspen	*Populus tremula*
Beech	*Fagus sylvatica*
Birch	
dwarf	*Betula nana*
downy	*B. pubescens*
silver	*B. pendula*
Box	*Buxus sempervirens*
Chestnut, sweet[1]	*Castanea sativa*
Crab apple[2]	*Malus sylvestris*
Elm	
wych-	*Ulmus glabra*
English	*U. procera*
smooth-leaved	*U. minor*
Field maple	*Acer campestre*
Hawthorn	
common	*Crataegus monogyna*
Midland	*C. oxycanthoides*
Hazel	*Corylus avellana*
Holly	*Ilex aquifolium*
Hornbeam	*Carpinus betulus*
Juniper	*Juniperus communis*
Linden (lime)	
small-leaved	*Tilia cordata*
large-leaved	*T. platyphyllos*
common[3]	*T. vulgaris*
Oak	
pedunculate	*Quercus robur*
sessile	*Q. petraea*
holm[4]	*Q. ilex*
Turkey[5]	*Q. cerris*
Pear, common[6]	*Pyrus communis*
Plum[7]	*Prunus species*
Poplar	
black[8]	*Populus nigra*
white[9]	*P. alba*
grey[10]	*P. canescens*
Lombardy[11]	*P. niara*
Rowan (mountain ash)	*Sorbus aucuparia*
Scots pine	*Pinus sylvestris*
Sycamore[12]	*Acer pseudoplatanus*
Whitebeam	*Sorbus aria*
Wild service	*S. torminalis*
Yew	*Taxus baccata*

Sessile Oak

Holm Oak

Field Maple

English Elm

Wych Elm

Sycamore

Hazel

Hornbeam

Beech

Silver Birch

Linden

White Poplar

Sweet Chestnut

Ash

Rowan

1 Introduced during the Iron Age, now naturalised.
2 Possibly native, or introduced in Neolithic times.
3 Common linden is a hybrid of the small-leaved and large-leaved species.
4 Holm or evergreen oak was introduced, possibly early in the Iron Age, and is now naturalised.
5 Introduced, now naturalised.
6 Probably introduced in Neolithic times, now naturalised, and the ancestor of all domesticated pears.
7 Probably introduced before the Iron Age, fully naturalised, and the ancestor of all domesticated plums and damsons. There are many species, subspecies and varieties.
8 Probably native, but not certainly so. Also known as downy poplar.
9 Probably introduced and now naturalised, but not certainly so. Also known as abele.
10 Hybrid between white poplar and aspen, naturalised in some places.
11 Introduced in the eighteenth century from northern Italy as one tree, from which all British Lombardy poplars have been produced by cuttings, so they are all clones of a single individual.
12 Introduced, probably in the fifteenth or sixteenth century; now naturalised.

Grimes Graves, Norfolk, are extensive and, in some places, deep.

Clearing the wildwood

By the end of the Atlantic Period, when Britain had become separated from the rest of Europe, humans were already well on their way to modifying the wildwood. People have lived in Britain for a very long time: they lived here during the Hoxnian period, for example. In those days they obtained their food by gathering wild plants and by scavenging meat from animals that had died or been killed. They also did some hunting, and made hand axes from flint, some of which have been found in Essex and Suffolk. They belonged to what archaeologists called the Acheulian or Clactonian culture, and lived here well over 100,000 years ago. It was only during the very coldest periods of full-blown ice ages that humans departed altogether, and even that is open to doubt.

The people living here 5000 years ago were more advanced. They were farmers and pastoralists, who needed food for their livestock and open ground on which to grow crops. They were also the first British industrialists and created the country's first industrial land-scape. It is still there to be seen, as are their 'factory' and mine, at Grimes Graves on the border between Suffolk and Norfolk, and in the Breckland around Hockham Mere, not far from there. In about 3000 bc Grimes Graves was a flint mine, where professional miners and flint-knappers dug out large pieces of flint and fashioned them into tools which they supplied to the farming community, and probably traded far and wide.

The tools were much more sophisticated than the hand axes that could have been used by the Acheulian people only as weapons or for digging out roots. The farmers used the new tools to clear the forest, and it never returned to the Breckland, which is now an open, heath-like area. The clearance of the wildwood had begun.

Decline of elm and lime

The first evidence of the clearance was a great reduction in the number of elm trees that occurred at about this time throughout Europe. Probably several factors contributed to the elm decline, but the most likely main cause was the use of elm foliage for feeding livestock. The early farmers could not allow their animals to wander freely through forests populated by rival tribes, packs of wolves and other competitors. They cleared an area by felling certain trees that would bring down others as they fell, setting fire to the smaller twigs as soon as they had dried, thus starting forest fires that opened the land and encouraged grasses to grow. They penned their animals in the clearings they had made and brought food to them. Elm leaves and shoots, including young seedlings, are very palatable to many herbivorous animals and were collected regularly, year after year and century after century, by chopping off the top part of the trees. When a tree is cut in this way it does not die, but grows many small shoots from the top of the stump, and these small shoots provided food in subsequent years. The technique is called *pollarding*, and a version of it is used to this day, not to provide food for livestock, but either to prevent trees, often on city streets, from growing too tall, or to supply small poles to make fencing, handles for tools, or other articles. It does mean, though, that the elms were never allowed to flower or set seed, which is not particularly important because they reproduce mainly from suckers. This increased the amount of fodder that each tree produced, so fewer trees were needed.

As the elms were seen to be growing on the better land, and land was needed for growing crops, elms were destroyed to free areas for

Pollarding. A crop of poles is cut, leaving a naked 'boiling', from which new shoots grow.

cropping. Lime trees suffered a similar decline, probably for the same reason, and the disappearance of elms and limes was associated with an increase in stinging nettles, plantains and other plants typical of ground that has been disturbed. Holly, on the other hand, was left to flourish. Once established, it is very difficult to destroy and animals prefer not to graze it. It had its uses, however. It makes excellent fuel, its foliage burning even when it is green, and its leaves could be collected and used as feed for cattle and deer in winter if no other food was available.

The wildwood began to open out into a landscape more like park land. In most places the change was not dramatic or sudden. Even the elm and lime decline may have taken centuries. Yet here and there the cleared forest never returned and the land still remains much as it must have been three or four thousand years ago. The chalk downs of southern England are the clearest example. There the soil is thin and although it lies over chalk it tends to be acid. When the trees were cleared grasses grew, and ever since the grassland has been used to graze livestock. Indeed, until about the eighteenth century its fertility was 'mined' by local farmers so that some areas lost their soil entirely, exposing the chalk. Sheep were allowed on to the downs during the day-time to graze, but were brought back to the farm every evening. They manured the land close to the farm by ridding themselves of the residues of the food they had eaten on the downs, thus transferring nutrients from the downs, which became less fertile, to the farms, which became more fertile. This loss of fertility prevented vigorous, aggressive plants from dominating the downs and so allowed a great diversity of species to flourish. It is this history of past use that gives the downlands their great botanical value today.

Medieval landscapes

When the Romans came they turned Britain into a major agricultural country, exporting food and materials to the rest of the Empire. By the time they left, three and a half centuries later, most of the wildwood had gone and Britain was a land of open country with patches of forest. The Normans began to conserve what remained of the forest, partly by reserving large areas of it in the name of the Crown for the raising of game. This was a serious method of food production, besides providing amusement for those who hunted. The largest areas of medieval royal forest remaining today are in the New Forest, Epping Forest, the Forest of Dean and the Wyre Forest. In time, however, that form of land management disappeared too. Some of the forests were converted to the production of small wood, by coppicing or pollarding, and timber. Others were cleared entirely. It became impractical to try to combine the production of trees with the production of livestock, and the rich, even royalty, learned to eat meat from farmed animals.

The treeless forest

Wood-fired furnaces for smelting iron and the building of wooden ships made further inroads into the remaining forests over succeeding centuries, although the effect of these activities should not be exaggerated. The Industrial Revolution, for example, used first water and then coal as its principal sources of energy, and made little use of wood. The threat to British timber imports during the First World War led to the establishment of the Forestry Commission in 1919, charged with managing all the Crown forests and with providing the country with a regular supply of timber. Today there is more tree-covered land in Britain than at any time during the last thousand years, although most of it is plantation conifer forest rather than natural broadleaved forest, and none of it is wildwood.

Yet most of Britain remains one large forest, at least potentially. We have cleared the trees to grow our crops, and through grazing livestock and regular ploughing we keep our farm land in cultivation. But if we stopped farming, what would happen? Weeds would grow, those small opportunist herbs whose seeds lie around waiting for a chance to germinate on ground from which other plants have been cleared. Then, among the weeds, a few woody shrubs would start to grow, and a few tree seedlings. In a few years the farm land would have given way to fairly dense scrub. Among the scrub would be trees, growing tall and shading the ground. Their shade would defeat many herbs and shrubs, and little by little forest would reappear. It would not be the original forest, or anything closely resembling it in composition, but it would be forest. How can we know that this is what would happen? Because in most places it is what does happen when land is left undisturbed for a few years.

Parks

Land that was enclosed for the purpose of raising game, especially deer, was called a *park*, a word that originally meant enclosed, cultivated land lying between the in-fields and out-fields in the ancient farming system. Deer are woodland animals, but they need some open space, and so do the people hunting them on horseback. A deer park that was fairly open, with trees dotted around singly or in small clumps on what was otherwise grassland, produced a landscape which came to be regarded as typically British.

Park woodland, which is another name for it, can still be seen, but its most dramatic expression is in the deliberately manufactured countryside contrived and engineered by the great landscape gardeners of the eighteenth century. They were inspired by this essentially medieval landscape and sought to reproduce it, with improvements, and mainly as ornament. They were delightfully uninhibited by any idea of historical or botanical precision. They made lakes where lakes could not exist naturally, they planted exotic tree species, and for good measure they often added small buildings, usually temples, built in the architectural style of Greece and Rome, but of different materials and in different colours. Some of their parks remain around large country houses, and since many are owned by the National Trust you can visit them. Most of the trees, however, are now some two hundred years old and near the end of their lives. Unless they are replaced an essential component of these historically interesting landscapes will soon be lost.

Britain may be a former forest and potentially forest still, but meanwhile it is actually a farm. When you visit the countryside you will see fields growing crops, or open country where sheep or cattle graze. You will see farms, even high in the hills. You will also see forests, it is true, but most of them will be commercial plantations, growing trees as a crop – and forestry, after all, is farming of a kind. If you are to understand what is going on around you now, as well as what happened in the past, you must learn a little about farming.

A man-made landscape. Parkland in Petworth Park, Sussex.

8

OVER THE HEDGE

As you travel through the British countryside you will see many forests. You can hardly avoid them, for commercial forestry occupies something like 10 per cent of the total land area, consisting mainly of rather more than two million hectares (nearly five million acres) of commercial plantation. Of that total, 947,000 ha (2,340,000 acres) are in Scotland, 855,000 ha (2,112,705 acres) in England and 235,000 ha (580,685 acres) in Wales. In addition, England has 90,000 ha (222,390 acres) of woodland that is not being cropped commercially, Scotland 70,000 ha (172,970 acres) and Wales 10,000 ha (24,710 acres).

It is misleading to suggest that most of this land is growing conifers. The Forestry Commission grows far more conifers than broadleaved trees, but not all woodlands are owned by the Commission, and more than half the privately owned woodlands in England grow broadleaves. A larger proportion of conifers is grown in Scotland, but Scotland is very close to the geographical limit for most broadleaved species and in many parts of the country they do not thrive. In Britain as a whole, 1,440,000 ha (3,558,240 acres) of productive woodland are planted with conifers and 557,000 ha (1,376,347 acres) with broadleaves.

The proportion of the total area of Britain that is devoted to growing trees, about 10 per cent, may seem large, but most countries are much more densely forested. The world average is 31 per cent, which is the area occupied by forests in the USA, but in Japan they occupy 68 per cent of the total area and in Finland 76 per cent. The USSR has more than 2,000 million hectares of forest, amounting to 41 per cent of its vast area. The average for the EEC countries is also about 31 per cent, and only the Netherlands (9 per cent, which is the same as the UK figure because Northern Ireland has few forests) and Ireland (5 per cent) have as small or an even smaller forest area than Britain. So we have little cause for complacency.

Identifying trees

The broadleaved trees you see growing in forests are most likely to belong to one of the species listed on p. 98. Conifers are more difficult to identify, because one conifer is more like all other conifers than is the case with broadleaved species. There are identifying features, however, if you look closely enough.

Identifying common conifers

1 Can you see the wood of the branch clearly among the needles or leaves, or are these clustered so tightly to the branch as to hide it? If you cannot see the wood, go to 3. If you can see the wood, or it is winter and the branches have no leaves or needles at all, go to 2.

2 Do the needles grow in bunches of 20 to 30, with a small woody 'knob' at the base of each bunch or, if it is winter, are the branches quite bare? If so, go to 6. Are the needles grouped in twos, threes or fives? If so, go to 7. Do the needles grow singly, but are they of different lengths, some short and some long? If so, go to 8.

3 Feel the tip of one of the twigs that bears leaves, look at the general colour of the tree, and crush a few leaves and smell them. If the tip feels fleshy and smooth, the tree gives an impression of being a yellowish green, and the crushed leaves have a sweet, fruity smell, go to 4. If the tree looks rather red and the tip is thin and hard, and the crushed leaves smell of resin, go to 5.

4 The tree is most likely to belong to the genus *Thuja*, the cedars, which come from North America. Western red cedar (*T. plicata*) is the species most commonly grown commercially.

5 The tree is most likely to belong to the genus *Chamaecyparis*, the cypresses, and probably it is the Lawson cypress (*C. lawsoniana*), a tree from North America. It is grown widely for ornament, but not commercially for its timber, and it looks much like a cedar.

6 The tree belongs to the genus *Larix*, the larches, of which several species are grown commercially. Are the twigs a pale yellow colour with very green needles? If so, go to 9. Are the twigs reddish in colour and the needles rather blue? If so, go to 10.

7 Is the bark of the tree orange or red, and are the needles rather blue and no more than about 4 cm (1.5 inches) long? If so, go to 11. Are the needles about 7.5 cm (3 inches) long, the colour of sage, and twisted, and does the bud at the end of each branch start fairly broad but narrow to a point? If so, go to 12. Is the bark dark, almost black, and divided by narrow grooves into what look like small plates, and are the needles green, rather than grey or blue? If so, go to 13. If the tree is not like any of these, look at the base of a needle. Does it grow from a small wooden peg-like structure, and if you break off a needle does the 'peg' come with it, leaving behind a scar? And if you look at the bark, are the 'pegs' left from where needles have fallen naturally? If so, go to 14. If there are no pegs, either at the base of each needle or standing out from the bark where earlier needles have fallen, and if small, round scars are left when needles fall or are removed, go to 15.

8 The tree is most likely to be a hemlock, probably *Tsuga heterophylla*, western hemlock, a tree from western North America.
9 The tree is most likely to be *Larix decidua*, European larch, a tree native to the mountains of central Europe but grown widely in Britain.
10 The tree is most likely to be *Larix kaempferi*, Japanese larch, native to Japan, or *L. eurolepis*, hybrid larch, the latter being a cross between Japanese and European larch (see 9). Both are grown widely in British plantations.
11 The tree is most likely to be *Pinus sylvestris*, Scots pine.
12 The tree is most likely to be *Pinus nigra*, Corsican pine. Native to Corsica it is grown in Britain only as far north as the Midlands.
13 The tree is most likely to be *Pinus contorta*, lodgepole pine, the North American tree much favoured by Indians for making the frames of their wigwams.
14 The tree is most likely to be spruce, of the genus *Picea*. Are the needles very green and does the tree look like a Christmas tree? If so, go to 16. Are the needles rather blue and very sharply pointed? If so, go to 17.
15 The tree is most likely to be a fir. Look at the buds at the growing tips of branches. Are they very pointed, brown, and apparently covered in scales? If so, go to 18. Are the buds short and rather stumpy, and if you crush one does it smell of resin? If so, go to 19.
16 The tree is most likely to be *Picea abies*, Norway spruce, which comes originally from continental Europe but is grown widely in Britain and can spread naturally, from its own seed, so it seems to be naturalising itself.

Needles leave a round flat scar.

17 The tree is most likely to be *Picea sitchensis*, Sitka spruce, from western North America.
18 The tree is most likely to be *Pseudotsuga menziesii*, the Douglas fir, named after the Scottish botanist David Douglas who sent the first seed from North America to Britain in 1827.

needles fall naturally peg remains.

19 The tree is most likely to be a silver fir, of the genus *Abies*. Crush a few needles and smell them. If they smell of tangerines, go to 20. Do the cones have an almost feathery look because the bracts (modified leaves at the base of flowers) are very long and point downward? If so, go to 21.

Needles leave round scars when pulled off.

20 The tree is most likely to be *Abies grandis*, the grand fir, from western North America.
21 The tree is most likely to be *Abies procera*, the noble fir, from western North America. In Britain it is more commonly grown for ornament than for its timber.

Juniper and yew, two native conifers already mentioned, are not grown commercially in Britain so you are unlikely to see them in forest plantations. Juniper is usually a shrub, has leaves that are almost blue, and berries that smell and taste strongly of gin, which is not surprising since juniper is used to flavour gin. You are most likely to see yews in churchyards, although they do occur in some natural woodland, and they, too, produce berries. The flesh of yew berries is edible, but the seeds, leaves and bark are very poisonous.

Commercial conifer plantations grow pines, larches, spruces, firs, cedars and hemlock (the tree, not the poisonous herb), but there is much confusion in the use of these common names. Scots pine is sometimes called Scots fir, for example, and botanically all the commercial species belong to the pine family (Pinaceae). To tell which tree is which examine a mature side-branch, ignoring young seedlings and new growth because these may not be typical of the plant. Now follow the numbers in the guide (see pp. 106–7), which describes the most commonly grown commercial conifers. It is not complete, of course, but at least it should allow you to identify most genera and many of the species you are most likely to see.

Identifying farm types

Apart from urban areas and the tops of the highest mountains, almost all the British countryside is either growing forests or is farmed. There are several types of farming. If the farmer grows vegetables, fruit, flowers or crops of this kind the farm is either a market garden or growing 'cash crops'. Flowers and some vegetables are often grown in large fields, on farms rather than in gardens. If the farmer grows cereals, root crops such as potatoes or sugar beet, or some vegetables, such as peas for freezing or canning, his is called an *arable farm*. If the farm produces some crops but also some livestock, it is a *mixed farm*. If it only raises livestock, but grows some crops for use as livestock feed, it is a *pastoral farm*. If it grows only grass to raise livestock it is known as a *stock farm* or, in the uplands, a *hill farm*.

The farmer's decision as to which kind of farming he will pursue is circumscribed by three outside forces: economics, climate and soil. If you look over the hedges and see what kind of farming is being practised you will be able to deduce quite a lot about the local effects of those forces and, from that, about the way people live, because each type of farming produces a distinct way of life (see pp. 110–11).

Farm soils

The richest, most fertile British soils are the fen and basin peats. They are black, deep, and will grow large crops of almost anything. The best of them are to be found around the Wash, in East Anglia, and they produce cash crops that sell for high prices. They are so valuable that the flat land is wide open, with every last corner being

Land use and way of life

Extremely large fields, with few hedges. Fields ploughed or growing crops.	Arable land, probably in East Anglia or East Yorkshire, the Midlands, eastern Scotland, especially Fife. Climate cold in winter, warm in summer, with low rainfall. Farms employ few workers, so local population density low unless there is other employment within commuting distance of villages and hamlets.
Extremely large, open cultivated fields, very dark soil, growing crops. Flat landscape.	Highly intensive fenland farms growing high-value crops, probably near The Wash or in Cambridgeshire. Climate dry and cold in winter, hot in summer. Farming mechanised, but nevertheless labour-intensive because of care taken with expensive produce.
Fields with hedges or fences, some fields growing grass, others ploughed or growing crops.	Mixed farming, with some arable crops and some animals. Probably in north-east Scotland, North Yorkshire, the Midlands or south of England, but patches elsewhere. Climate fairly gentle, with moderate rainfall. Well-populated countryside because of labour needed to tend stock.
Small fields with hedges, some or all of which are growing vegetables you can recognise.	Market gardening. Could be anywhere, but probably near a large town, or at least within easy reach of one by road or rail. Very labour-intensive, with small holdings, but the total scale also small. If there are many glasshouses, they will be growing crops out of season.
Mainly small fields growing grass, with hedges, probably with trees.	Livestock farming, most probably mainly dairying. Probably on the western side of Britain. Climate mild in winter, warm in summer, wet throughout the year. Labour-intensive, so large villages and hamlets, close together.
Open hillside, heath or moorland.	Hill farming, raising some cattle, mainly for fattening on better land at a lower altitude, and sheep. Climate harsh, with long, cold winters, cool summers, and high rainfall throughout the year. Farming is labour-intensive, but because the land is so poor the farms are small and widely scattered, with farmers sharing the upland grazing.

used and no space wasted on such trivia as hedges. So the landscape tends to be bleak and dull, the farming is prosperous, and the farmers probably get ulcers worrying about their profits.

Brown and grey-brown soils are good, but sometimes rather acid. They can support most kinds of farming and you find them in various parts of the country, including the north of Caithness, down the east side of Scotland and northern England, around the Solway Firth, and in west and south Wales.

The calcareous (chalk) soils of the downs are inclined to be acid, but they are also shallow, which restricts their use, although they can grow crops with a bit of encouragement. They are used mainly for grazing sheep.

The mountains have soils that lie very thinly over rocks, sometimes with rocks outcropping at the surface, and they cannot be cultivated. Where the soil is deeper it is often waterlogged and impractical to drain, so from a farming point of view it can grow only tough grass.

Farming and climate

Most British weather arrives from the west, off the Atlantic, and since we have high ground all along the western side of the country as far inland as the Pennines, incoming air loses most of its moisture over the south-western peninsula of England, Wales, Lancashire and the Lake District, and western Scotland.

Soil must be fairly dry before it can be ploughed or it simply turns into a quagmire that dries into large, hard lumps. It is thus generally easier to cultivate soils in the east of the country than in the west.

Arable crops need warm, dry, sunny weather in late summer to ripen them, but in much of western Britain July and August are wet months, so arable crops grown there are unreliable. Pasture grass, on the other hand, likes mild, moist conditions, although a spell of dry weather is needed for making hay or silage in late spring or early summer, when the grass is at its nutritional best.

For reasons of climate and soil, therefore, it has always been easier to grow arable crops on the eastern side of the country, to raise sheep and beef and dairy cattle on lush pastures in the west (hence the cream, clotted cream, butter and cheeses of western counties), and to raise young cattle and hardier breeds of sheep on the rough grazing in the hills.

Farming and economics

A farmer can produce almost anything almost anywhere, but if he departs from the pattern his produce will cost more. If arable crops ripen patchily, yields will be low compared with those in more favoured areas. Animals will produce less and grow more slowly on inferior pastures. At one time the problem had to be endured because some of the arable produce was needed to supplement the grass fed to livestock, and livestock manure was needed to fertilise the arable land. Mixed farming was therefore common. Today, when industrially produced fertilisers have replaced much of the animal manure used and feed can be transported conveniently by road or rail, specialisation is the norm.

When the nutritive cycle was broken it became possible for arable farmers to rid themselves of livestock and grass and to concentrate on their more profitable arable crops, and for livestock farmers to buy in the feed they needed and give up their attempts to grow crops. The prices paid to the farmer today are such that only the most productive farms are profitable. That is why the tendency to specialise has intensified until today farmers can afford to produce only those commodities for which their farm is best suited. The arable farms are in the east, the livestock farms are in the west, and idiosyncratic farmers who go their own way are either independently wealthy or taking a short cut to bankruptcy.

There are exceptions, of course, but this is the general pattern, and when people criticise modern farming for over-producing they are criticising its success. Yields per hectare of arable crops are about ten times higher in Britain than they are in the USA.

Armed with all this information you can learn a great deal, at any time of year, simply by looking at the way the land around you is being used.

A use for poor, sandy soil. Tentsmuir Forest, near Dundee, Tayside, with harsh, intrusive edges. Map no. 59.

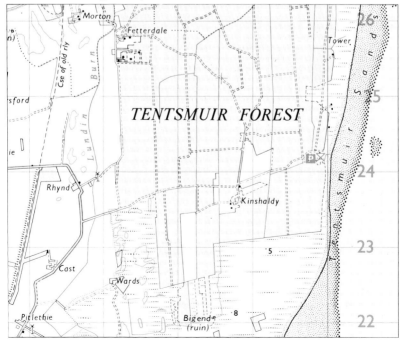

Identifying farm crops (1)

The crops you see growing in fields are either broadleaved or have narrow leaves, like grass. On hillsides or on high ground, and occasionally in old meadows on low ground, the grass will be 'unimproved'. This means it grows naturally and has not been sown by the farmer. Grass-like and broadleaved crops are here dealt with separately. It is extremely difficult to identify grasses except when they are in flower, and this includes the usual cereal crops. So the following guide can be only approximate for grasses and for cereals unless they are almost ripe.

Grass-like crops

Grass looks rough. There appear to be many species. Clumps of grass stand out higher than other grass. Some of the grass has thin, wiry leaves.

'Unimproved' grassland, probably on high ground or ground too steep for wheeled vehicles.

Land is level and low-lying, probably close to a river on the valley floor. Grass looks rough and among it there are larger grass-like plants, dark green, with coarse, round leaves.

Poorly drained land, liable to flooding. The dark, grass-like plants are sedges, not grasses. The ground may be marshy. Used to graze livestock for part of the year, but may carry liver flukes, parasites which cause illness in cattle and sheep and spend part of their life-cycle in the body of a species of freshwater snail.

Grass looks lush and is all more or less the same height. There appear to be one or two, or at most only a few, grass species.

'Improved' grassland, the grass having been sown by the farmer on land that has been ploughed. The pasture will consist of no more than two or three species, probably mainly a ryegrass, and after a few years the pasture may be ploughed and either resown with grass or used to grow other crops. Such pastures are used to raise dairy cattle or to fatten beef cattle or sheep prior to marketing.

Plants look like grass, but are paler and have rather broad leaves. You can see the tilled earth between each small group of plants.

A cereal crop, of wheat, oats, barley or rye. At this stage it is impossible to tell which, but rye is rarely grown, and then only on the poorer land, and oats are little grown except in Scotland.

Cereal crop, nearly ripe and so becoming golden in colour. Stands about 60 cm (2 ft) tall. Ears consist of many grains in their husks all around the stem. There may be no *awns* (hair-like extensions of the husks) but if awns are present they look wispy and stand away from the ear.

Wheat.

Cereal crop, nearly ripe and so becoming golden in colour. Stands about 60 cm (2 ft) tall. Ears consist of many grains in their husks, almost hidden by the long, rigid, strong, spike-like awns which lie parallel to one another pointing upward.

Barley.

Cereal crop, nearly ripe and so becoming golden in colour. Stands about a metre (3 ft) tall, but may be taller. Ear consists of many grains in their husks, almost hidden by short, rigid, coarse, spike-like awns sticking outward from the stem.

Rye.

Cereal crop, nearly ripe and so becoming golden in colour. Stands about 60 cm (2 ft) tall. The grains, in their husks, are separate from one another and each dangles from its own small stem away from the plant.

Oats.

Densely planted green crop that stands up to 2 m (6 ft 6 in) tall, each plant consisting of a single stem with large, grass-like leaves growing out from it all the way to the top.

Maize, the plant known in America as corn. It is grown in Britain on a field scale as feed for livestock and is harvested before it sets seed. The animals eat the foliage. Sweetcorn is a variety of the same plant, but grown as a horticultural crop. It is actually a grass.

Identifying farm crops (2)

Broadleaved crops

Green crop up to 90 cm (3 ft) tall, with broad but small, deeply lobed leaves, green at the base but rather blue near the top. The flowers are brilliant, intense yellow, making the whole field look yellow. When the crop ripens the leaves fall, and you can see many long, narrow seed pods.

Rape, also known as cole, or coleseed (*Brassica napus*). It is a relative of the swede, which it resembles in its foliage, and belongs to the same family as the cabbage. It used to be grown to feed livestock, which grazed it in winter when there was no grass. Today it is usually allowed to flower and set seed. The seeds are crushed for their edible oil and the 'cake' left after pressing is fed to livestock. Rape is grown widely and is the only important British crop which yields edible vegetable oil.

Green crop consisting of rosettes of broad leaves growing up to 30 cm (1 ft) tall.

Either turnip or mangels, grown to provide winter feed for livestock or, in a few areas, mainly in East Anglia, sugar beet. Sugar beet is our only sugar crop but it can be grown economically only within a short distance of the factories that process it, which is why its range is restricted.

Green crop, about 90 cm (3 ft) tall, whose white, inconspicuous flowers have a very sweet, almost sickly smell. When ripe the whole plant turns brown, loses its leaves, and you can see many small seed pods, about the length of pea pods, but narrower.

Field beans, grown to feed livestock. The beans are rich in protein.

Green plant, up to 60 cm (2 ft) tall, with broad leaves growing out from the single stem.

Kale, grown to feed livestock, which are allowed to graze it in winter.

In addition to these, you may see peas being grown on a field scale. When ripe they will be harvested by machine and taken to a factory for shelling, sorting and then freezing. You may also see cane fruits (mainly raspberries) and other soft fruits such as strawberries grown on a field scale, and tree fruits (apples, pears, plums, etc.) grown in orchards.

Wild plants and the law

The Wildlife and Countryside Act 1981, Section 13, states:

1 Subject to the provisions of this Part, if any person –
   a intentionally picks, uproots or destroys any wild plant included in Schedule 8; or
   b not being an authorised person, intentionally uproots any wild plant not included in that Schedule, he shall be guilty of an offence.

2 Subject to the provisions of this Part, if any person –
   a sells, offers or exposes for sale, or has in his possession or transports for the purposes of sale, any live or dead wild plant included in Schedule 8, or any part of, or anything derived from, such a plant; or
   b publishes or causes to be published any advertisement likely to be understood as conveying that he buys or sells, or intends to buy or sell, any of those things,
   he shall be guilty of an offence.

3 Notwithstanding anything in subsection **1**, a person shall not be guilty of an offence by reason of any act made unlawful by that subsection if he shows that the act was an incidental result of a lawful operation and could not reasonably have been avoided.

4 In any proceedings for an offence under subsection **2a**, the plant in question shall be presumed to have been a wild plant unless the contrary is shown.

Schedule 8 is a list of 61 plants. The law means that you may remove weeds from your garden or from land you own or rent because on your own land, or working under instructions from or with the permission of the landowner or tenant, you are an 'authorised person'. However, if the plant is listed in the Schedule you must not remove or damage it deliberately. If it is destroyed unavoidably as a consequence of another lawful operation, that is not an offence, but you must be able to show that any injury was accidental.

As a visitor to the countryside, you must not uproot or destroy any wild plant.

Alison, Small	Gentian, Spring	Orchid, Fen	Spearwort,
Broomrape, Bedstraw	Germander, Water	Orchid, Ghost	Adder's-tongue
Broomrape, Oxtongue	Gladiolus, Wild	Orchid, Late Spider	Speedwell, Spiked
Broomrape, Thistle	Hare's-ear,	Orchid, Lizard	Spurge, Purple
Calamint, Wood	Sickle-leaved	Orchid, Military	Starfruit
Catchfly, Alpine	Hare's-ear, Small	Orchid, Monkey	Violet, Fen
Cinquefoil, Rock	Heath, Blue	Pear, Plymouth	Water-plantain,
Club-rush, Triangular	Helleborine, Red	Pink, Cheddar	Ribbon leaved
Cotoneaster, Wild	Knawel, Perennial	Pink, Childling	Wood-sedge, Starved
Cow-wheat, Field	Knotgrass, Sea	Sandwort,	Woodsia, Alpine
Cudweed, Jersey	Lady's-slipper	Norwegian	Woodsia, Oblong
Diapensia	Lavender, Sea	Sandwort, Teesdale	Wormwood, Field
Eryngo, Field	Leek, Round-headed	Saxifrage, Drooping	Woundwort, Downy
Fern, Dickie's Bladder	Lettuce, Least	Saxifrage, Tufted	Woundwort, Limestone
Fern, Killarney	Lily, Snowdon	Solomon's-seal,	Yellow-rattle, Greater
Galingale, Brown	Marsh-mallow, Rough	Whorled	
Gentian, Alpine	Orchid, Early Spider	Sow-thistle, Alpine	

9

ANIMALS

As you travel the countryside you are certain to see farm animals and you may wish to identify breeds of cattle, sheep and poultry. These days most pigs and poultry are raised indoors, and are therefore a rather uncommon sight, except where farmyard chickens, kept to supply the family rather than on a commercial basis, play their traditional role and forage for food among the spilled grain, scraps from the table, and such grass as may grow within their reach. You are most likely to see them when they wander into the road in the course of their explorations of the verges. You will see few pigs or poultry, but many cattle and sheep, and now that demand for goat's milk is growing, you will see goats.

The origin of farm animals

Identifying breeds is more difficult than it may seem because domesticated animals are to a large extent man-made, and as needs change old models are traded in for new ones which may or may not look different. They retain many of the general characteristics of their original wild ancestors, of course, but that is about all, and they may have more than one wild ancestor. Closely related races, subspecies or even species from different parts of the world may have been pressed into human service. They will have produced descendants of varying shapes and colours, but descendants that can interbreed.

Domestication itself brought important changes. Modern poultry are recognisably related to the Asian jungle fowl from which they are descended, although they are usually a different colour, but mammals are more difficult. You might not associate a farmyard pig with a European wild boar, for example, and indeed the domestic

*European mouflon (Ovis musimon),
an ancestor of domesticated sheep.*

Identifying farm livestock (1)

Pigs

Appearance	Breed
Black and white, spotted, ears pointing forward	Gloucester Old Spots
Black with white forelegs, the white extending as a band across the shoulders, ears pointing forward	Saddleback[1]
Black with white forelegs, the white extending as a band across the shoulders, ears erect	Hampshire
White, ears erect	Large White
White, ears pointing forward[2]	Landrace[3]
	Welsh

1 Also known as Wessex Saddleback.
2 Animals may belong to either of these breeds, which are virtually identical in appearance.
3 Also known as Yorkshire.

pig is only distantly related to the wild boar. It is descended much more closely from Chinese pigs, first domesticated in Asia and introduced to Europe in the last century. The modern pig may have four species of wild ancestor or even more.

Domesticated mammals are usually smaller or larger than their wild relatives. The shape of their skulls may change, and so may their horns if they ever had any, because in most cases the animals retain throughout their lives certain juvenile characteristics that make it possible for them to tolerate close association with humans. From birth, a young mammal spends much of its time in close physical contact with its mother and its litter-mates. A small kitten or puppy, for example, cannot urinate or defecate without help from its mother or some other adult. It has to be rolled on its back and stimulated by vigorous licking. Its mother will wash it frequently, and as it develops it will start playing with its brothers and sisters, and its games will involve much mock-fighting and romping. Like a human infant it will signal its discomfort insistently, but it will show no aggression towards adults and if it belongs to one of the species of mammals that live in social groups it will learn 'rules' of behaviour, involving ways of greeting others and avoiding or inhibiting potentially dangerous conflict, appropriate to its social status within the family group. At first its diet consists of milk, but it will be weaned on to food that is softer than the food eaten by adults, and that is often partly pre-digested by an adult and regurgitated. If it continues to be fed food prepared by humans that is easier to eat and digest than its natural adult diet, individuals will not suffer if their jaws and even their teeth fail to develop fully. In the wild state probably they would starve, but they have no difficulty eating the diet provided by humans. If people think it makes them more attractive, over many generations this can lead to a shortening of the jaw, and a shorter face, to some extent resembling the face of an infant, a juvenile characteristic. As a wild adult it will become much less tolerant of such intimate contact. In the course of domestication, humans select the more placid individuals for breeding, and their placidity is due largely to the fact that they continue to tolerate both close association with others and handling by humans. Essentially this is juvenile behaviour that extends into adulthood, but it must be reinforced by experience and most domesticated animals can revert readily to living without humans, as their own ancestors once lived. A puppy soon learns that the humans who handle it will not hurt it, but a puppy that is not handled frequently in the first three months of its life may never adjust completely to living with humans. It will be nervous, and possibly aggressive, because it is often frightened. It is this retention of juvenile characteristics that makes animals 'tame'. If they had horns, for example, they may lose them entirely, or, more correctly, the horns may never erupt.

Wild sheep did not have the woolly coats all sheep have today. Their coats consisted of two layers, one of short hair next to the skin with a layer of long, lank hair, much like the coat of a goat on the outside. Indeed, at one time it was difficult to distinguish sheep from goats. The Bible refers to this, and archaeologists still have difficulty when they have only a partial skeleton on which to base an identification. The two animals are very similar. The fleece is a product of domestication and is something of a biological mystery. Sheep were domesticated in the first place for their milk and meat. They began growing wool later.

Selective breeding

Once the animals were domesticated, selection could begin. Individuals were allowed to breed only if they possessed traits considered desirable by their human owners. This divided the original stocks into breeds, with different breeds being produced in different places, perhaps from different wild stocks. Later these different stocks were interbred in order to transfer traits from one strain to another, and this process continues. As often as not the desirable traits were purely cosmetic. Some animals were held to look better than others. There was much trading in animals, and some curious case histories, none more curious than that of the turkey.

The wild turkey from which all domestic turkeys are descended lives in North America. Early settlers sent specimens to Britain, where they were bred in captivity, domesticated, and the first commercial breeds were developed. Domesticated turkeys were

Identifying farm livestock (2)

Poultry

Appearance	Breed
Black, with short legs	Orpington
Black, with yellow or dark legs	Leghorn
Black, with dark or black eyes, slaty-blue or black legs	Minorca
Black and white speckled, with red eyes	Blue Andalusian
Spangled black and white, gold or silver	Hamburgh
Blue-black, barred	Maran
Slaty blue	Orpington
Slaty blue or black, with red eyes	Blue Andalusian
Brown	Leghorn
Brown, speckled, with black neck	Indian Game
Buff	Leghorn
Buff, with white legs	Orpington
Gold or silver, with some black	Wyandotte
Greenish, with white tips to the feathers and yellow legs	Ancona
Greenish, with light bars like rings around the body, silvery neck, slaty-blue legs	Campine
Grey, speckled or barred, yellow legs	Plymouth Rock
Reddish brown	Rhode Island Red
White[1]	Light Sussex
	Leghorn
	Orpington
	Plymouth Rock
	Wyandotte

1 Could be any of these.

then exported from Britain to North America, where they became established on farms and in American culture, as the source of meat for festive occasions – the sort of occasions at which the British ate beef, goose or some other meat. It is only quite recently that turkeys have become the most popular Christmas bird in Britain, and the turkeys bred for the purpose are descended from domesticated stock imported from North America.

Other poultry has taken this route, though in less spectacular fashion. The Plymouth Rock breed of poultry takes its name from Plymouth, New Hampshire, not Plymouth, Devon. Wyandottes are also American, and the Maran breed, noted for the dark brown eggs it produces, is French. Most modern commercial poultry, living indoors, does not aspire to anything so grand as a breed name. The birds belong to cross-breeds, known simply by numbers.

The development and 'improvement' of breeds accelerated during the last century until eventually there were hundreds of breeds of cattle, sheep, pigs and poultry, and every breed of cattle had a society dedicated to its promotion and the preservation of its so-called genetic purity. Today, at least with commercial farm animals, looks are of little importance. What matters is the efficiency with which they convert the food they eat into something the farmer can sell. This has led, sadly, to the rejection of many of the older breeds and the extinction of some, as the number of breeds of any importance has been reduced. At the same time there has been much interbreeding, so the animal you see today is very likely to be a cross-breed.

The reason for breeds

Commercial breeding is less whimsical than it may appear. Each type of farm animal yields several different products: poultry produce eggs and also meat; cattle produce milk and meat, with hides as a by-product; sheep produce meat and wool; pigs produce only meat, with hides as a by-product, but the meat that is cured to make bacon is different from meat sold directly, as pork. So the animals themselves must be specialised. Cattle may be bred to produce milk, or meat, or rather less of both. Poultry may be bred to lay eggs or grow large for their meat, or to do rather less well at both. High production of a particular commodity is achieved by breeding an animal that devotes a relatively high proportion of the food it eats into producing that commodity.

Cattle provide the best example of what happens. A dairy cow must produce milk, and lots of it. There is no benefit to the farmer if the cow grows large and muscular. So the perfect dairy cow is a bundle of skin and bones that converts most of its food into milk. A beef animal, on the other hand, must be solid and muscular, but it is not asked to produce any more milk than is needed by its own calves. So it will yield very little milk, but will be heavy and solid. Cross a good dairy animal with a good beef animal and if you are lucky you may produce calves which will grow up as all-purpose beasts. The heifers (female calves) will grow up to join the dairy herd and the bullocks (male calves) will be fattened for beef.

Dairy cows are either pregnant or lactating. That is how they spend their lives, and like all mothers they must eat well. They need rich, luscious grass. You will find them in the lowlands, mainly in the west of Britain where it is more profitable to grow grass than arable crops. Beef cattle are raised more slowly. They are fattened for market on rich grass, but may spend their youth on poorer pastures, sometimes on rather higher ground. Sheep, too, may spend part of their lives on poor upland pastures and the rest of it being fattened in the lowlands, but there are sheep breeds specially adapted for life in one kind of environment or the other. The land, and its climate, affect the kind of farming and the animals being raised, and if you know something about one you can infer something about the other (see p. 109).

Identifying farm livestock (3)

Cattle

Appearance	*Breed*
Variable colour, very shaggy coat, long horns, small	Highland[1]
Black, stocky, even squat	Aberdeen Angus[1]
Black, curly hair[2]	Galloway[1]
	Welsh Black[1]
Black or red, very small indeed[2]	Kerry[3]
	Dexter[3]
Black, curly hair, and white band around shoulders	Belted Galloway[1]
Black and white patches	Friesian[3,4]
Black and white patches, but distinctive white face	Friesian-Hereford[5]
Brown with patches of fawn	Simmental[1]
Brown, from very dark to almost cream, with dark patches around eyes and muzzle	Jersey[3]
Brown with white patches, small	Guernsey[3]
Brown with white patches, large	Ayrshire[3]
Reddish-brown and white, with white face	Hereford[1]
Red	Devon[5]
Red, roan, sometimes white or with white patches	Shorthorn[6]
White, large	Charolais[1]

1 Beef breed.
2 Animals may belong to any of these breeds, which are virtually identical in appearance.
3 Dairy breed.
4 Also known as Holstein-Friesian or British Friesian.
5 All-purpose breed, females raised for dairying, males for beef.
6 Different versions of the same breed have been selected for beef (Shorthorn), dairying (Dairy Shorthorn), or both.

Goats

Appearance	*Breed*
Colour variable, large floppy ears, 'Roman' nose	Anglo-Nubian
Black and white	British Alpine
Golden shaggy coat	Golden Guernsey
White[1]	Saanen
	British Saanen
White and silvery brown, long coat	Toggenburg
White and silvery brown, short coat	British Toggenburg

1 Could be either of these.

Identifying farm livestock (4)

Sheep
The identification of sheep is more difficult because there are so many breeds and crosses and most sheep have a white fleece. The guide is therefore subdivided into groups according to the main distinguishing characteristics, taken in order. Look first to see whether the animal has horns. Then see whether its fleece extends over its forehead, as a fringe, or on to its face. See whether the fleece itself is short and tightly curled, or loose and shaggy. Look at the colour of the face. Finally, because sheep breeds are still found more commonly in the areas where they were first developed, consider the part of the country in which you see them. Compare the list in each of the five subdivisions to find a breed that answers to the description of the one you are examining.

Horns
Blackface
Dalesbred
Dorset Horn
Exmoor Horn
Jacob[1]
Lonk
Rough Fell
Swaledale

Wool on face

1 *With wool, on face or as fringe*
Clun Forest
Dartmoor
Devon Closewool
Devon Longwool
Dorset Down
Dorset Horn
Exmoor Horn
Hampshire Down
Kerry Hill
Leicester
Lincoln Longwool
Llanwenog
Lonk
Oxford Down
Romney
Ryeland
Shropshire
South Devon
Southdown
Teeswater
Wensleydale

2 *No fringe, no wool on face*
Blackface
Black Welsh Mountain
Border Leicester
Cheviot
Dalesbred
Derbyshire Gritstone
Herdwick
Jacob[1]
North Country Cheviot
Radnor
Rough Fell
Shetland
Suffolk
Swaledale
Welsh Mountain
Whiteface Dartmoor

Fleece
1 *Long, loose or shaggy*
Blackface
Border Leicester
Cheviot
Dalesbred
Dartmoor
Derbyshire Gritstone
Devon Longwool
Herdwick
Jacob[1]
Leicester
Lincoln Longwool
Romney
Rough Fell
South Devon
Swaledale
Teeswater
Wensleydale
Whiteface Dartmoor

2 *Short, tightly curled*
Black Welsh Mountain
Clun Forest
Devon Closewool
Dorset Down
Dorset Horn
Exmoor Horn
Hampshire Down
Kerry Hill
Llanwenog
Lonk
North Country Cheviot
Oxford Down
Radnor
Ryeland
Shetland
Shropshire
Southdown
Suffolk

Face colour
1 *Mainly black or brown*
Blackface
Black Welsh Mountain
Clun Forest
Dalesbred (black and white patches)
Dorset Down (grey to brown)
Hampshire Down (dark brown)
Llanwenog
Lonk (black with white patches)
Oxford Down
Radnor (grey)
Shropshire
Southdown (greyish brown)
Suffolk
Swaledale (black with grey muzzle)
Welsh Mountain

2 *Mainly white*
Border Leicester
Cheviot
Dartmoor (white, mottled with black or grey)
Derbyshire Gritstone (white with black patches)
Devon Closewool
Devon Longwool
Dorset Horn
Exmoor Horn
Herdwick
Jacob (white with black patches)[1]
Kerry Hill (white with black nose)
Leicester
Lincoln Longwool
North Country Cheviot
Romney
Rough Fell (white with black patches)
Ryeland
Shetland
South Devon
Teeswater (white or grey)
Welsh Mountain
Wensleydale
Whiteface Dartmoor

Sheep breeds

Location

Anywhere	Jacob[1]
Eastern England, East Midlands	Lincoln Longwool
	Suffolk
English–Scottish borders, Cheviots	Border Leicester
	Cheviot
English–Welsh borders	Clun Forest
	Kerry Hill
	Radnor
Lake District	Herdwick
	Rough Fell
Lowlands generally	Clun Forest
Midlands of England	Oxford Down
	Ryeland
	Shropshire
Northern England	Leicester
	Teeswater
	Wensleydale
Northern Scotland	North Country
	Cheviot
Pennines	Dalesbred
	Derbyshire Gritstone
	Lonk
	Swaledale
Shetlands	Shetland
South of England	Dorset Down
	Dorset Horn
	Exmoor Horn
	Hampshire Down
	Romney
	Southdown
Wales	Black Welsh Mountain
	Llanwenog
	Oxford Down
	Radnor
	Welsh Mountain
Uplands generally, but especially in Scotland and northern England	Blackface
	Border Leicester
West of England	Dartmoor
	Devon Closewool
	Devon Longwool
	South Devon
	Whiteface Dartmoor

1 The Jacob has large, thick horns and may have two or three pairs of them. Its fleece has large brown patches.

Wild animals

Wild vertebrate animals are easier to identify, but much more difficult to observe. They are sensitive to disturbance, which is why hides are used by those who wish to study them closely. Fish, amphibians and reptiles are extremely shy, and will hide if so much as a shadow falls across them, and most of our mammals are either wholly or partly nocturnal. A bright full moon will deter a wood mouse from foraging. If you plan to look for wild animals, therefore, you need a great deal of patience.

You need a field guide, especially for birds, and even more for butterflies and moths and other insects and invertebrates. A field guide is also helpful in identifying mammals, but there are a few general principles to help you distinguish between species you are likely to see which might be mistaken for one another.

Do not attempt to handle any live wild mammal, even if it seems small and harmless. You may injure it, and even a mouse can bite. It is an offence to injure or interfere with any wild animal. Those classified as vermin can be destroyed, but only by properly authorised persons and in carefully specified ways. The fact that an animal is a 'pest' does not mean the law permits it to be treated cruelly.

Even when armed with a field guide you will need to know where to look, and here your maps will help. At one time animals moved freely between Britain and what is now continental Europe, but when the sea-level rose and Britain became an island, immigration ceased for those species which cannot fly. The post-glacial colonisation of Britain was still incomplete, so we have rather fewer native species than are found on the Continent. Species entered from the south and moved across Britain to the Isle of Man and Ireland, but not all of them completed the journey before the Irish Sea flooded in, thus the Isle of Man and Ireland have fewer species than Britain. That is why Britain has three species of snake but Ireland has none, and why you will find field voles, common shrews, moles, harvest mice and weasels in Britain but not in the Isle of Man or Ireland, but stoats and pygmy shrews in both. The stoats and pygmy shrews made the crossing before the sea rose, but the other species were too late.

The colonisers came from forested Europe to forested Britain. They are essentially animals of the forest, although many have adapted to more open countryside. You will find the richest variety of wildlife, therefore, in mixed woodland, and especially close to the woodland edge or in farmed countryside where there are plenty of hedges linking areas of woodland. You will recognise such areas on the 1:50,000-scale map, or more easily on the 1:25,000 map, which shows field boundaries and gives more information about vegetation.

Telling one mammal from another

Rabbits and hares Rabbits and hares look generally similar. Hares are larger, have markedly larger ears, and when disturbed they run for cover, often weaving back and forth as they go, rather than heading for a burrow. Hares do not dig burrows.

Mice, voles, shrews, moles The wood mouse has large ears, a very long tail and soft brown fur. It looks clean and well groomed. A vole has a shorter tail, smaller ears and a coarser, greyer coat. If the animal is mouse-like, very small indeed, dark in colour and has a long, very mobile snout, it is a shrew. If it is dark, larger than a mouse, with shovel-like limbs and eyes so small you can hardly see them, it is a mole.

Stoats and weasels The stoat is larger than the weasel. If the animal you see has a black tip to its tail, a straight, sharp division between its brown upperside and white underside, or in winter is wholly or partly white on its upperside, it is a stoat. The weasel does not turn white in winter, the division between its brown upperside and white underside is irregular, it has no black tip to its tail, and it may have white feet. If you see two or more weasel-like animals together, they are stoats.

POLECAT.

HARE

RABBIT

Mink, otters, polecats You might mistake a mink for an otter. If the animal is dark brown all over and has a slightly bushy tail, it is a mink. The otter is larger, has a pale chin and chest, and a very long tail that is very thick at the base, where it joins the body. In Wales you might see a mink-like animal with rather coarse fur, paler on the upperside than on the underside, and with pale markings on the face. It is a polecat, the wild ancestor of the domesticated ferret.

Deer If you see deer, they are most likely to be red deer, fallow deer or roe deer. If the adults have pale spots they are probably fallow deer, but could be sika deer. The antlers of the male fallow deer are palmate: each antler grows into a blade-like shape, with 'fingers' pointing rearward from the edge of the blade. The sika deer have smaller, simpler antlers, with few branches and no blades. Make sure you are looking only at the adults, because young deer of other species are spotted. The red deer stands 120 to 150 cm (48 to 60 in) tall at the shoulder; the roe deer 65 to 75 cm (26 to 30 in). A very small deer, about 60 cm (24 in) tall at the shoulder, with no antlers but tusks pointing downward from the mouth, is the Chinese water deer. The muntjac is an even smaller deer, only about 50 cm (20 in) tall at the shoulder, with very small antlers. You may hear it barking, rather like a dog.

Mammals that have been introduced

In addition to the native animals, there are those which were introduced by humans and have established themselves in the wild. The rabbit was introduced, probably first to the Scillies in the twelfth century, was common locally in the fifteenth century, but did not become fully established over the whole of mainland Britain until the eighteenth and early nineteenth centuries. The reason Robin Hood killed deer rather than rabbits is that in his day there may have been no rabbits in his part of Nottinghamshire.

The house mouse was also introduced, probably in pre-Roman times, and both brown and black (ship) rats are introductions. Other introductions were more recent. The grey squirrel arrived in Britain in the last century, the edible dormouse that now lives in Hertfordshire in 1902, and the red-necked wallaby escaped from captivity in the 1930s and now lives wild in the Peak District and in part of Sussex.

In a few parts of the country you may catch a glimpse of a porcupine. They, too, have escaped from captivity and established themselves in the wild. The porcupine does not shoot its long quills at people, like arrows, but the quills can be detached easily, so the presence of quills is usually the first evidence anyone has of the presence of porcupines.

An animal that was once domesticated but has taken to living more or less independently of humans is called 'feral'. You may see feral horses in the New Forest, Dartmoor, the Gower Peninsula and elsewhere. There are feral goats in some places.

The coypu, a large South American rodent, was introduced to Britain in 1929 to be farmed for the soft fur, called nutria, that lies next to its skin beneath its outer coat of coarse hair. The first coypus escaped and took to living in the wild in 1932. Mink were introduced in 1929, also to be raised in captivity for their fur. Some escaped almost at once and there has been a feral population ever since.

Signs left by mammals

Most of our mammals can be detected by signs of their presence rather than by actual sightings. A badger set, for example, has large openings into a bank, in dry ground, and you may often see excavated earth and a pile of dry bracken or grass, discarded bedding, near the main entrance. Look along the bottom of hedges and you may see tunnels through the vegetation, large enough for a terrier-sized dog to pass. They could be badger pathways.

A burrow with a smaller mouth may be occupied by a fox, although foxes and badgers sometimes share their accommodation, and one still smaller will have been dug by rabbits. Beware of very small burrow entrances, especially those between the stones in stone walls. They could conceal an adder, or a weasel, and small though it is a weasel is quite fearless and can deliver a savage bite.

There are other tunnels, too, at ground level around large tussocks of grass. They are made by voles.

Mice and voles often carry food to a particular place off the ground where they can eat it in safety. Look in hedgerows or on banks for small level areas at about chest or head height that might serve as feeding platforms for very small animals. You may see a few seeds there, left by a vole because voles eat the flesh of small fruits and discard the seeds. Or you might find the remains of the fruits left by a mouse, because mice eat the seeds and not the flesh.

Where the ground is clear of vegetation and soft you may find footprints. If they are clear enough you should be able to identify them using the illustrations in your field guide. You may also find droppings. They, too, can be used for identification.

Animal tracks may be identified by footprint and stride when seen in mud or snow.

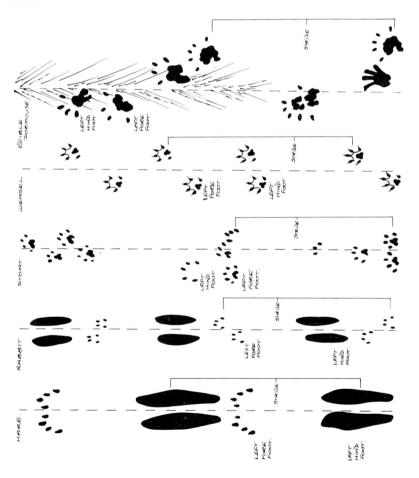

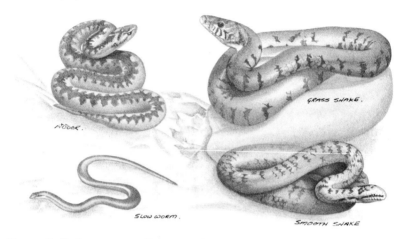

ADDER.

GRASS SNAKE.

SLOW WORM.

SMOOTH SNAKE

Amphibians and reptiles

There are few species of amphibians and reptiles. Toad spawn is laid in strings; frog spawn is laid in massive clumps. Frog and toad tadpoles are indistinguishable. Toads are generally more rough-skinned than frogs. A toad with a distinct yellow mark along its back is a natterjack toad: you may find it near the coast.

Newt tadpoles are small and more or less transparent. There are three British species of newt, the great crested, the smooth and the palmate, the great crested being the largest and the palmate the smallest.

If you find a lizard about 15 cm (6 in) long, generally brown but with attractive though subtle markings, it will be a common or viviparous lizard. If it is a little larger than this and on its underside it has dark rings with spots at the centre, it will be a sand lizard. Male sand lizards are greenish in colour during the mating season.

You may come across a snake-like animal, up to 60 cm (24 in) long, fawn or almost pink in colour and with dark lines running along the sides. This is a slow-worm, a legless lizard, and if you watch it for a while it may reveal its lizardness by blinking at you. Lizards have eyelids; snakes do not. It is quite harmless, but be careful if you handle it for it may shed its tail as a defensive mechanism. It will grow a new tail, but the new one is rarely as handsome as the old.

There are three native British snakes. The most common is the grass snake, which you are most likely to encounter not far from water. The adder also likes water, but you may find it in forests, on the upland moors or on heathland. The much rarer smooth snake occurs only in parts of southern England. Only the adder is venomous.

Reptiles like to bask in the sun on stones, often in or on top of walls, but they also need shade. They rely on basking and finding shade or water to regulate their body temperature. Look for them in summer, soaking up the early morning sunshine.

Birds

Britain has few native mammals, and even fewer amphibians and reptiles. Except in the case of bats, where you will be lucky to get a clear view of the animal, it is not too difficult to distinguish one species from another. With birds it is more difficult, because more than 400 species of bird either live here throughout the year or are seasonal migrants. However, 400 to 500 species is still a number small enough to be contained within a single compact guide. As an amateur you can learn to recognise species of bird. A good guide will not only tell you what to look for, but also where to look. Birds are often very particular in their requirements, and a knowledge of its habitat and a map to locate places where that habitat may be found will increase your chances of seeing any particular type of bird that may interest you.

Insects and other invertebrates

It is not possible to produce a small guide with descriptions of all the insects you may meet. There are more than 20,000 species native to Britain and recognition sometimes depends on small anatomical details. Butterflies can be listed in a guide, because there are less than 400 species of them in the whole of Europe. Like birds, flying insects may be carried long distances by the wind – the English Channel is no more than a minor obstacle – and so to be useful a guide must include European as well as British species.

In Europe you can tell a butterfly from a moth. If the insect has antennae which end in small clubs, flies by day, rests with its wings folded vertically together above its back, and has two pairs of wings held together by their own shape rather than by small hook-like structures linking the forewings to the hindwings, it is a butterfly.

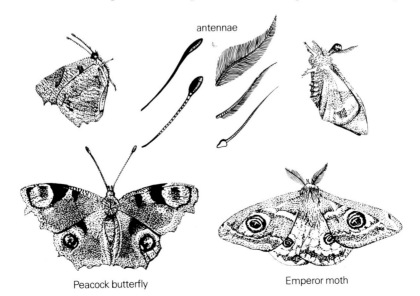

antennae

Peacock butterfly   Emperor moth

These guidelines do not apply throughout the world. There are many exceptions to them; it just so happens that none of the exceptions occurs in Europe.

In Britain there are more than 2000 species of moth, about five species of moth to every species of butterfly. This makes the task of moth identification sound impossible, and so it is if you include the vast list of small, sometimes minute, vaguely pale-coloured, undistinguished moths. If you restrict your list to the larger, more colourful species most of the difficulties are overcome, but if you wish to study living moths you will have to do it at night.

In addition to the insects there are many invertebrates that might interest you but whose positive identification requires some specialist knowledge. There are centipedes and millipedes, for example, woodlice which are crustaceans and not insects, and mites, spiders and harvestmen. Then there are the molluscs, the snails that can be identified by their shells, and the slugs that can only be identified approximately by their appearance: to be positive you need to dissect the specimen.

It all sounds hopeless, but it is far from impossible. All you need is boundless enthusiasm, patience and a willingness to learn the principles of identification as these are outlined in popular field guides, and you can make a start. The mistake is to try too much, to attempt to cover the whole field of vertebrates and invertebrates together. That can lead to discouragement. The professionals specialise and the more expert they become the more they have to narrow their field. Some are authorities on wasps, others on ants, some on spiders, and ornithologists often specialise in passerines (birds that perch), waders, sea birds, owls, or some other group.

The important thing is to experience the countryside, to enjoy it, and to remember that it teems with life even though much of that life may be hidden from you.

PART III
LANDSCAPES

10

MOUNTAINS

The word 'mountain' is used to define any large, elevated feature of a landscape that is more than about 300 m (1000 ft) high. This definition says nothing about the shape of the feature, however, or about the gradients you may encounter as you try to climb or cross it, and because it says nothing about shape and gradient it implies nothing about the vegetation growing there or about the animals feeding on that vegetation or on one another.

A mountainous region is one with many steep gradients rising to high elevations, certainly rising to more than 300 m and often to twice that height or more. Some of the gentler slopes and high plateaux will be grassed, but there will be many rocky outcrops and sheer rock faces and screes. There will be small rivers flowing rapidly down the slopes and into steep-sided, flat-bottomed valleys, many of which will be glacial features. These valleys are much wider than could possibly have been cut by their present rivers.

Maps of mountains

You will find such landscapes in the Outer and Inner Hebrides, mainland Scotland north-west of a line from the Tay to the Clyde, in the Southern Uplands, a belt extending across the Scottish–English border region and joining the Pennines to the south, in the Lake District, the Pennines, and North and Mid-Wales. The relevant OS Landranger sheets are:

Outer Hebrides 8; 13; 14; 18; 22; 31
Inner Hebrides and adjacent west coast of Scotland 23; 24; 32; 33; 39; 40; 46; 47; 48; 49; 55; 60; 61; 62; 63; 68; 69
Highland Scotland 9; 10; 15; 16; 17; 19; 20; 25; 26; 34; 35; 36; 41; 42; 43; 44; 50; 51; 52; 53; 56; 57; 58
Southern Uplands 73; 74; 76; 77; 79; 80; 81
Lake District 85; 86; 89; 90; 91; 96; 97; 98
Pennines 104; 105; 110; 111; 119; 120; 128
North and Mid-Wales 115; 116; 123; 124; 125; 135; 136; 146; 147; 160; 161

The mountains of the Lake District, Peak District, Snowdonia (North Wales) and Brecon Beacons (Mid-Wales) are inside the boundaries of national parks. There are no national parks in Scotland. National parks provide planning protection from inappropriate development and encourage forms of land management that preserve the scenic quality, but they confer no special rights of public access.

Necessary precautions in the mountains

You can visit the mountain areas of Britain by road, and much of the best of their scenery can be seen from car parks, laybys or within a short, easy walk of villages or visitor centres. If you plan a more adventurous excursion, away from roads, you must take great care and follow the advice given in Part I. Go nowhere unless you have the appropriate map. Remember that rainfall is higher in the mountains than elsewhere, that temperature falls as you climb and wind speed increases, and that even in summer weather conditions can deteriorate rapidly. You will be safe enough if you take sensible precautions and travel prepared, recognising that the mountains of Britain can be extremely dangerous and are full of traps for the unwary. Do not be deceived by the relatively small scale of the British landscape. A fall of several hundred metres will cause as much damage to the human body in Britain as it would in the Alps or the Himalayas.

Except for the highest peaks and areas of bare rock, most of the British mountains are farmed. On the higher ground you will find coarse grasses used as pasture, mainly for sheep but in better areas for cattle as well. On the lower ground, especially in the wide glacial

High mountains sheltering a fertile, farmed valley, with a country park. Invershiel, Highlands. Map no. 33.

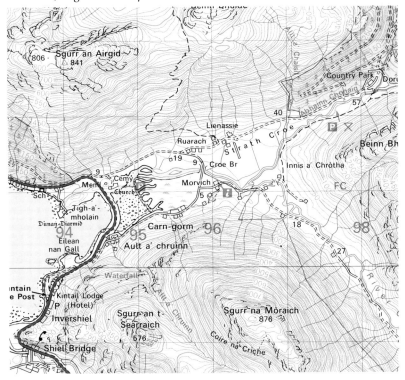

Coire an t-Sheachda, in the Cairngorms.

valleys, even at high altitudes, you will find ploughed fields and farm crops, much of them grown to feed livestock through the winter when most of the animals are kept in yards. The mountains are scenically beautiful, but they are hard places to live and farm incomes are well below those in the gentler lowlands. Tourism brings in much needed money, and is welcome, but as a visitor you must remember that even in the national parks local communities must continue to farm the land, and you must respect their right to do so and observe the Country Code and Access Charter.

The Grampians

The most majestic of the British mountain ranges, the Grampian that lies between the Highland Boundary and Great Glen Faults and forms the heart of the Scottish Highlands, is ancient and most of it has disappeared. It was formed when rocks being thrust from the south-east encountered the older, very solid rocks to the north-west and were folded upward. In their youth, some 400 million years ago, the Grampians stood higher than the Himalayas stand today. They have been eroded by the weather, and the extent of that erosion bears dramatic witness to the eternal remorseless power of ice, water and wind.

The range, including minor ranges such as the Cairngorm, still contains our highest mountains, including Cairn Gorm itself (1245 m, 4084 ft) and Ben Nevis (1343 m, 4406 ft). Apart from its ski slopes and associated tourist facilities, Cairn Gorm lies on one side of the Cairngorms National Nature Reserve, between Cairn Gorm and Ben Macdui (Beinn MacDuibh), at 1310 m (4296 ft) the highest peak in the Cairngorm range. The Reserve covers almost 26,000 hectares (64,000 acres), making it the largest nature reserve in Britain and one of the largest in Europe.

To the north and north-west the Grampians are formed from older sedimentary rocks which have eroded in a fairly uniform way, so the mountains there are generally lower, more rounded, and have more plateaux than those further south. Volcanoes and the intrusion of granites have added to the scenic grandeur and geological complexity of the central and southern Highlands.

It is in this region that you will find the clearest evidence of the ice sheets. Apart from such obvious glacial features as U-shaped valleys, there are large surface boulders and screes which also indicate the work of glaciers. Moving ice sheets ripped away projecting rocks and carried them as boulders, while the expansion of water as it froze in cracks in the peaks protruding above the ice caused more boulders and smaller fragments to break free and fall.

In parts of the Highlands you will find what remains of the Caledonian Forest, of pine and birch, but if you want to see a display containing 60 per cent of the plants typical of an arctic–alpine habitat you should visit the Ben Lawers National Nature Reserve (NG reference NN 6138), which you can reach by travelling south-west from Aberfeldy along the A827 road, beside Loch Tay. The mountain itself rises to 1215 m (3984 ft). There is a nature trail and you can go on a guided walk from the visitor centre which is open from Easter to the end of September.

You may see a golden eagle in the remoter parts of the Highlands. The only bird with which you might confuse it is the buzzard, but not if you are familiar with buzzards. A golden eagle is half as large again as a buzzard, and when seen from below it has a much more prominent head and a longer, rather square tail.

Red deer are fairly common throughout the Highlands, and in the Glen More part of the Cairngorms, near Loch Morlich to the east of Aviemore, you may see reindeer. A herd was introduced there from Sweden in 1952 and is now fully established. The reindeer is much like the red deer, but smaller, standing about 1 m (40 in) tall at the shoulder. Adults of both sexes have antlers (in red deer only males have antlers) and the main beam of the antlers is rather flattened in cross-section; in red deer it is round. Reindeer are very variable in colour but in winter they are almost white. The animals are domesticated, although they roam freely in search of food. There is an information centre at Glenmore Lodge (NG reference NH 9909).

Southern Uplands

The Southern Uplands, including the Cheviot Hills on the eastern side, are less rugged than the Highlands, but provide the most beautiful and dramatic entrance to Scotland if you follow the A68 northward. Precisely at the Border you pass Carter Bar (418 m, 1370 ft) and have a view across miles of green, rolling hills. The view to the south, into England, is blocked by higher ground.

The central part of the Uplands forms a massif, with summits rising to more than 750 m (2500 ft). This separates the Midland Plain, containing the main Scottish coal-mining and industrial belt, with Glasgow at the western end and Edinburgh at the eastern, from the Solway Plain running across northern England, with Newcastle upon Tyne at its eastern end. At one time the hills were much higher. They are of the same age as those of the Lake District and North Wales, but lack the hard granites and volcanic rocks that slowed the process of erosion in Wales and Cumbria, so the Border hills are gentler, almost featureless. The summits that stand above the lower hills are made from massive grits, harder than the surrounding greywackes, mudstones and flagstones, but even they are rounded. Almost everywhere the hills are grassed, and sheep have grazed them for centuries.

Moffat Water, with the hanging valley and waterfall at Roundstonefoot. Map no. 78.

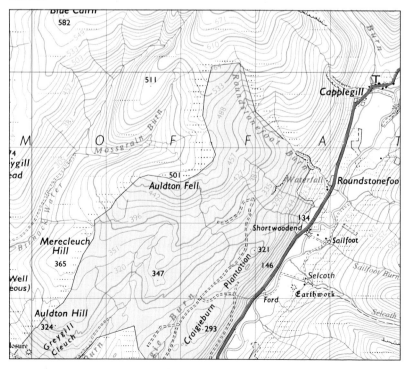

Grey Mare's Tail waterfall at Roundstonefoot.

It is a glacial landscape, once buried deep beneath its own ice sheet, and the evidence is still to be seen. Follow the A708 road between Selkirk and Moffat and you will travel along one side of a glacial valley through which Moffat Water meanders between hills that rise steeply to over 300 m (1000 ft). Look out for the waterfall from a hanging valley at Roundstonefoot (NG reference NT 139085).

The wildlife is similar to that of the Highlands, and you may see a golden eagle, peregrine falcon or merlin. If you see a bird that looks like a crow but is much larger it will be a raven. You may also see red-throated and black-throated divers in the lochs. This is the furthest south that either species breeds.

Lake District

The high ground of the Lake District was raised at the same time as the Pennines, about 24 million years ago, when the Alps were forming in central Europe and active submarine volcanoes were ejecting the rocks from which Snowdon was being built. Many of the peaks are more than 750 m (2500 ft) high and Scafell Pike (a 'pike' is a peak) is the highest mountain in England (NG reference NY 216071) at 978 m (3210 ft). In the north around Skiddaw (NG reference NY 260290) the hills are made from sedimentary rocks, sandstones and muds that have been heated and compressed to make slates, then squeezed and folded. To the south, around Scafell and Helvellyn, the landscape has been made in the first place by volcanoes. There are beds of lava, rocks and ash ejected by volcanic explosions, and some of the ash has formed mud and then slate. The southern slate, originally made from volcanic ash, makes good roofing material. The slate to the north occurs in thick slabs and is used to make walls around fields. Today the volcanic region is a range of hills, but at one time most of it was simply high rolling land that over the years has been cut and eroded by ice and water until it assumed its present form. Further south still, around Lake Windermere and Coniston Water, the landscape is gentler, more rolling, over sandstones, grits and slates.

Although the entire region is geologically young, it has been severely eroded, mainly by ice. When it formed, what is now the entire Lake District was domed and rivers flowed outward from the centre. When the ice came glaciers tended to follow existing river valleys, moving outward from the centre, deepening and widening the valleys. When the ice melted some of the valleys flooded, forming the present lakes. A glance at a map shows the lakes as long and narrow, and radiating outward from a centre somewhere near Grasmere. Further evidence of their origin as glacial valleys is provided by the hanging valleys that enter some of them. You may find a good example at the north-western end of Buttermere (NG reference NY 173162), but the whole of the Lake District should be seen as a glacial landscape with many of the features you would expect.

Most of the Lake District is grassed, although there is a great deal of bracken, a plant that thrives by being burned, is almost impossible to clear except by aerial spraying with a herbicide, and that most farm animals find unpalatable. The Herdwick sheep will eat it, however. Look out for this breed. Beatrix Potter, who lived in the Lake District, was very active in improving and promoting it. Look out, too, for golden eagles, peregrine falcons and ravens. If you are a keen lepidopterist you may be fortunate enough to find the mountain ringlet (*Erebia epiphron*), an alpine butterfly found nowhere else in Britain.

The Pennines

The Pennines run like a line of vertebrae along a north–south line through the centre of northern England. Ashbourne lies at the southern end and the highest ground is found near Edale and Hayfield, between the A624 and A57 roads running south and east from Glossop. Kinder Scout (NG reference SK 0987) rises to 636 m (2088 ft) and the peak of Bleaklow Hill (NG reference SK 0996), north of the A57, is 633 m (2077 ft). Much of the area is on limestone rocks, and local water is rich in minerals. Ashbourne water is now bottled and sold in supermarkets, and Matlock and Buxton are spa towns. The limestone has been worn away below ground to form potholes and caves, attracting many potholers, but the ease with which in dry weather the rivers move to underground courses has caused difficulties for local people. The Manifold, for example, appears and disappears in so complicated a fashion that for many years no one really knew its complete course. The Manifold Valley, to the west of the more famous Dovedale, runs through Ilam (NG reference SK 1451). Because of the unreliability of their water supply, villages in the district tend to crowd along the sides of dependable streams.

Herdwick sheep and, holding the prize certificate, Beatrix Potter. The man is Tom Storey, her shepherd.

Wales

The Welsh mountains form a continuous massif, but can be divided into three sections. In the south the Brecon Beacons, with the Black Mountains to both east and west, have peaks at 886 m (2906 ft, NG reference SO 0222) and 763 m (2504 ft, NG reference SO 0621). Waun Fâch (NG reference SO 2129) rises to 811 m (2660 ft) and several others reach almost to that height. They are formed mainly from Old Red Sandstone.

To the north-west, the Cambrian Mountains are made from slates and shales, rocks that erode easily to produce a gentler landscape. The ground remains high, however, and Pumlumon Fawr (Plynlimon, NG reference SH 7987) rises to 752 m (2467 ft). The Cambrian Mountains are the only place in Britain where you may see the red kite (*Milvus milvus*), a bird of prey that was once fairly common.

The mountains of North Wales, dominated by Snowdon (NG reference SH 6155), rising to 1085 m (3559 ft), are volcanic, but eroded by glaciers into rough, jagged peaks and screes separated by deep glacial valleys. The A4086 road from Capel Curig to Llanberis follows one of the best examples, the Llanberis Pass.

Llanberis Pass, Snowdonia, a deep glacial valley. Map no. 115.

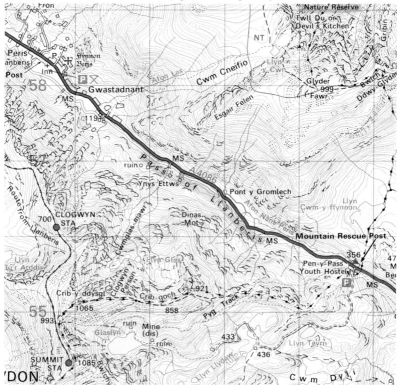

11

HILLS, HEATHS, MOORS AND DOWNS

The words 'heath' and 'moor' are often used interchangeably, but there is a difference. A heath may develop in the lowlands on a sandy or depleted, usually acid soil. A moor forms on high ground and is often wet, in places with bogs or marshy areas. This means that heaths and moors differ in their vegetation, and thus in the animals they support, as well as in the conditions they provide for walkers.

Hills may be no more than small mountains, but as the word is used here they are grassed all the way to the summit and offer splendid scenery with generally gentle walking conditions, although some gradients may be steep. The Downs are quite distinct, developed over low, gently rolling, chalk hills.

Heaths

A heath is a region with few or no trees, having a cool, moist climate. In summer the average temperature during the hottest month is rarely more than 17°C (63°F); it rains on two days out of three, with rainfall distributed fairly evenly throughout the year, and the total rainfall is usually between 60 and 110 cm (24 to 43 inches).

Often heathlands occur in the mountains, but you can find them in the lowlands, too, and in Britain they may develop almost anywhere given the opportunity. That opportunity depends upon the prevention of colonisation by trees. Left to itself, lowland Britain would revert to forest. Heaths are potentially forests, places where trees are not allowed to grow. Despite their lack of trees, however, heaths may be called 'forest', because at one time they were retained for hunting. By the time the legendary Robin Hood roamed Sherwood Forest, in the twelfth century, it was mainly heathland developed over sandy soil, with trees or clumps of woodland here and there.

Wherever you find heathland the original forest was cleared to provide land on which to graze livestock, and subsequent grazing has kept the area treeless. Sometimes the original clearance took place a very long time ago. The Breckland was cleared around 5000 years ago and parts of the Sussex and Hampshire Downs were cleared up to a thousand years before that, but the main clearance and early development of heathland occurred during the Bronze

The view north into Westerdale on Danby High Moor, North York Moors National Park.

Age, which began in Britain about 3000 years ago. Grazing prevents recolonisation by trees, but for heathland to develop something must also prevent farmers from ploughing and growing crops. In many cases the emerging heath was common land, at first not needed for crop cultivation and then, when the management of common land became formalised, barred from any use that would preclude the rights of the commoners. In other places, such as in North Yorkshire, repeated clearance of forest accompanied by the burning of wood and surface vegetation depleted the soil and left it too acid for cultivation. Most heaths have acid soils.

Farm livestock would have destroyed tree seedlings, but the cattle and sheep had competitors. When the trees were removed and the ground surface was exposed to direct sunlight, grasses and herbs flourished. These attracted large herbivorous wild animals, such as deer, whose numbers increased in response to the large food supply. Great herds of deer may have trampled or eaten such young trees as the cattle missed, and in modern times sheep and rabbits have maintained heathland landscapes. Today we find those landscapes attractive, but had there been any Bronze Age, Roman or Saxon environmentalists they might have campaigned against such devastation of the countryside. Heathlands are derelict landscapes.

As its name implies, the most common plant on most heaths is heather, also known as heath or ling. There are six species native to Britain, although some occur only locally. The most common is heather or ling itself (*Calluna vulgaris*), with tiny pale pink or purple flowers. The plant most people regard as Scottish 'purple' heather is bell-heather (*Erica cinerea*), which grows in many parts of Britain, but there is a species with deep purple flowers that really is confined to the Scottish mountains. It is blue heath (*Phyllodoce coerulea*).

Heather has distinct phases in its growth. At first it is a small, pyramid-shaped plant. Where plants have grown from seed they will be scattered, but where they have developed from the roots of older plants they form clumps. Branches then grow outwards until the plant is dome-shaped. By the time the plant is about twenty-five years old the branches have become crowded, their outward growth has slowed, and a gap appears in the centre. The gap widens and branches start to collapse to the sides and those at the centre die, while new plants emerge around the edges from roots produced by the horizontal branches.

Grouse feed on heather, and in areas where grouse are hunted the heather is managed for their benefit. Such an area of managed heather is called a grouse moor.

In addition to heaths and heathers you may find bilberries (also known as whortleberries), broom and gorse. The surface vegetation provides good cover for small mammals, which attract predators, especially kestrels, and in summer you should see many butterflies.

Heaths are best developed on well-drained ground in the south of England, although there are some good examples as far north as Cheshire. You can visit heathlands in the areas covered by the following OS Landranger sheets (the NG references relate to visitor or information centres or points of access).

Cheshire *Little Budworth Common Country Park* (NG reference SJ 590655) 117; 118. *Thurstaston Common* (NG reference SJ 244853) 108
Cornwall *The Lizard* (NG reference SW 701140) 203
Devon *Chudleigh Knighton Heath* (NG reference SX 838776) 191
Dorset *Studland Heath* (NG reference SZ 034836) 195
Dyfed *Dowrog Common* (NG reference SM 769268) 157
Glamorgan *Ogmore Down* (NG reference SS 897762) 170
Hampshire *Yateley Common Country Park* (NG reference SU 822597) 186
Hereford and Worcester *Devil's Spittleful* (NG reference SO 810747) 138. *Hartlebury Common* (NG reference SO 820705) 138; 139
Leicestershire *Bradgate Park* (NG reference SK 523116) 129
London *Wimbledon Common* (NG reference TQ 2271) 176
Nottinghamshire *Sherwood Forest Country Park* (NG reference SK 627677) 120
Staffordshire *Cannock Chase* 127; 128
Suffolk *Cavenham Heath* (Breckland) (NG reference TL 757727) 155. *Dunwich Common* (NG reference TM 476685) 156
Surrey *Thursley* (NG reference SU 915399) 186
West Midlands *Sutton Park* (NG reference SP 103963) 139

Moors

Moors occur on poorly drained, fairly level ground in the uplands. Bogs are characteristic of moorland. They develop where ground becomes waterlogged, and this produces anaerobic (airless) conditions in which the decomposition of dead plant material is very slow. The material accumulates, the soil becomes very acid, and this limits the plants that can survive to those adapted to a humid, acid soil. There are few nutrients available to the plants, so you often find species with unusual means of sustenance, such as the carnivorous sundews (*Drosera*) which trap insects. Despite being so wet, evaporation from the surface may be high and so desiccation is always a risk. The several species of bog mosses (*Sphagnum*) are able to absorb and retain large amounts of water, and thrive to become the most common plant in many bogs.

You will find moors throughout the upland areas of Britain, but the most spectacular examples are listed below, with their relevant OS Landranger sheet numbers and NG references where appropriate.

Clwyd *Moel Famau Country Park* (NG reference SJ 171611) 116
Cornwall *Bodmin Moor* 200; 201
Cumbria *Moor House* (NG reference NY 730325) 91
Derbyshire *Longshaw* (NG reference SK 267800) 110; 119
Devon *Dartmoor National Park* 191; 202. *Exmoor National Park* 180; 181
Dumfries and Galloway *Galloway Forest Park* 76; 77. *Silver Flowe* (NG reference NX 470820) 77
Glamorgan *Blaenrhondda Waterfalls Walk* (NG reference SN 922021) 170
Highland Region (Sutherland) *Ben More Coigach* (NG reference NC 085040) 15. *Strathy Bog* (NG reference NC 790550) 10
Isle of Man Centre and south of the island, 95
Northumberland *Harbottle Crags* (NG reference NT 927048) 80
Powys *Lake Vyrnwy* (Llyn Efyrnwy) (NG reference SH 985215) 125
Shropshire *Long Mynd* (NG reference SO 425945) 137
Somerset *Exmoor National Park* 180; 181
Strathclyde *Braehead Moss* (NG reference NS 955510) 72
Yorkshire *North York Moors National Park* 94; 100; 101

Downs

The downs are low, rolling, grass-covered hills developed over chalk that in some places has been exposed, sometimes by men cutting away the thin layer of turf to make pictures, sometimes by natural erosion. Some of the man-made designs, such as the Cerne Abbas Giant in Dorset (NG reference ST 6802), or the White Horse near Uffington, Berkshire (NG reference SU 3086), are very ancient. The White Horse is 114 m (374 ft) long and no one knows who carved

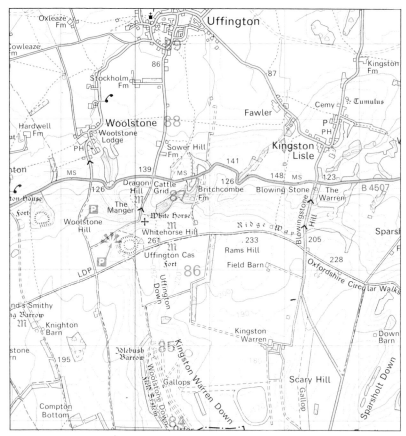

Ridgeway and Whitehorse Hill, Oxfordshire. Map no. 174.

it, or why or when, although, like similar horses carved elsewhere on the downs, it is believed to date from the Iron Age, more than 2000 years ago. The Cerne Abbas Giant was carved much later, in Romano-British times. Other carvings are more recent. Military badges not far from Wilton, Wiltshire, are a modern reminder of the association between the Army and nearby Salisbury Plain.

Apart from imposing some restrictions on public access, the Army exerts a generally beneficent influence on Salisbury Plain, as it does in the case of most of its firing ranges. It prevents any other form of land use and controls the movement of people. This allows the wildlife to flourish, so these areas are so rich in species that were the Army to leave, the only sensible alternative would be to establish nature reserves on them. Salisbury Plain is now the largest continuous area of uncultivated downland in Britain, and there is another large area not far away, at Porton Down.

There are remains of many ancient settlements dotted all over the downs. Stonehenge is the most famous, but it is only one of innumerable sites. Clearly the early inhabitants of these islands found the downs attractive places to live, and it is not too difficult to see why they were among the first areas to be deforested. Imagine Britain with a warmer, wetter climate than it has today. The lowlands, and especially the valleys, are forested. The Downs are also forested, but there, over the chalk, the soil is thinner and the trees easier to clear. Once cleared, the land commands good views over long distances. It is easy to see parties of people approaching but it is also much easier to find your way from one settlement to another if you keep to the tops of the hills, and people needed to travel in order to trade. The thin downland soil was light and could be easily cultivated before the heavy iron plough was introduced, so crops could be grown there. Where the ground remained uncultivated, grass grew to feed livestock, and grazing prevented recolonisation by bushes and trees.

Eventually the downland settlements were abandoned and people moved to lower ground, probably in response to a deterioration in the climate, but the downs were never abandoned. They remained in use, and when sheep farming became economically important they were a convenient source of plant nutrients. Sheep were turned out to graze on the downs but brought back to the farm in time for them to complete the digestion of their feed. The grass was removed from the high ground and the manure was deposited on the lower ground. The system was ingenious, but the downs were severely depleted of plant nutrients. In some places this deliberate over-grazing removed the turf entirely, and exposed the chalk. Where a covering soil remained it was rich in humus, but despite the underlying chalk it was, and is, acid.

The impoverishment of the soils meant that very fast-growing, 'aggressive' plants were unable to dominate the sward, for such plants need good feeding. Annuals were uncommon, because they must grow rapidly to complete their life-cycles within a single season. A great variety of species flourished, more modest in their requirements but intolerant of shade, and in modern times rabbits joined the sheep to help maintain the unusual downland habitat.

Today it is more difficult to maintain the grassland of the downs with its great variety of herbs. Sheep farming has declined and myxomatosis periodically reduces the rabbit population, so there is a tendency for scrub to invade as the first stage in a return to woodland. In addition, the profitability of arable farming has encouraged some farmers to plough the thin soils for cereals.

The downs are famous for their orchids, which include the bee orchid (*Ophrys apifera*). This orchid takes six to eight years to produce a flower bearing a startlingly lifelike resemblance to a bumblebee. It might seem that the idea is to trick male bumblebees into mating with the flower so that they collect pollen and transfer it to the next bee-like flower with which they try to mate. As an example of evolutionary ingenuity it leaves something to be desired,

Bee orchid (Ophrys apijera).

however, because the bee orchid pollinates itself. Perhaps the real reason is quite different, or the resemblance is pure coincidence and exists, like beauty, only in the eye of the human beholder. In addition to orchids you may find wild herbs such as salad burnet, basil, thyme and marjoram, and where there are bright flowers and strong perfumes you will find insects, including butterflies.

The downs occupy a broad sweep of southern England. If you plan to visit all of them you will need OS sheets 173, 174, 184, 185, 186, 196, 197 and 198.

Hills

Britain has so many ranges of hills that it is impossible to list all of them, while to suggest that some are more interesting, more attractive, or in some other way more noteworthy than others would be less than fair. However, it may be helpful to mention a few of the better-known ranges, a visit to which may encourage the intrepid explorer to search more deeply into the British countryside. In each case the relevant OS Landranger sheet numbers are given.

Brendon Hills Somerset 181
Cotswolds Gloucestershire-Oxfordshire 162; 163
Forest of Bowland Lancashire 97; 98; 103
Malvern Hills Hereford and Worcester 150
Mendip Hills Somerset 182
Moorfoot and Lammermuir Hills Lothian-Borders 66; 67
Ochill Hills Fife 58
Pentland Hills Lothian-Borders 66; 72; 73
Quantock Hills Somerset 181; 182
Yorkshire Dales National Park (south Pennines) 92; 98; 99

12

FORESTS

We cannot know what the British part of the original Atlantic Forest, the 'wildwood', was like. There are woods in Britain, now open to the public, that have been undisturbed for a long time, but that means for hundreds rather than thousands of years. Even had humans not wrought changes, the climate has fluctuated over the centuries. It is much cooler now than it was when the Atlantic Forest was in its prime and the Little Ice Age that lasted from the Middle Ages until late in the last century brought even harsher conditions than those we experience now. Natural communities are not static. They may change little over several human generations, but over long periods their structure and composition adjust in response to many influences.

Today there is a larger total area of woodland in Britain than there has been for a very long time, perhaps for a thousand years. This fact does not re-create a landscape typical of a Saxon landscape, of course, for much of the forested area consists of plantations containing a limited number of exotic species, and the farming landscape is quite unlike any in which a Saxon farmer would have felt at home. It does mean, though, that there are many forests you can visit, of a wide range of types; and all forests support many species in addition to trees.

Woodland as a community

As you walk through a wood it is not too difficult to see how the community manages its affairs, at least in a general kind of way. To the layman the area is obviously dominated by trees. But to the specialist the word 'dominant' is used in three senses. To the ecologist, studying communities of plants and animals, the dominant species is the one that exerts the greatest influence over the community as a whole. To the botanist, interested only in plants, the dominant species is the most influential one in each part of the community, so a wood will have dominant tree species but also dominant shrubs and herbs. To the forester, a dominant is a tree that towers above its neighbours, the tallest tree, and perhaps one that will soon be felled.

The trees dominate a wood because they are larger than other plants and also because they live for much longer. There are oaks believed to be more than one thousand years old, and even short-lived trees can reach ages of a century or more. The trees account for

Forest of Dean, Gloucestershire – a large area of plantation and ancient woodland. Map no. 162.

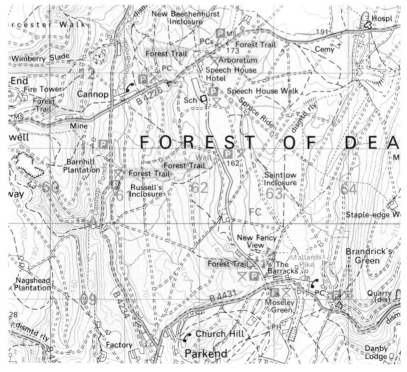

Where light shines directly on the woodland floor small herbs flourish, but they cannot tolerate shade.

a very large amount of plant material. In one hectare of a mature conifer plantation the trees may consist of about 400 kg of cones, 5.5 tonnes of needles, more than 9 tonnes of wood and nearly 1.5 tonnes of bark in the branches, and 41 tonnes of wood and more than 4.5 tonnes of bark in the stems, a total of around 62 tonnes (about 25 tons in an acre). In one hectare of broadleaved woodland about 25 million leaves fall to the ground each autumn (about 10 million to the acre).

As the trees shed material – needles, broad leaves, fruits, twigs, branches, pieces of bark and so forth – food is supplied to species living at ground level, but much of it consists of celluloses which animals cannot digest. The material is attacked by bacteria and fungi, which support a community of small plants, and the animals that feed on them. Rummage carefully in the top 10 centimetres (4 inches) or so of a small area of woodland soil and if you manage to collect a good sample, and if you have access to a microscope, you could find tens of billions of organisms.

The living trees also provide food and shelter for fungi such as bracket fungi, climbers such as ivy, mosses, lichens and ferns, for insects that feed on leaves, shelter in cracks in the bark, bore into the wood, or parasitise leaves to produce galls, and for micro-organisms. They provide buds, fruits and seeds for birds and such small mammals as squirrels and some mice, while birds also feed on the insects.

How trees influence other plants

A tree takes water from the soil, transports it to all its branches and twigs, and allows it to evaporate through its leaves (the needles of conifers are leaves). This makes the air surrounding the tree moist, but the soil beneath the tree rather dry and depleted of nutrients. The trees provide shelter from the wind, so temperatures within a wood fluctuate less than they would in open country. But the trees also shade the ground, in summer making it cooler than more exposed ground might be. They also shelter the ground directly beneath them from rain and snow, so that precipitation is distributed unevenly. You may find that when the open paths through the wood are wet and muddy the ground is much drier deep inside the wood, among the trees.

Trees also modify the chemistry of the soil around them. The litter they deposit on the surface makes the soil more acid, but some trees create more acid conditions than others. Oaks produce a very acid soil, for example, and conifers tend to produce a more acid soil than broadleaved species. Only plants tolerant of an acid soil can grow in the immediate vicinity of trees. The distribution of those plants reveals the direction of the prevailing wind, for it is the material falling from the tree that makes the soil acid; although the wind seldom blows strongly deep inside a wood, falling material inevitably drifts a short distance downwind, so the soil is more acid on the downwind side of the tree. If you can recognise acid-tolerant plants, you may be able to work out the direction of the prevailing wind from the plants growing near trees.

All green plants must have light, but different plants need different amounts, so you can tell something about the extent of shading from the plants you see growing on the ground. If there are no green plants you may be sure little light penetrates. A thin covering of moss can survive on rather more than one-tenth of the intensity of light you would find in open country on an overcast day. If there is a great deal of moss the light intensity will be about one-quarter that of an overcast day in the open. Grass can grow with about the same amount of light, but it will not really thrive unless it receives nearly half the light it would have on an overcast day in the open. Heathers need rather more than that.

Obviously the intensity of light is greater in direct sunshine, but inside a wood there is actually more light on a cloudy day. Direct sunlight travels in straight lines, creating deep shadows as well as brilliant illumination, but clouds scatter the light, so it enters at many different angles and illuminates a larger area. You could check this with a photographic light meter.

Woodland fungi

Fungi are not classified as plants at all, but are placed in a category of their own. They need no light, and they are very efficient at extracting nutrients even from severely depleted soils, so they flourish in woodlands.

Many of them are intimately associated with the trees, and not merely as parasites. A fungus consists of a *mycelium*, a network of filaments through which the fungus obtains nutrients. When the time comes for the fungus to reproduce it grows a *fruiting body* within which spores develop. The spores are then shed, to be carried on the wind to places where new fungi can grow. Many fungi are microscopically small and their fruiting bodies are barely visible to the naked eye. Others produce large and in some cases edible fruiting bodies. The mushroom or toadstool you see in late summer or autumn is a fruiting body. It disappears as soon as its spores have been shed, but the fungus remains as the hidden mycelium. Many species of fungus always appear close to trees of particular species. This may mean no more than that the tree and the fungus have similar requirements. In some cases, though, the relationship is much closer. The mycelium grows among the roots of the tree, and trees with fungal mycelia grow faster and stronger than those without. This is a *mycorrhizal* relationship in which the fungus obtains sugars directly from the tree and the presence of the fungus makes it easier for the tree to take up mineral nutrients from the soil, so both benefit.

The poisonous but beautiful fly agaric (Amanita muscaria).

Where you find fly agaric (*Amanita muscaria*) or the striking purple *Cortinarius violaceus* you will usually find birch trees nearby. The sickener (*Russula emetica*) grows near pine trees. The false chanterelle (*Hygrophoropsis aurantiaca*) grows where there are both birch and pine. *Tricholoma albobrunneum* prefers beech, but its relative the bright yellow sulphur toadstool (*Tricholoma sulphureum*) likes oak.

There are many species of fungus which produce large fruiting bodies. Many are very beautiful, some are edible and taste delicious. However, there are many more whose edibility is uncertain, or that are edible when cooked but not raw, like the sickener which causes vomiting if you eat it uncooked. Some are poisonous, and among those there are some which are deadly. Unless you are very sure you have identified the species correctly and know what you are doing, never eat a wild fungus.

Squirrels

The most familiar woodland mammal is the squirrel. The grey squirrel (*Sciurus carolinensis*) was introduced from North America about a century ago, just as the population of the native red squirrel (*Sciurus vulgaris*) was declining. No one knows why its population fluctuates, although the destruction of its habitat may be an important cause and disease epidemics probably contribute. The success of the grey during a time when the red was depleted may have prevented the red from returning, but contrary to popular belief the grey squirrel did not drive away the red, and from time to time it suffers from disease epidemics of its own.

On the whole the red squirrel prefers conifer woodlands and the grey squirrel broadleaved woodlands, although each of them can make a living in woodland of either type and grey squirrels have made themselves at home in town parks. Both are capable of causing serious damage to trees, but at present the comparative rarity of the red squirrel means that it is not regarded as a pest, whereas the grey squirrel is.

You are unlikely to find grey squirrels in northern Scotland or on any offshore islands. Red squirrels are more or less confined to north-west Scotland, North Wales and parts of northern and eastern England, and you may find them on some islands, including the Isle of Wight and Anglesey.

Age of woodland

Woodlands are classified by ecologists according to their age. Age is important because of the time it takes for a full, rich community of plants and animals to develop. The older the woodland the greater diversity of species you are likely to find in it. This does not mean the woodland must remain untouched – indeed, management can improve it. What matters is that it remains woodland and at no stage are all the trees cleared from a large area which is then turned over to another use.

Primary woodland occurs on a site which is known to have been wooded since the first human records were kept. Because of the nature of the historical record this implies that the area has been wooded since its original colonisation by the wildwood. Secondary woodland is known to have been planted at some time in the past, or to grow on land that has not always been wooded. If the site was wooded before about 1600 it is called 'ancient' woodland.

Bratley Wood ancient woodland, New Forest.

Traditional woodland management

As already noted, you cannot find woodland that you can be sure is identical to the 'wildwood', although in Scotland what remains of the Caledonian Forest comes close. Elsewhere you can find areas that closely resemble medieval forest, because by the Middle Ages the management of the trees was well established in ways that ensured they yielded a reliable crop of wood and timber year after year.

The boundaries of the area belonging to a particular owner were marked, often with a ditch and bank to keep out grazing animals, and with pollarded trees. These are trees from which the tops are removed at a height of about 3 m (10 ft) so that many thin, straight stems grow up from the stump (see pp. 101–2). Within the wood itself certain trees were allowed to grow to their full height, as standards but never to the full girth of a really old tree, before being felled to provide large timber. When a tree was felled another young tree was allowed to grow up to take its place, but trees were not planted deliberately. The other trees were *coppiced*. A coppiced tree is cut close to the ground, leaving a low stump from which many thin, straight stems develop. These are cut, usually after about twelve years, and used to make fencing, legs for furniture, handles for tools, and a wide variety of articles that are small enough not to need large pieces of timber, and the whole area is worked in rotation so that there is a crop each year. The initial growth is rapid from a coppice stump, and coppicing exploited this speed of growth. The system was called 'coppice-with-standards'. It largely died out as coal became the most important fuel and concrete and iron the most important construction materials, but it is being reintroduced, mainly for conservation reasons, and you can see its effect. At one time most British woodlands were managed in this way.

There are far too many areas of woodland, distributed throughout the entire country, for them all to be listed. Those listed here are particularly good or interesting examples of their type of woodland. The relevant OS Landranger sheet number is given in each case and the NG reference to a point of access where appropriate.

Berkshire *Windsor Great Park,* ancient woodland (NG reference SU 953735) 175

Cambridgeshire *Aversley Wood,* ancient woodland (NG reference TL 158815) 142

Devon *Shaptor and Furzeleigh Woods,* coppice-with-standards (NG reference SX 818794) 191

Essex *Epping Forest,* ancient woodland (NG reference TQ 412981) 166; 167; 177. *Stour Wood,* ancient woodland very rich in wildlife (NG reference TM 190315) 168

Gloucestershire *Cotswold Beechwoods,* reminiscent of original Cotswold forest and probably ancient (NG reference SO 894131) 162; 163. *Forest of Dean National Forest Park* (NG reference SO 615080) 162

Grampian *Glen Tanar,* remnant of Caledonian Forest (NG reference NO 480910) 44

Gwent *Wentwood Forest,* ancient woodland and modern plantation (NG reference ST 436936) 171

Gwynedd *Coed Dinorwic,* ancient woodland (NG reference SH 586603) 115. *Coeddyd Aber,* ancient woodland (NG reference SH 662720) 115. *Coedydd Maentwrog,* natural oak woodland (NG reference SH 652414) 124

Hampshire *The New Forest,* ancient woodland (NG reference SU 300080) 195; 196

Hereford and Worcester *Nunnery Wood,* ancient woodland (NG reference SO 877543) 150. *Pepper Wood,* coppice woodland (NG reference SO 937747) 139. *Wyre Forest* (NG reference SO 759766) 138

Highland *Glen Affric,* Scots pine and birch (NG reference NH 2424) 26. *Strathfarrar,* remnant of Caledonian Forest (NG reference NH 270375) 25; 26

Kent *Denge Wood,* ancient woodland probably never cleared, with coppice-with-standards management, and a yew wood (NG reference TR 105525) 189. *Earley Wood,* coppice-with-standards (NG reference TR 122504) 189. *Park Wood,* coppice-with-standards (NG reference TR 043527) 189

Rannoch Forest, Tayside. Map no. 42.

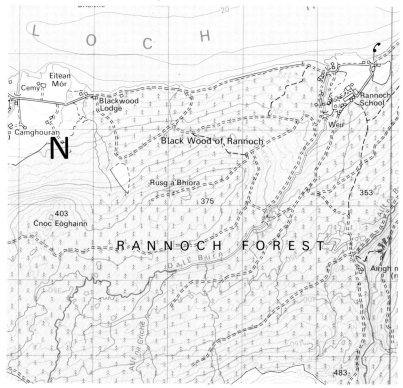

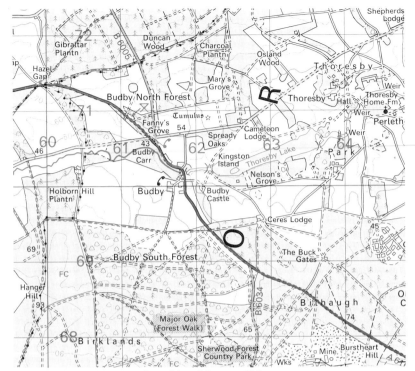

Sherwood Forest, Nottinghamshire. Map no. 120.

Leicestershire *Swithland Woods*, ancient woodland (NG reference SK 538129) 129

Merseyside *Dibbinsdale* (NG reference SJ 345827) 108

Northamptonshire *King's Wood*, ancient woodland (NG reference SP 864874) 141. *Stoke Wood*, coppice-with-standards (NG reference SP 802864) 141

Northumberland *Border Forest Park*, Kielder Forest, the largest plantation forest in Britain (NG reference NY 633935) 79; 80

Nottinghamshire *Sherwood Forest Country Park* (NG reference SK 627677) 120

Powys *Pwll-y-wrach* (NG reference SO 163327) 161

Suffolk *Bradfield Woods*, coppiced and pollarded ancient woodland (NG reference TL 935581) 155. *Croton Wood*, ancient woodland with coppiced small-leaved lime (NG reference TL 977432) 155

Sussex *The Men's*, ancient woodland (NG reference TQ 024236) 197. *Kingley Vale*, 'the finest yew wood in Europe' (NG reference SU 824088) 197

Tayside *Black Wood of Rannoch*, remnant of Caledonian Forest (NG reference NN 570550) 42

Yorkshire *Forge Valley Woods*, ancient woodland growing in a steep-sided gorge, the woodland composition changing with height on the sides of the valley (NG reference SE 985860) 101

13

LOWLAND FARM LAND

In rural Britain there is no land which belongs to no one. A large amount of land is owned by the state and managed by such statutory bodies as the Forestry Commission or the regional water authorities, or by government ministries (most notably the Ministry of Defence), but most is owned privately. The important thing is that all of it, every last corner, belongs to some person or institution. Since the land is owned, most of it is expected to earn money. Apart from nature reserves, country parks and other areas dedicated as amenities, and land used for military training, almost all the rest is managed in ways designed to yield a return. Reservoirs hold water collected from the surrounding area. Mines and quarries occupy land, producing fuel or minerals. The land may grow heather to feed grouse that are then shot, it may produce other game, or it may be forested; but most of it is farmed. The national parks are farmed or forested, as is much of the land owned by the National Trust. Farming is by far the most widespread way in which our countryside is used.

Indeed, farming is so widespread that we tend to overlook it, as though farm land were not really countryside at all. After a first sigh of appreciation at the sight of so much greenery after leaving the city we rush past the miles of fields in search of the 'real' countryside of mountain, moor, non-commercial forest or coast. Not only does this give us a distorted impression of our own landscapes, it also reflects a very recent fashion in what is scenically attractive.

Farms and wilderness

Many of us today contrast farmed land unfavourably with 'wilderness', which is land for which humans have found no use, but until the eighteenth century most people regarded wilderness with considerable distaste: it contained wild animals, natural and supernatural monsters and devils, and offered no possibility of sustenance. People died in its harshness. Beautiful countryside was countryside that either had fields and was farmed, or had the potential for this. The first European explorers in North America viewed that continent in the same way. 'It is a well-cleared country, pretty and pleasant, and crossed by streams which empty into the great lake. There is no ugly surface of great rocks and barren mountains such as one sees in many places in Canadian and

Algonquin territory. The country is full of fine hills, open fields, very beautiful broad meadows bearing much excellent hay . . .,' wrote Father Gabriel Sagard about part of Quebec in 1632. It was much like European farm land. Our own farming systems developed from earlier ones in which unenclosed land was called 'the waste' (see pp. 77–9).

The modern view has much to support it, but essentially it is an urban view. Large urban populations need areas in which to relax, to get away from crowds, to wander freely. Perhaps they need to escape temporarily from the over-protective environments made by humans for the convenience and safety of humans. The world as a whole needs wilderness areas to provide space for plants and animals which have no commercial value and which necessarily would be excluded from land that was being managed productively. If we believe the world would be the poorer for the loss of its wildlife, then we must allow that wildlife space in which to live, and so we must protect the wilderness. Yet the view remains urban. Many country-dwellers might agree with it in principle, but not in practice as it might apply to their own surroundings. They would prefer their landscapes to be tidy, well ordered and producing lavishly the commodities on which their livelihoods depend. The ecologist regards a wild, uncultivated region as attractive, but the farmer does not. You cannot live off the scenery.

Dartmoor, a region of granite tors and high, treeless, exposed country. This is Blackslade Mire.

The myth of the 'golden age'

Part of this urban view derives from a romanticised picture of rural life, of sun-drenched hayfields, buxom dairymaids and happy, well-fed, hard-working, simple rustics. Alas, they are creatures of myth. There never was a 'golden age'. Farmers were often poor and their workers led a miserable existence. During the Industrial Revolution many of them sought escape by moving to the expanding cities. Appalling though conditions were in the factories and slums of nineteenth-century industrial Britain, they were an improvement on the grinding poverty, hunger, illness and squalor the poor had known in the countryside. When you visit the farmed landscapes of Britain it is no bad thing to remember the story of the people who have lived in them and wrested a living from them. The beauty and apparent tranquillity of this landscape is deceptive. It has been fashioned by humans through centuries of hard labour.

Farmers domesticate their soils. After many years of cultivation a farm soil is as different from its 'wild ancestor' as any domesticated plant or animal. Like them, it is more productive. Not all soils can be cultivated, and so over the centuries, as farmers have worked their lands in the most productive ways they could, great differences have emerged between farms in favoured areas and those in less favoured areas. The favoured areas have terrain that is not too steep for cultivation, a benign climate, and soil that is, or has been made, deep, fertile and well drained.

Farming areas of Britain

Domesticated soils are found in the lowlands or in valleys, amid orderly, 'tame' landscapes. You can find such landscapes throughout Britain, from Caithness to Cornwall.

North-east Scotland *OS Landranger sheets 11, 12, 17, 21, 27, 28, 29, 30, 37, 38*

In the north-east of Scotland a belt of lowlands extends from eastern Caithness south as far as Aberdeen. North of Tain the soil is developed mainly from Devonian and Old Red Sandstones. To the south it is developed from schists and granites.

The climate is cool and moist. The average temperature in July is around 13°C (55°F) and in January around 3°C (37°F). The total rainfall over the year averages about 760 mm (30 in), and it is wetter to the south of the area than in the north. Late summer is an especially wet time.

Grass is the main product, used principally to fatten cattle, especially around Aberdeen. You will find dairy farms that supply nearby towns. Some arable crops are grown. The growing season for plants begins in late April and ends in October. Root crops do well because the rain in late summer suits them, but this makes it difficult to ripen cereals. In the south of this area you may see oats

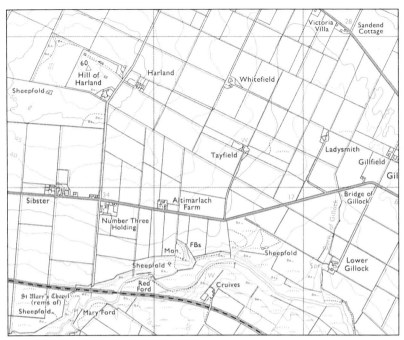

Farming pattern near Wick, in the far north of Scotland. Pathfinder Map no. ND 25/35.

Farms near Pitmedden, Grampian Region. Pathfinder Map no. NJ 82/92.

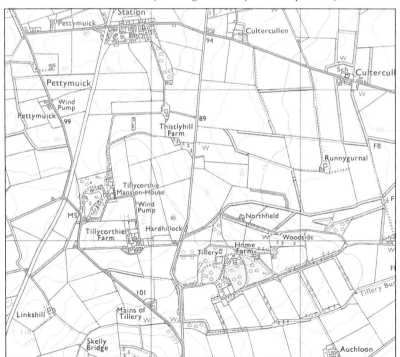

Arable farming landscape in Fife.

being grown, but in Caithness, where it is rather drier, some barley is grown for distilling to make whisky.

Eastern Scotland from the border to Aberdeen *OS Landranger sheets 45, 54, 58, 59, 65, 66, 67*

From the northern part of Fife northward the soils are developed mainly from Devonian and Old Red Sandstones. In south Fife and around Edinburgh they are developed mainly from limestones and sandstones rich in calcium, and there are also coal measures, worked in the Fife and Lothian coalfields.

In July the average temperature is around 15°C (59°F), and in January around 3.5°C (38°F). Total annual rainfall is about 750 mm (29 in). Spring is a dry season, which allows farmers to till their fields in time for the start of the growing season for plants, in late March. Days are long in summer, which helps in the ripening of cereal crops, and the growing season does not end until November. July and August, however, are wet months. The area is intensively farmed and grows arable crops, especially cereals, but the climate is not good for barley.

Central Lowlands *OS Landranger sheets 56, 57, 63, 64, 70, 71*

Apart from the coal measures around Glasgow and Ayr, the soils are mainly developed from limestones and sandstones rich in calcium. The average July temperature is around 15.5°C (60°F) and that for January around 3.5°C (38°F). Average rainfall over the year is about

1000 mm (41 in). The mild, wet climate is good for growing grass, and apart from some horticulture around Ayr the region is devoted mainly to dairying.

Lancashire and Cheshire *OS Landranger sheets 97, 102, 103, 108, 109, 117, 118*
The region has a great variety of soils left behind by glaciers, some heavy to work, others light, but all fertile. North of Liverpool they include some of the most fertile soils in Britain. Temperatures in July average about 15°C (59°F) and in January nearly 4°C (39°F), and total rainfall exceeds 900 mm (35 in).

In the south, where soils are heavy, the region is devoted mainly to dairying, and Cheshire is renowned for its cheeses. Elsewhere arable crops are grown, especially potatoes, but also wheat.

North-east England from the border to Middlesbrough *OS Landranger sheets 75, 81, 88, 93*
There are coal measures in County Durham, to the south of this area. Elsewhere the soils are derived mainly from limestone, sandstones rich in calcium, or millstone grit. The soils vary in texture and this affects the way they are used. In general, the lighter soils grow arable crops and the heavier soils grow grass used to fatten cattle. The average temperature in July is around 16°C (61°F) and in January 3.5°C (38°F). Annual rainfall is about 670 mm (26 in).

In the north of the region the land is used mainly for fattening cattle, with some mixed farms. Further south there is rather more dairying, and arable farming becomes important, based mainly on root crops and barley.

North-west Midlands from Wrexham south to Shrewsbury *OS Landranger sheets 117, 118, 126, 127*
The soils are derived mainly from sandstones, in the south approaching close to the Staffordshire coal measures. They are mainly heavy, but well drained and very fertile, and the climate is gentle. In July the average temperature is around 16°C (61°F) and in January around 4°C (39°F). Average annual rainfall is about 650 mm (26 in). Dairying is the main farming enterprise, with some arable farming in the south.

South Midlands including Hereford and Worcester, Gloucestershire, Warwickshire and north Oxfordshire *OS Landranger sheets 138, 139, 149, 150, 151, 162, 163, 164*
The soils are derived mainly from limestone and sandstones rich in calcium, and vary widely in quality, although heavy clays are common. In July the average temperature is around 17°C (63°F) and in January around 4.4°C (40°F). Average annual rainfall is about 650 mm (26 in). Arable farming is the most common enterprise, but around Hereford and in the Vale of Evesham fruit-growing is important and there are many orchards and market gardens.

The Vale of Evesham enjoys a slightly lower rainfall than that elsewhere in the region, is sheltered, and has sloping land that is

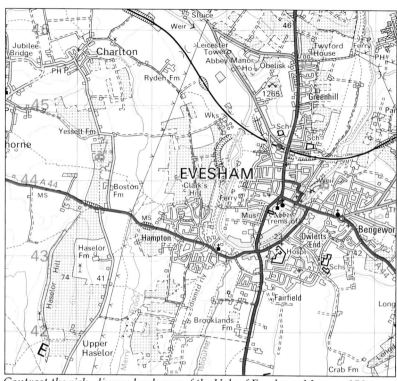

Contrast the rich, diverse landscape of the Vale of Evesham, Map no. 150, (above) with the flat, open area around Methwold Fens, Norfolk, Map no. 143.

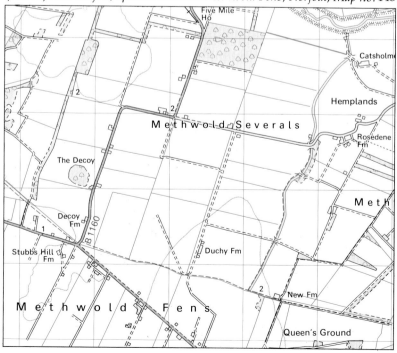

relatively free from frost. It has been intensively cultivated for fruit and other horticultural produce, at least since the late eighteenth century, but its enterprises expanded greatly when Gloucester, Birmingham, Evesham and Worcester were all linked by rail in the middle of the nineteenth century. The industry began on the light soils of river terraces but spread to heavier soils. About one-third of the total British output of asparagus is produced in the Vale.

East Midlands from Newark south to Bedford *OS Landranger sheets 120, 129, 140, 141, 152, 153*

The soils are developed mainly from limestone and sandstone, with some thick, heavy clays, and they vary greatly from place to place because much of the material from which they are made was carried by glaciers. The average temperature in July is 16.8°C (62°F) and in January 3.8°C (39°F). Average annual rainfall is about 650 mm (26 in). The farming is based either on fattening cattle, and some sheep, or on cereal-growing, with farms of all three types situated side by side.

Eastern England from the Humber south to the Thames *OS Landranger sheets 112, 113, 121, 122, 130, 131, 132, 133, 134, 141, 142, 143, 144, 152, 153, 154, 155, 156, 165, 166, 167, 168, 177, 178*

This vast region contains the richest arable lands in the country. The Fens, around the Wash, from south Lincolnshire south to Ely in Cambridgeshire, are flat and composed in some places of black peat and in others of silt, on land reclaimed from the sea. The other soils of the region are made mainly from glacial deposits, including those derived from limestone, and chalky boulder clays. The climate is warm in summer, cold in winter, and dry. In July the average temperature is around 16.8°C (62°F) and in January around 3.7°C (39°F). Annual rainfall is about 600 mm (24 in).

Some cattle are fattened on the heavier soils in the north and there is some dairying close to the large towns, but with these minor exceptions the region is given over to the growing of arable crops and you will see few farm animals. Barley, wheat and, locally near the processing factories, sugar beet are the main crops. Fields are large, with few hedges even bordering the roads, and at cereal harvesting time the combine harvesters work three abreast. If you think of arable farming as an industry, then this is the factory floor. The farming is highly mechanised and therefore capital-intensive, and farms employ few workers. This means that beyond the commuting belts from the cities the human population density is very low. Villages and hamlets are small and widely scattered.

The Fens are worked even more intensively, growing some arable crops but mainly vegetables, bulbs and flowers that sell for higher prices than cereals. Much of the area is below sea-level and must be kept drained by networks of ditches from which water is raised by pumps. It is possible that the farming in the Fens will have to change in years to come since the fertility of the peats and silts has been exploited to the very limit and beyond, so they are becoming exhausted. Crop diseases and pests cause serious problems, exposed soil dries out and blows in high winds, destroying germinating seeds and choking the ditches, and deficiencies of mineral nutrients occur in the overworked soils.

The light Breckland soils, to the east of the Fens, are mainly forested, but where they are farmed, usually to grow barley, they, too, are suffering from over-exploitation and erosion.

South-west England from Cheddar to Land's End *OS Landranger sheets 172, 180, 181, 182, 183, 190, 191, 192, 193, 194, 200, 201, 202, 203, 204*

Apart from the moorland areas, the soils are derived mainly from Old Red Sandstone in the west and south, millstone grit and greensand in the north and east, and slates over much of the low ground in Cornwall. The climate is mild and wet. In July the average temperature is around 17°C (63°F) and in January around 6°C (43°F). Annual rainfall is about 1000 mm (40 in). The soil temperature tends to be higher than the air temperature, however, because much of the region is open to winds from the ocean that have little effect below ground level, and a few centimetres below the surface temperatures rarely fall below 5.6°C (42°F), the minimum needed for plant growth. Thus plant growth ceases for only a very short time during the coldest part of winter, and sometimes not even then, and the growing season begins early. Early flowers and vegetables are produced in sheltered areas in the west of the region, and the main British cider-producing areas are found in the east. Cider apples are not grown in Cornwall, however, except very locally and on a small scale.

Apart from horticulture and fruit-growing the region is one of small fields, grass, sheep, and beef and dairy cattle. Arable crops are confined to particular areas where the climate is a little drier.

Southern England from Dorchester to Eastbourne and north to the Downs *OS Landranger sheets 195, 196, 197, 198, 199*

The soils are varied, but mainly clays or rather acid, infertile sands. In July the average temperature is around 17°C (63°F) and in January around 5.3°C (42°F), but the average annual rainfall is much greater in the west (about 980 mm, 39 in) than in the east (700 mm, 28 in). The farms are devoted mainly to dairying, for there are many urban areas to supply, and there is some general arable farming.

South-east England east Sussex south of the Downs, and south Kent *OS Landranger sheets 179, 188, 189*

The region lies to the south of the Downs mainly on sands and gravels in the east and clays in the south. The Romney and Pevensey areas are reclaimed marshes, similar to the Fens in most respects. In July the average temperature is around 16.7°C (62°F) and in January 4°C (39°F). Severe frosts are fairly uncommon. Average annual rainfall is around 770 mm (30 in).

Reclaimed marshland on Romney Marshes, Kent.

The farming in the region is dominated by the proximity of London and the prosperous towns of the south coast. There is still some hop-growing in Kent, although the flowers are now harvested by machines, and the 'garden of England' still grows fruit, but land that could be used to grow wheat or barley spends at least part of the time growing vegetables which sell for a much higher price in the London markets. This is also the land of rich landowners from the city who spend their weekends in such enterprises as the raising of pedigree cattle. The Romney Marshes have their own breed of sheep, however, which have nothing to do with such hobby farmers. They were bred to thrive on rich grass growing luxuriantly on wet land and are resistant to foot rot. They are stocked very densely during the summer and moved to the Downs in winter. The Pevensey Levels have better supplies of drinking water and are used rather more for fattening cattle. However, these fen-like soils are being used more and more for intensive horticulture.

14

WETLANDS

A wetland is a lake, pond, marsh or swamp, an area of still, open, fresh water which in the case of a marsh or swamp may be almost hidden by the plants growing in it. Many people worry about the rate at which important natural habitats on dry land are being lost, but aquatic habitats are under even greater threat, for they are extremely vulnerable. They are easily polluted, either deliberately by people who regard the nearest open water as a suitable place to dispose of their rubbish, or inadvertently by substances washed into them from surrounding land.

Pollution is only part of the problem, however. Wetlands are easily destroyed. Many are shallow and in their existing state have little or no commercial value. It is not too difficult to drain them and provide land for farming or even for building. Small ponds were once needed as places where farm animals could drink. These days we have piped water supplies for the animals, ponds may become foul or dangerous to children, and it often seems sensible as well as convenient to fill them in with harmless but bulky wastes, such as rubble from building sites.

Wetlands made by industry

Once an area of wetland has been drained or filled it is lost, but if this is the negative side to the story there is also a positive side. Many hollows can be flooded to make new wetlands, and our industries manufacture many suitable artificial hollows. Gravel pits, worked to provide material for making concrete, are often flooded when they are exhausted or the local demand for concrete falls, and with careful planning and management they can be transformed within a few years into lakes that are almost indistinguishable from natural lakes. Reservoirs are not natural and are not allowed to become so, but they often support considerable wildlife and provide valuable and attractive recreational facilities for local people.

Many of our most treasured wetland areas were made in the first place by humans. The Norfolk Broads is the most famous example. At one time it was marsh, swamp and peat bog, and the layers of peat were extremely deep. The peat was used as fuel, obtained in the way peat is always obtained, by digging it from trenches. The trenches were cut wider and deeper, one joined with the next to give an open-cast effect, and one by one the hollows filled with water to make lakes. It is estimated that in the Middle Ages people cut more than 25 million cubic metres (900 cubic feet) of peat. By the fourteenth century most of the workings were filled with water. Then the sea-level rose, the water-level in the wetlands rose, and the Broads were completed. They were made a long time ago, but they were made by people. Like the Breckland, the Broads is a derelict industrial landscape.

The life-cycle of a lake

Running water will usually recover from pollution, however severe, but still waters run an additional risk because the most common form of pollution has the effect of accelerating their own evolution, and it is the fate of most shallow fresh waters to turn eventually into dry land. Pollution ages them.

Imagine a typical, but newly formed lake. It is fed by one or more rivers and discharges its surplus water into another river. Less water leaves the lake than is fed into it because of the amount that evaporates from the open surface. The water reaching the lake contains minute particles of minerals collected in its travels and carried in suspension. Some of the particles leave in the outgoing water, but since more water enters than leaves, more particles also enter than leave. The surplus settle to the bottom of the lake as silt.

Thorpe Park, Surrey – old gravel workings turned into a valuable amenity. Map no. 176.

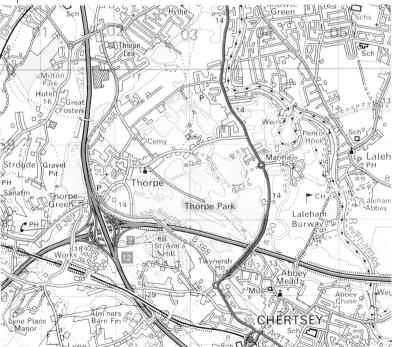

The silt accumulates over the years, forming a layer that grows ever thicker, and as it thickens so the depth of water is reduced. However, if this were all, it would take a very long time indeed for the lake to fill with silt completely.

The incoming water also contains chemical salts carried into it by water draining from surrounding land. These salts include compounds of nitrogen and phosphorus, essential nutrients for plants, and they, too, accumulate in the lake. They are soluble in water, so the outgoing water contains them, but when water evaporates the salts are left behind. Thus the difference between the amounts of incoming and outgoing water allows the lake to become enriched with nutrient salts. Around the edges of the lake, where the water is shallow, plants are able to root themselves with their leaves above the surface. They can photosynthesise while also obtaining ample mineral nutrients. Other plants, which need no roots, can float in the upper waters of the lake. If you collect a sample of fresh water and it looks green, the colour is due to the presence of countless millions of unicellular algae, microscopically small green plants. The plants provide food for animals, and so the lake becomes rich in wildlife.

At this stage the lake consists of an area of open water, surrounded by plants, typically reeds or rushes, and supporting fish as well as many invertebrates, and the birds that feed on them. You might see many species of duck, moorhens and coots, and warblers and other small birds among the tall shoreline vegetation. The lake is at its peak, but its story has not ended.

The plants follow their own life-cycles, and as each generation dies, vegetable matter falls into the lake. Around the edges the plants are large, and their remains form a layer of organic material that is soon deep enough to allow plants to root in it. So, year by year, the reeds and rushes advance into the open water. That, too, is becoming shallower because the accumulating silt has been joined by the remains of the small floating plants and the bodies of fish and other animals, so the bed is growing thicker all the time, and richer in plant nutrients because of the organic matter which rains down upon it. As the lake nutrients increase, plant growth becomes more vigorous, and as plant growth becomes more vigorous, so the accumulation of material on the bed accelerates.

The lake becomes shallower and more choked with vegetation until eventually the large plants extend across the whole of its surface. At this point a new factor becomes important. Growing plants take up water through their roots and it evaporates from their leaves. This is called *transpiration*, and it is the way plants move mineral nutrients to where they are needed, and the way non-woody plants remain rigid. Transpiration moves large amounts of water from the ground, or in this case from the lake, into the air. The loss of water by transpiration far exceeds the amount lost by

Reeds advancing into an ageing lake – Esher, Surrey.

evaporation from an open water surface, because the total area of leaves is far greater than the total surface area of water above which they grow. The lake has turned into a swamp or marsh.

This is but another stage in the story, however. The process continues, indeed accelerates, until quite small plants, such as sedges, can grow right out in the middle of what used to be the lake. It is a lake no longer, nor even a marsh, but water meadow, and the sedges are soon joined by grasses. Now it does not take long before the water meadow dries out completely and becomes an ordinary meadow, with a river running through it, that will be colonised by trees. In most of Britain lakes are destined to become woodland.

The process depends on the injection of plant nutrients from the water feeding the lake. The more nutrients there are, the shorter will be the life of the lake. If additional nutrients are supplied by humans, the lake will age more rapidly still. That is the risk posed by pollution from agricultural fertiliser and sewage.

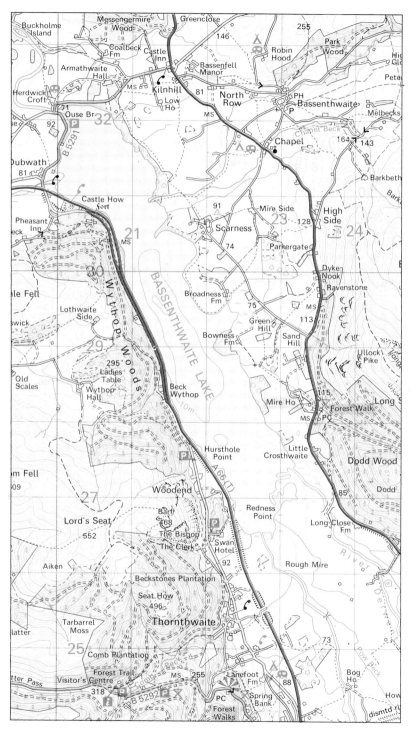

Bassenthwaite, Cumbria – an area with open lake and marsh. Map no. 168.

Tarns

There are some lakes in the uplands in which the rate of evaporation from the surface balances the rate at which water enters, so no rivers flow from them. These are called tarns. They are usually shallow, formed in glacial hollows, and they are always mysterious. There is a curious atmosphere about them. Local legend often has it that they are bottomless, because how else can we account for the fact that water enters, no water leaves, yet the lake never overflows? The myth surrounding Dozmary Pool, on Bodmin Moor, is typical: local legend claims that it is the lake from which the arm appeared offering the sword to King Arthur.

Rich lowland lakes and poor mountain lakes

If you visit some of our larger and more famous lakes, especially those in the mountains of Wales and Scotland, you will see many that appear not to conform to the pattern described above. They have existed for a long time, perhaps from the end of the last ice age, but their shores are rocky, with few plants, and their waters may be peaty but they are not green. No plants float on the surface. They seem different because they receive little in the way of plant nutrients. They are ageing, but at a very slow rate indeed.

Plant nutrients are derived partly from the air and partly from underlying rocks, and they occur in fertile soils. Before plant roots can absorb them they must be converted into compounds that are soluble in water, because plants take up their nutrients in solution. Soil bacteria play a vital part in changing insoluble mineral compounds into soluble ones. The soil receives its moisture from rain and snow, and also from the groundwater that moves below the surface. Surplus water drains from the soil, eventually into rivers, and dissolved nutrients go with it. This loss of nutrients is called *leaching*. Rivers carry plant nutrients, and that is how the nutrients reach lakes. If the soil is infertile, however, it may contain little nutrient. A river flowing down a mountainside, over bare rock, and draining an area of rock and at best a very thin covering of soil, will carry almost no nutrient. So the condition of a lake has a great deal to do with the kind of ground its rivers cross before they reach it.

In general it is true that where lakes occur in regions of hard, igneous (once molten) rocks such as granites they will contain little plant nutrient, supporting few plants and animals, and their waters will tend to be rather acid. Where lakes occur in regions of chalk or limestone their waters will tend to be rather alkaline and relatively rich in nutrients, especially in farming areas. They will be rich in wildlife. Deep lakes age more slowly than shallow ones because large plants are unable to root in the bed, and if the sides of a lake plunge steeply, there will be little opportunity for shore plants to establish themselves. Steep-sided, deep lakes are more common in mountainous areas than elsewhere. The combination of acid waters poor in nutrients, considerable depth and steep sides accounts for the longevity of mountain lakes.

The quality of the water may vary from one part of a very large lake to another. Loch Lomond, for example, is broad and shallow at its southern end, where it is fed by the river Endrick which flows across farm land, but narrow and deep at its northern end, where it is fed by small rivers flowing across hard rocks. The northern end is poor in nutrient and supports few plants, but the southern end is rich in plant life, and is ageing fairly rapidly.

Wetlands to visit

You can find ponds, lakes and even marshes in every part of Britain. Those listed below are just a very few of the better-known examples of particular types of wetland. In each case the National Grid reference is given for the point of access, and the number at the end is that of the relevant OS Landranger sheet.

Cambridgeshire *Fowlmere*, an area of water and reedbeds developed on what used to be watercress beds (NG reference TL 407462) 154. *Wicken Fen*, a large area of fenland with open water, reedbeds, marsh and scrub, managed in such a way as to prevent its development into woodland (NG reference TL 563705) 154

Central *Loch Lomond*, the largest freshwater lake in Britain, narrow, deep and supporting little wildlife at the northern end, but wider, shallower and much richer in life in the south (NG reference NS 420910, on the B837 which runs along the southern half of the eastern side, or NG reference NS 3204, at Tarbet on the A838, which runs along the northern part of the western side) 56

Cornwall *Dozmary Pool*, a tarn on Bodmin Moor that is associated in local legend with the ancient King Arthur myths (NG reference SX 192745) 201

Cumbria *Wast Water*, the deepest of the English Lakes, formed in a glacial trough, whose surface is more than 60 m (200 ft) above sea-level, but whose bed is more than 15 m (50 ft) below sea-level (NG reference, southern end, NY 143044) 89

Devon *Slapton Ley*, a freshwater lake, smaller pools, reedbed and fen (NG reference SX 826431) 202

Dumfries and Galloway *Loch Ken*, long, narrow lake stretching from just south of New Galloway almost to Castle Douglas, with marshes and water meadows (NG reference NX 638765) 77; 83. *Plantain Loch*, shallow loch rich in wildlife, including sundews and dragonflies (NG reference NX 841602, near Dalbeattie) 84

Dyfed *Bosherton Ponds*, a large area of open water, now rich in wildlife, made in the eighteenth and nineteenth centuries by damming three valleys (NG reference SR 966948) 158

Hereford and Worcester *Feckenham Wylde Moor*, an artificial lake amid fen marsh (NG reference SP 012603) 150

Advancing reeds and water lilies, Wicken Fen, Cambridgeshire.

Hertfordshire *Rye House Marsh*, small area of marsh, rich in wildlife (NG reference TL 386100) 166

Highland *Insh Marshes*, formed on a floodplain of the river Spey (NG reference NN 775998, near Kingussie) 35. *Loch an Eilein*, a Highland lake untypically rich in plant life, not far from Aviemore (NG reference NH 898085) 35. *Loch Maree*, deep, steep-sided lake lying in a glacial trough (NG reference NG 9568, on the A832 road which runs along the southern shore) 19

Humberside *Hornsea Mere*, a large freshwater lake close to the sea and bordered by reeds and fen, rich in wildlife and especially attractive to birds (NG reference TA 198473) 107

Kent *Stodmarsh*, a large area of open water, reedbeds and marsh formed by the flooding of subsided land above old coal mine workings, now very similar to the wetlands once common in the area (NG reference TR 222607) 179

Lancashire *Leighton Moss*, an area of open water, reedbeds and marsh, rich in wildlife, that is managed to prevent it evolving into dry land (NG reference SD 478752) 97. *Martin Mere*, a man-made mere, with marshes and water meadows, providing an important wintering ground for migratory arctic wildfowl (NG reference SD 428145) 108

Merseyside *Red Rocks Marsh*, small area of fresh to brackish marsh between two sand dunes (NG reference SJ 204884) 108

Norfolk *Broadland Conservation Centre*, where the natural history of the Norfolk Broads is described, is approached by a duckboarded path from the car park (NG reference TG 359146) 134

Northumberland *Blackaburn Lough*, south of Kielder Water, a lake that grades into acid swamp (NG reference NY 763796) 87

Tayside *Loch Leven*, a shallow lake that receives nutrients from surrounding farm land and is rich in wildlife, especially duck and other wildfowl (NG reference NO 150010) 58. *Loch of the Lowes*, a shallow lake and marsh fringed with woodland, supporting both lowland and highland wildlife species (NG reference NO 050440) 53

Tyne and Wear *Shibdon Pond*, an area of shallow open water and marsh caused by the flooding of subsided land (NG reference NZ 195628) 88

Warwickshire *Kingsbury Water Park*, a large area of flooded gravel workings and surrounding land, producing open water, reedbeds and swamp (NG reference SP 204958) 139

Yorkshire *Malham Tarn*, a lime-rich upland tarn with bog and fen, one of the best-documented nature reserves in Britain (NG reference SD 890672) 98

Blackaburn Lough, Northumberland. Map no. 87.

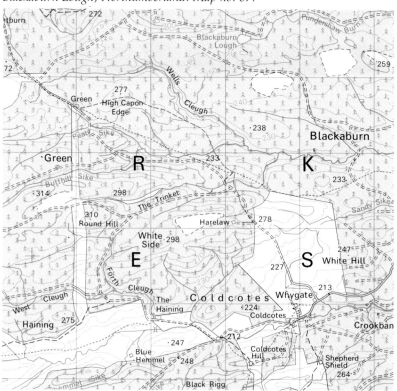

15

RIVERS AND ESTUARIES

British rivers tend to flow east or west from the mountains and they have but a short distance to cover before reaching the sea. We do not have the mighty rivers found on continents, but if you wish to see the important features of any river this is an advantage. Our rivers contain most of these features, but they are compressed. A single day trip by car is often long enough at least to glimpse all the stages through which some of our rivers pass.

The story of a river is very similar to that of a lake, except that it extends over distance rather than over time. Rivers do not die and turn into dry land as lakes do because the flow of water is maintained, but their quality and the amount and type of life they support change along their courses. A bright, sparkling mountain brook is a very different body of water from the tidal estuary it becomes at its mouth.

Sections of a river

The course of a river can be broken down into stretches, each of which has its own characteristics and supports its own distinct kind of plant and animal community. The division is somewhat theoretical, in that you may not see every stage marked clearly in every river, but it provides a useful general guide.

Near the source, most of our rivers flow down steep slopes over hard rocks and, of course, they carry little water. Because the slope is steep the flow is rapid, and because the rocks are hard and slow to erode there are many small waterfalls, and turbulence as the water flows over and around large stones. The bed is usually composed of pebbles or gravel, with some deeper, stiller pools. The water is cold. It contains little in the way of plant nutrient but is rich in dissolved oxygen. There are no aquatic plants, except perhaps a little blanket weed that can cling to stones against the force of the water, but there are some insect larvae, living in crevices or clinging to cracks, and insectivorous fish, usually trout. Salmon breed near the headwaters of certain rivers. The presence of salmon or trout means the river is unpolluted, but that is only another way of saying it can support little in the way of plant life. It is a harsh environment, almost the aquatic equivalent of a desert.

On lower land the river grows wider and deeper, but the current is still strong. The water is a little warmer, it has collected some plant nutrient, and there are sheltered places where a few aquatic plants

Ordnance Survey air photograph taken from a height of 11,750 feet of the River Arun, West Sussex. A mature river meandering to the sea. The ancient town of Arundel is in the north of the picture with Littlehampton and the marina in the south.

can grow. Still further downstream, after the river has collected more tributaries, silt begins to accumulate in protected hollows on the bed, the water is warmer, and more plants can grow. Herbivorous fish begin to appear and there is a richer invertebrate life. In the lower reaches, the river becomes wider, deeper, and because it now flows down very gentle slopes it flows slowly and may start to meander.

Floodplains

It is here, where the river meanders over almost level ground, that it may form a floodplain. The flow of water cuts a path for the river, but it cuts more easily and quickly through a soft surface than through a hard one. It takes the easiest course, and quite small obstacles are enough to divert it to one side or the other. Thus a series of meanders are formed. The river is now carrying much silt, especially when melting snow or heavy rain on the high ground near its source increases its flow suddenly and it is in spate. At the forward edge of each bend it cuts away constantly at the bank, while at the inside of the bend, where the water pressure is less, silt accumulates. Thus the front of the bend is being cut away, the bank on the inside of the bend is being built up, and very slowly the whole bend advances downstream. Extend this to the entire area over which the river meanders, and you will see that, given enough time, all the meanders will advance as far as they can go and new meanders will form behind them. The river will always look the same, but if you plot the actual position of its course you will find it moves. Since the inside banks, behind each bend, are formed from deposited silt, eventually the whole area will be covered with silt in a belt as wide as the furthest extremity of the bends on either side. This is called a floodplain, not because it floods, although it may do, but because at one time or another the course of the river occupies the whole of it. Its original soil is buried beneath a layer of gravel and silt, the gravel tending to accumulate at the upstream end, while the silt, which is fine-grained, is carried further. The silt carries with it nutrients that have drained from land along the whole length of the river, and where it is deposited an alluvial soil is formed.

Floodplains are sometimes very large, and usually they are banded on either side by raised banks, or levées. Where the plain is safe from periodic flooding caused by the river overflowing its banks, the land is extremely fertile and often farmed intensively.

Occasionally it may happen that a meander has such an exaggerated horseshoe shape as to allow the river to take a short cut across the end if the pressure of water is sufficient. Sooner or later, when the river is in spate, a new course will be cut across the ends of the 'horseshoe'. Later, when the river subsides, the new course will be maintained, the meander will advance, and the remainder of the horseshoe will be isolated, as an ox bow lake.

Estuaries

A floodplain can form anywhere along the course of a river, provided the river crosses almost level ground. Often, though, there is a floodplain in the lower reaches, not far from the mouth.

Below that floodplain the river begins to meet the sea, and it does so a little way inland because tidal salt water advances upstream. This addition of water widens the course and causes turbulence leading to the depositing of silt that is being carried downstream and sand being carried upstream as mudflats and sandbanks. The river becomes an estuary. Large rivers have very extensive estuaries in which the main water course may divide into many channels. The channels may meet and cross one another, giving a braided pattern, or may diverge to form a delta. Several of the larger British rivers probably had deltas at one time, but rising sea-levels drowned them. Today most of our estuaries are drowned river valleys, actually located some distance upstream from the original point at which fresh and salt water met.

An estuary is a harsh environment, but a rich one. Salt water and fresh water do not mix readily because their densities are different and usually they are at different temperatures. As the tide rises, the incoming salt water flows beneath the fresh water, so that water flows in both directions simultaneously. In some parts of certain

Colne Estuary, Essex. Map no. 168.

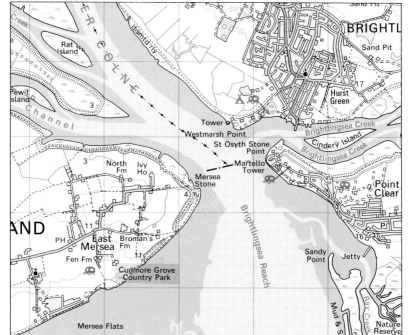

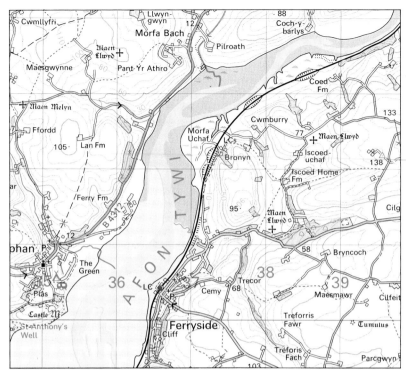

Afon Tywi Estuary, Carmarthen, Dyfed. Map no. 159.

estuaries wind, currents, or the shape of the bed may force the two kinds of water to separate into distinct channels flowing side by side. If you watch the movement of the water as the tide flows into an estuary you may see such channels quite clearly, side by side but moving in opposite directions. You should choose a day when there is little or no wind, however, because the wind makes waves on the surface of the water which can confuse the picture. You may see waves apparently moving in one direction while the water itself is really moving in the opposite direction.

Aquatic plants and animals may live in fresh water, or in salt water, but few can move readily from one to the other. Osmotic pressure, the force that makes water flow across cell membranes from a weak mineral salt solution to one that is stronger, is usually fatal. It causes dehydration in freshwater species moving into salt water, and distends or even bursts cells in salt-water species that move into fresh water. There are species, such as salmon and eels, which can tolerate either, and some which live in brackish water that is more salt than fresh water but less so than sea water. Some sea fish, such as flounders and grey mullet, move upstream, keeping close to the bottom, where the water is salt, and some river fish may move downstream, near the surface where the water is fresh. But most species keep to their own environment.

Knots flying above the mudflats where they feed, Kent.

The richness of the estuary is hidden, in the muds. Being silt, they are rich in nutrients, but few plants can tolerate the changes in salinity and water-level needed to exploit them. Instead they harbour immense populations of micro-organisms and such invertebrate animals as worms and molluscs. Waders, which are birds adapted to feeding on these animals, hunt in the mud at low tide.

How much life do the mudflats support? A tiny snail, *Hydrobia ulvae*, less than a centimetre long, is an important food item for many waders. In the muds of the Clyde estuary there are about 42,000 of these snails just below the surface of every square metre of mud. In the Dovey estuary there are around 63,000 *Corophium volutator*, a small crustacean, beneath every square metre of mud. This abundance of small animals accounts for the large estuarine bird populations. Some 20,000 oystercatchers have been counted in the Dee estuary, Cheshire, where there are also vast numbers of knot and dunlin as well as smaller populations of many other species.

Visiting rivers and estuaries

The sites listed below are just a few of the large number you might visit, for every river and estuary is worthy of examination. In each case the National Grid reference is given for the best point of access, and the number at the end refers to the relevant OS Landranger sheet.

Avon *Frome Valley*, a nature trail beside the fast-flowing river Frome, close to the centre of Bristol (NG reference ST 622765) 172

Central *Endrick Water*, the principal river feeding the southern end of Loch Lomond, rises on Carleatheran Hill (NG reference NS 6892) and the B818 runs close to it from Fintry (NG reference NS 6186) to Boquhan. The A811 crosses it south of Drymen (NG reference NS 4887) just as it begins to meander across the plain before entering the Loch. 57

Clwyd *Afon Dyfrdwy* (River Dee) meanders across the plain south of Holt (NG reference SJ 4254) and opens out into a large, deeply silted estuary, rich in wildlife, starting at Connah's Quay (NG reference SJ 3069) 108; 116; 117

Cornwall *River Camel*, which is tidal in that part of its lower reaches where it meanders across a small floodplain on which its course has been fixed by levees, becomes an estuary downstream from Wadebridge, with saltmarshes, sandbanks and mudflats attractive to waders. A disused railway line has been made into a public footpath beside the estuary from Padstow to Wadebridge, and beside the river from Wadebridge for some distance upstream (NG reference SW 980735) 200

Devon *Exe Estuary*, south of Exeter, a large area of mudflats, saltmarsh and open water almost closed near the mouth by a sand spit formed by the longshore drift at Dawlish Warren, is rich in wildlife. It can be seen from Powderham (NG reference SX 973845), just off the A379 north of Starcross on the western side, or from Lympstone (NG reference SX 992836), off the A376, on the eastern side. 192. *Lydford Gorge*, where the river Lyd, a tributary of the Tamar, plunges through a series of pools and falls in a narrow, wooded gorge on its way from Dartmoor. There is a car park at the entrance just outside Lydford village (NG reference SX 508842) 201

Dumfries and Galloway *Caerlaverock* and *Eastpark*, one of the largest areas of natural saltmarsh in Britain, of major international import-ance for wildlife, and especially for barnacle and other geese, on the Scottish side of the Solway Firth, south of Dumfries (NG reference NY 052656) 84; 85

Durham *Eden Dean*, the 5-km (3-mile) long, narrow, wooded valley of the river Eden, cutting through the coastal limestone plateau and glacial silt south of Peterlee until it meets shingle banks thrown up by the sea. The valley is rich in wildlife (NG reference NZ 410387) 88

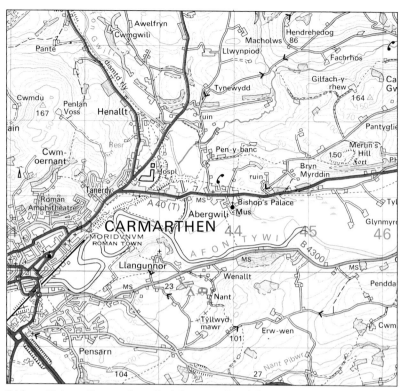

Bishops Palace, Carmarthen, Dyfed – an ox bow lake. Map no. 159.

Dyfed *Bishop's Pond*, a pond which in fact is an ox bow lake that was formerly part of the river Tywi. The B4300 passes close to it (NG reference SN 446212) 159

Essex *Colne Estuary*, a large expanse of open water, mudflats, grazing marshes and saltmarsh, west of Clacton-on-Sea and St Osyth (NG reference TM 085154) 168

Fife *Eden Estuary*, noted for its ducks, including eider, and waders, is sandy at the seaward end but muddier further inland. You can reach it most conveniently by walking north along the West Sands from St Andrews to Out Head (NG reference NO 495199) 59. *Firth of Tay*, a large estuary where the wintering wildfowl are said to include 20 per cent of the British population of eider ducks. They can be seen best at high tide (because at low tide too large an area of sand and mud is exposed and the birds are too distant from the shore) from Kingoodie on the northern side (NG reference NO 339293) or Balmerino on the southern side (NG reference NO 358249) 59

Glamorgan *Taf Fechan*, a river whose steep valley, near Merthyr Tydfil, is cut through rocks ranging from hard millstone grit to much softer limestone, producing a variety of natural habitats in a small area. The A470 approaches close to the valley at Cefn-coed-y-cymmer (NG reference SO 045097) 160

Gloucestershire *Slimbridge Wildfowl Sanctuary*, a large area of mud-flats, saltmarsh, meadows and lagoons on the southern side of the Severn Estuary, just off the A38 about half-way between Thornbury and Gloucester (NG reference SO 723048) 162

Grampian *River Dee*, which rises in the Grampian Mountains and enters the North Sea at Aberdeen. The A93 runs beside or at least close to it all the way from Braemar (NG reference NO 1692) not far from the source, past Balmoral, Ballater, Aboyne and Banchory, to Aberdeen. 38, 43, 44, 45. *Sands of Forvie*, beside the estuary of the river Ythan, are an important breeding site for eider and other ducks, and provide nesting grounds for terns and wintering grounds for waders. The A975 from Aberdeen passes a picnic site from which much of the Sands can be seen (NG reference NK 025275) 38

Gwent *Goldcliff*, south of Newport, is an area of tidal flats, used by many migratory birds, on the north side of the Severn Estuary (NG reference ST 385825) 171. *Peterstone Wentlooge*, on the north side of the Severn Estuary, just off the B4239 about half-way between Newport and Cardiff. A sea wall has protected the area on the landward side from salt water, allowing it to develop as grassland and scrub, while on the seaward side there are mudflats and saltmarsh (NG reference ST 278807) 171

Peterstone Wentlooge, on the Severn Estuary. Map no. 171.

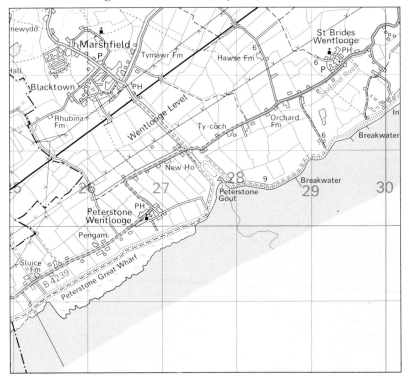

Highland *Cromarty Firth*, the large estuary of the river Conon, starting at Dingwall. The A9 runs along the north side as far as Alness, then the B817 leads to Invergordon and the beginning of *Nigg Bay* (NG reference NH750720), an important wintering and resting ground for migratory waders and wildfowl. On the southern side, *Udale Bay* (NG reference NH710675) is equally important. The B9163 from Conon Bridge to Cromarty runs close to it. 21

Lancashire *Ribble Marshes*, the estuary of the river Ribble, starting downstream from Preston, comprising extensive (dangerous) salt-marshes and mudflats that attract many birds. The best view is from the unclassified coastal road between Southport and Crossens (NG reference SD360210) 102; 108

Merseyside *Gayton Sands*, on the north side of the Dee Estuary, support saltmarshes and attract many birds. There is a picnic site from which the Sands can be viewed (NG reference SJ273786) 108; 117

Staffordshire *Manifold Valley*, north of Ilam, where the river flows over limestone containing 'swallet holes' so it is partly underground. In dry weather there is insufficient water to provide a flow above ground and in some places the river disappears (NG reference SK1451) 119

Strathclyde *River Clyde*, which rises not far from Roberton, where the A73 crosses and then runs a short way beside it (NG reference NS9529), flows northward around the Tinto Hills to the *Falls of Clyde* (NG reference NS880415), a stepped gorge whose sides are rich in mosses, ferns and other plants watered by the spray. A local beauty spot, the river at this point once powered the mills of New Lanark, owned by Robert Owen. 72

Tayside *Montrose Basin*, where the river South Esk has flooded a wide, circular area behind the higher ground on which stands Montrose, forming an estuary that is almost sealed at its mouth. The Basin provides vast mudflats broken by small channels feeding water to the main course of the river, which is on the southern side, and it is an important feeding ground for waders (NG reference NO694575) 45; 54

· 16 ·
COASTS

Great Britain has a coastline whose total length is probably more than 9000 km (5600 miles), and that does not include the many offshore islands. It is exposed to the Atlantic Ocean, the Irish Sea, the North Sea and the English Channel, and the combination of different sea conditions, climates and rocks has produced every type of coastal scenery and wildlife of which our latitudes are capable.

In general, the older, harder rocks on the western side of the country have produced rocky cliffs and coves with sandy beaches, while the softer sedimentary rocks to the east are revealed in flatter landscapes, where sea and land merge – in places almost imperceptibly – rather than clash. Yet there are exceptions. Morecambe Bay is a vast area of shallow water over a bed of sand and mud that is revealed at low tide, and Flamborough Head, near Bridlington, offers dramatic cliffs.

The coast is always changing. Winter storms can scour away entire beaches, or deposit sand to build out a coast, so that while coastal erosion is a familiar problem in some places, in others, less spectacularly perhaps, the land is extending itself seawards.

As you visit the coast, watch for signs of change. Look for evidence of former sea-levels. In Cornwall, for example, many of the rivers end as valleys drowned by the rising sea. In many parts of Britain you will find raised beaches, places now high above the sea but that once bordered it. At low tide, or after a storm, you may see the remains of forest, drowned when the sea rose.

Visiting the coast

It is impossible to provide a short description that does justice to the whole coastline of Britain. You must visit it for yourself. When you do, however, always remember that no matter how benign it may look, the sea will kill you if it can. Never approach the edge of a cliff when it is windy. People are rarely blown from cliffs by a wind blowing off the land: they are plucked away by gusts eddying up cliff faces. Check the tide table before venturing into areas where you could be marooned by water that can rush inland faster than you might think possible.

The list below describes just a few sites, selected because they are interesting or typical of the coastal region in which they occur. The coast itself has been divided into sections, starting at Land's End and going right around the country in a clockwise direction. Within each section the sites are arranged in alphabetical order of the counties or regions in which they occur. The numbers of the relevant OS Landranger sheets are given for each section, and sections always end at the edge of a sheet. This means that some counties are broken apparently arbitrarily, but the divisions make some geographical sense. Devon, for example, appears at both ends of the list, but its north coasts, facing the Bristol Channel, are very different from its south coasts, which face the English Channel. National Grid references are given for points of access.

South-west England Land's End to Bristol 203; 204; 200; 190; 180; 181; 182

Devon *Braunton Burrows* (NG reference SS 464326), on the north side of the mouth of the river Taw, formed where sand slopes very gently into the sea, have developed into a large system of dunes, with bare sand near the sea and a wide variety of plants, with shingle and still pools, further inland. Access is by minor roads from Braunton village, near Barnstaple. *Northam Burrows* (NG reference SS 444298), on the south side of the mouth of the Taw, has a sandy beach, rock pools, sand dunes and saltmarsh. Access is from Northam village, near Westward Ho! and Bideford.

South Wales Cardiff to Cardigan 171; 170; 159; 158; 157; 145

Dyfed *Pembrokeshire Coast National Park*, extending along 270 km (168 miles) of coastline from Saundersfoot, near Tenby, to Cardigan, is our smallest national park, but the only one set entirely along the

A sea storm releases vast amounts of energy – and can be extremely dangerous on shore as well as at sea.

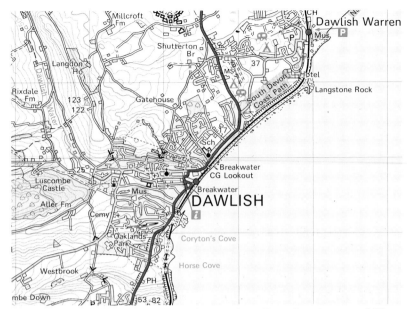

Dawlish, Devon, where storms can damage the railway line. Map no. 192.

coast. Its scenery includes cliffs, islands, estuaries, saltmarsh and, inland, lakes, heaths and woodlands.

Glamorgan *Gower Peninsula*, south-west of Swansea, is a limestone coastal plateau, covered in grassland, scrub and woodland, and ending in cliffs that have been worn into bays, coves and caves. The A4118 from Swansea to Port-Eynon and minor roads leading from it provide access. *Kenfig Pool* and the sand dunes around it are rich in vegetation. The village of Kenfig (NG reference SS 802815) is just north of Porthcawl.

Cardigan Bay and North Wales Aberaeron to Rhyl 146; 135; 124; 123; 115; 116

Dyfed *Ynyslas Dunes*, north of Aberystwyth, is a large system of sand dunes rising from a shingle beach. The dunes support much wildlife, and a petrified forest lies just offshore, visible at low tide. Access is from the B4353 (NG reference SN 610940).

Gwynedd *Great Ormes Head*, on the peninsula north of Llandudno (NG reference SH 780832) has high cliffs and supports a wide variety of plants and birds. There are nature trails through the limestone grassland and along the cliff tops.

North-west England Liverpool to Workington 108; 102; 97; 96; 89

Cumbria *Bardsea Country Park*, near Barrow-in-Furness, overlooks the mudflats of the northern side of Morecambe Bay, where oak and ash coastal woodland stands just above the mud and shingle of the shore. Bardsea village (NG reference SD 300742) is south of Ulverston on the A5087. *St Bees Head*, south of Whitehaven, has sandstone cliffs which provide nesting sites for countless sea birds.

Bempton Cliffs, Humberside, the highest chalk cliffs in Britain.

The B5345 from Whitehaven to St Bees village passes close (NG reference NX 960118). *South Walney*, at the southern end of the Isle of Walney (NG reference SD 215620), is the place where heaped glacial deposits covered by blown sand separate the Furness peninsula from the tides of Morecambe Bay. There are sand dunes, rough meadows, freshwater marsh, saltmarsh, mudflats, open pools and shingle, and South Walney supports one of the largest colonies of herring and lesser-black-backed gulls in Europe, as well as many other birds and an interesting plant community. The Isle is closed on Mondays, except for Bank Holidays, and is reached by road from Barrow-in-Furness.

Lancashire *Morecambe Bay*, a vast tidal plain of sand and mud where well over 100 species of bird, including about one-quarter of the entire British wintering population of bar-tailed godwit, knot, oystercatcher and turnstone, spend the winter. The A5105 runs close to the shore north of Morecambe (NG reference SD 468666). At *Ainsdale*, south of Southport, and further south to *Formby* there are large areas of sand dunes. You need a permit to leave the public paths. The A565 passes through Formby and Ainsdale.

South-west Scotland Dalbeattie to Oban 84; 83; 82; 76; 70; 68; 62; 63; 55; 49

Strathclyde *Carradale* is a village overlooking Kilbrannan Sound and Arran, about half-way down the Kintyre peninsula, with a beach where otters, porpoises, two species of dolphin, and killer whales

Sand dunes at Caithness.

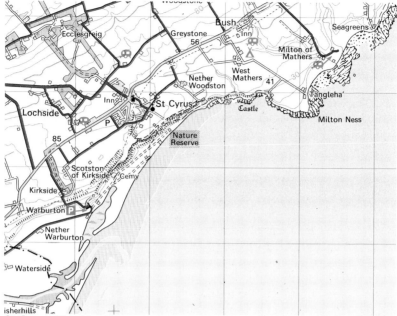

St Cyrus, Tayside. Map no. 45.

are frequent visitors, and land behind it where white feral goats can be seen grazing. The B842 runs parallel to most of the eastern coast of the peninsula and the A83 follows the western coast (NG reference NR 815375). At *Ballantrae* there is a flat, shingle spit overlooking the North Channel with a series of brackish lagoons behind it where the fresh water of the river Stinchar meets salt water. The area attracts sea birds and supports an interesting plant community. The A77 passes through Ballantrae village (NG reference NX 085825).

North-west and North Scotland Sound of Mull to Melvich 47; 40; 33; 24; 19; 15; 9; 10

Highland *Invernaver*, near the long sandy beach at Bettyhill, is a place where northerly gales have carried sand far inland to build up dunes over what was formerly acid heathland. Watch the sea along this part of the coast and you may be able to see the line where water from the Atlantic meets water from the North Sea. Access is from Borgie along the A836 (NG reference NC 681612).

North and North-east Scotland Thurso to Dundee 11; 12; 17; 21; 27; 28; 29; 30; 38; 45; 54

Grampian At *St Cyrus*, on the A92 north of Montrose, 4 km (2.5 miles) of sandy foreshore are backed by dunes and a relict cliff, marking a former sea-level. There are also saltmarsh, dune pasture, areas of blown sand, and the cliffs themselves are of geological interest. The area is noted for its wild plants, insects and birds (NG reference NO 745645).

South-east Scotland St Andrews to Eyemouth 59; 66; 67

Borders *St Abb's Head* is a small headland north of Eyemouth, where tilted volcanic rocks are exposed in spectacular cliffs topped with grassland that in places extends all the way to the shore. The area is very rich in bird life and supports a wide range of plants. The coast to the south is kept unpolluted by strong tides, and kelp forests grow just offshore (NG reference NT 914693).

Lothian Along the *East Lothian coast*, between Prestonpans and Dunbar, mudflats, saltings and sand dunes support large numbers of birds that roost on lagoons where ash is dumped from the coal-fired power station at Cockenzie and generally seem undisturbed by the holidaymakers visiting the beaches, caravan and camping sites and golf courses, or by heavy industry that includes a cement works. The A198 from Edinburgh to East Linton runs more or less parallel to the coast, and through North Berwick (NG reference NT 5585) which is a convenient centre for exploration.

North-east England Berwick-upon-Tweed to Skegness 75; 81; 88; 93; 94; 101; 107; 113; 122

Humberside *Bempton Cliffs*, the highest chalk cliffs in Britain, towering more than 120 m (400 ft) above the sea, are the site of the largest colony of sea birds, with more than 65,000 pairs of nesting kitti-wakes, and the only gannetry on the British mainland. The cliffs continue for 8 km (5 miles) and support a wide range of lime-loving

Bempton Cliffs, Humberside. See the photograph on p. 192. Map no. 101.

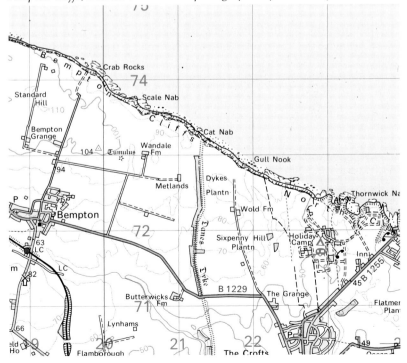

plants; they are dangerous and you must keep to the paths. The cliffs (NG reference TA 197740) can be reached from the B1229 near Bempton village. *Spurn Peninsula*, leading to Spurn Head on the northern side of the mouth of the Humber, is a long, narrow stretch of shingle and sand that has been washed away by the sea at least three times in the last three centuries. At low tide a large area of mudflats and saltmarsh is exposed. The sand dunes support many interesting plants and the Peninsula provides refuge for many species of migratory bird. Access is by minor roads leading from Easington on the B1445 (NG reference TA 417151).

Lincolnshire *Gibraltar Point*, just south of Skegness, is a marshy area with sand dunes made from material washed in by the sea and blown by the wind, so the coast is extending itself. You can see the whole process, from the accretion of sand to the formation of unstable dunes. The area is rich in wildlife. Access is by the minor road leading south from Skegness through Seacroft (NG reference TF 556581). From *Saltfleetby to Theddlethorpe* there is a stretch of shingle, sand dunes, mudflats, freshwater marsh and saltmarsh, with a wide range of wildlife, where you can see how a coastline is built by constant deposition of sand and silt, providing habitats to be colonised. Access is from the A1031 (NG reference TF 465924). *Donna Nook* (NG reference TF 421998), north of Saltfleet, also off the A1031, has sand dunes, mudflats, saltings and sandflats, and 250 species of bird have been seen there.

The gentle coastline at Spurn Head, Humberside.

Holy Island, with Lindisfarne Castle, Northumberland.

Northumberland *Lindisfarne*, or Holy Island, is a low island set amid a large expanse of mudflats that are exposed at low tide, when the island is linked to the mainland by a causeway. Wind and tides have built a breakwater from shingle and sand behind which large flocks of wintering birds find shelter on the sand dunes and saltmarsh, making the island a site of international importance to naturalists. Access is from the A1 by a minor road through Beal, and to the causeway (NG reference NU 095430).

Tyne and Wear *Marsden Cliffs*, on the southern side of South Shields, is where the Pennine limestone crops out at the coast. The cliffs are rich in plant life and attract many sea birds. The A183 from South Shields to Whitburn passes close (NG reference NZ 397650).

Eastern England Boston to Dover 131; 132; 133; 134; 156; 169; 168; 178; 179

Lincolnshire *Frampton Marsh* is a large expanse of creeks, saltmarsh and mudflat beside The Wash, where you can see a wide range of plants and waders, as well as common seals. Check the tides first because the area floods rapidly. Access is south from Boston but involves a long walk, and the area can be extremely cold and bleak in winter (NG reference TF 390385).

Norfolk *Blakeney Point* is a long spit of shingle and sand, formed by wind and waves, with dunes and saltmarsh nearby. Be careful not to get cut off by the rising tide. Access is from the A149, but it is a long

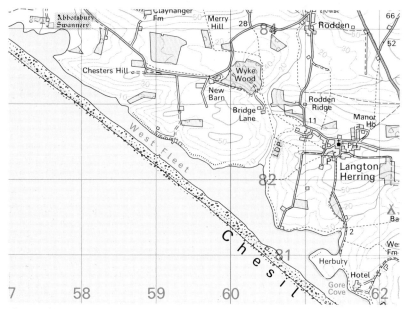

Chesil Beach, Dorset. Map no. 194.

walk (NG reference TF 001464). *Holkham*, to the west (NG reference TF 892447), where there are dunes, saltmarsh, sandflats and mud-flats, is more easily accessible by a minor road leading north from the A149 at Wells-next-the-Sea to an information centre and camp-ing and caravan site.

Suffolk *Landguard* is a shingle bank formed by the sea and contain-ing a fort built to guard the entrance to Harwich harbour, compris-ing a pebble beach with a narrow plain behind it. There are many interesting plants and the nearby scrub and woodland provide nesting sites for many migratory birds. Landguard (NG reference TM 285319) is just south of Felixstowe.

Southern England Folkestone to Falmouth 189; 199; 198; 197; 196; 195; 194; 193; 192; 202; 201; 204

Cornwall *The Lizard* is a peninsula of great geological complexity, providing a range of habitats and consequently of great botanical importance as well as scenic splendour. *Kynance Cove* (NG reference SW 688132) is on the western side of the peninsula. The A3083 leads south from Helston to Lizard village (NG reference SW 701140), with minor side-roads.

Devon *Wembury Marine Conservation Area* (NG reference SX 507484) is a 6-km (3.7-mile) stretch of rocky foreshore and the shallow water offshore, with tidal pools. Access is by minor roads leading from the A379 near Plymstock, on the outskirts of Plymouth.

Dorset *Chesil Bank and the Fleet*, a shingle storm beach stretching more than 25 km (15.5 miles) north from the Isle of Portland, with the Fleet, a brackish-water lagoon, behind it, is renowned for its swannery, at Abbotsbury, and for the other birds which spend the winters there. Access is from the B3157, halfway between Abbotsbury and Weymouth (NG reference SY 568840). *The Isle of Portland*, ending at Bill of Portland (NG reference SY 680685), is connected to the mainland by Chesil Beach and is an important staging post for migrating birds. *The Isle of Purbeck*, which is not an island but was once joined to the Isle of Wight, is the only place in Britain where chalk and Jurassic limestone are exposed side by side, but this is only part of its geological interest. To the west it joins the Kimmeridge clays and then oil-rich shales. The cliffs themselves have been eroded into coves, caves and wave-cut platforms and part of the beach and the seabed up to 1 kilometre (0.6 miles) from the shore form the *Purbeck Marine Reserve*. The A351 from Wareham to Swanage crosses the Isle and there are many minor roads from it.

Kent *Dungeness* (NG reference TR 063196) is a vast shingle plain looking like a desert, said to be the largest shingle ridge in Britain and possibly in Europe. Despite its barren appearance it supports a number of plants, but its value lies mainly in its location, as the first landfall for birds migrating from the south. Access is by minor roads from Lydd or New Romney.

Sussex *Cuckmere Haven* (NG reference TV 519995), south of the A259 east of Seaford, at the mouth of the Cuckmere River, provides access to the Seven Sisters Heritage Coast, part of which is inside the Seven Sisters Country Park. There are high chalk cliffs, renowned for their plants, and many sea birds.

Bournemouth today, Map no. 195. Compare this with the map on p. 12.

·17·

ISLANDS

Great Britain is an island, but one surrounded by smaller offshore islands. In most cases the islands derive their characteristics from a combination of the geology of the neighbouring mainland area and a climate strongly influenced by the proximity of the sea. Most are important staging posts for migratory birds.

So far as humans are concerned, the story is rather different, for the isolation resulting from a stretch of open water that may be narrow but also likely to be dangerous, has led to the development of very self-reliant communities. Islanders often have a distinct culture of their own, and in Britain this is even more marked than in other parts of the world. The Outer Hebrides have remained strongly Celtic, but the northern isles, the Orkneys and Shetlands, were Scandinavian during the period in which their culture flowered. The Orkneys were pledged to Scotland in 1468 and the Shetlands in 1469 by Christian I of Denmark as the dowry with which his daughter, Margaret, married James III of Scotland, but the dowry was not paid. Both island groups were annexed by Scotland in 1472, but the Danes continued to make claims on them for a further three centuries. Today, although the Orcadians and Shetlanders speak English (but not Gaelic, which they have never spoken), their place names and cultural affinities are mainly Norse.

Islands have an attraction all their own, and there are too many of them close to our shores for a complete listing to be practicable. Those mentioned below are the better known and more accessible ones. In each case the relevant OS Landranger sheet number is given, as well as the sea route to them and the length of the voyage in distance or time.

The list begins in the south-west, with the Isles of Scilly, and proceeds in a clockwise direction around Britain, ending with the Isle of Wight.

Visiting islands

Isles of Scilly 203. Sail to Hugh Town, St Mary's, from Penzance (40 km, 25 miles). Vehicles are carried. The Isles were once a continuation of the Land's End peninsula, but were isolated when the sea-level rose. They are rich in plant life, are an important staging post for migrating birds, and are especially interesting for their marine life, which includes corals.

Lundy Island 180. Sail from Ilfracombe (40 km, 25 miles). Vehicles are not carried. The island is a granite outcrop, but the granite is younger than that of Dartmoor. It is a place of high cliffs, valleys and coves, with a rich vegetation and bird population. The waters around the island are a marine nature reserve, with sea slugs, sea anemones and corals.

Ramsey, Skokholm and Skomer 157. From June to September boats sail daily to Ramsey from St Justinian's. Skokholm, Skomer and the smaller islands associated with them lie within the Pembrokeshire Coast National Park, and in summer details of visits to them can be obtained from the Park authorities. You cannot take vehicles to any of these islands. Ramsey (NG reference SM 700235) is at the northern end of St Brides Bay and the Skomer group at the southern end. *Ramsey* has a large population of grey seals and choughs. The *Skomer* group have big colonies of sea birds, and Skomer also has a marine nature reserve. Sailings to all the islands should be arranged in advance.

Bardsey Island (Ynys Enlli) 123. The island is an important staging post for migrating birds and also supports a variety of plants. Rabbits keep the grass short. There are resident sea birds, and grey seals are frequent visitors. Bardsey is a nature reserve, closed to the

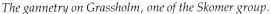

The gannetry on Grassholm, one of the Skomer group.

public. You can visit it only if you obtain a permit from the Bardsey Island Trust (telephone Newton Abbot 68580), but the island (NG reference SH 120215) is clearly visible from the southern end of the Lleyn Peninsula.

Anglesey 114. Access by road across the Menai Strait, on the A5, or over the Menai Bridge from the A487. Most of the island is a low-lying plain, but at the South Stack (NG reference SH 205823), west of Holyhead, there are high cliffs with large colonies of sea birds. *Cemlyn Bay* (NG reference SH 336932), off the A5025 west of Amlwch, is a shingle bar made from pebbles thrown up by storms, with a brackish pool behind it. The plants are specialised, with each group adapted to its very local environment.

Isle of Man 95. Sail from Heysham (4 hours) or, in summer only, from Fleetwood (3 hours) or Ardrossan (6 hours). Vehicles are carried on all routes. Once high ground standing above a plain, the Isle of Man was isolated as rising sea-levels flooded the plain to form the Irish Sea, and it has a more limited range of plants and animals than mainland Britain. There are no badgers, foxes, moles, squirrels or voles, for example. The island is composed mainly of slates, flags, grits and conglomerates overlying granites, with an area of lime-stone in the south. The highest point is *Snaefell* (620 m, 2034 ft). *The Ayres* (NG reference NX 438039), at the northernmost point of the island, is an area of sand dunes noted for its lichens. Access is by minor roads leading north from the A10 between The Lhen and Bride. Near the southernmost tip of the island, at *Cregneish* (NG reference SC 185675) on the A31 south of Port Erin and Port St Mary, there is the site of a Celtic farming settlement, perhaps 2000 years old, with a museum describing it.

Ailsa Craig 76. A dome-shaped rock, 350 m (1150 ft) high, with vertical cliffs rising to 150 m (500 ft), Ailsa Craig (NG reference NS 020000) lies about 16 km (10 miles) offshore from Girvan and is clearly visible from the A77. You cannot visit it because it is the most important sea-bird site in the area. It has about 35,000 birds, half of them gannets but the rest including kittiwakes, guillemots, razor-bills, gulls, fulmars, black guillemots and puffins.

Arran 69. Sail to Brodick from Ardrossan (1 hour). Vehicles are carried. The largest of the islands off the mouth of the Clyde, Arran lies on the Highland Boundary Fault and is partly highland, Goat Fell rising to 875 m (2868 ft), and partly low-lying and mainly forested. The island is rich in wildlife and the Nature Centre at Brodick provides detailed information on the animal and birdlife you might expect to see.

Bute 63. Sail from Skelmorlie to Rothesay (30 minutes). Vehicles are carried. A popular holiday resort, Bute has a mainly rocky shoreline, and is richer in wildlife than most islands, its mammal population including roe deer and feral goats. The Natural History Museum in Rothesay provides details.

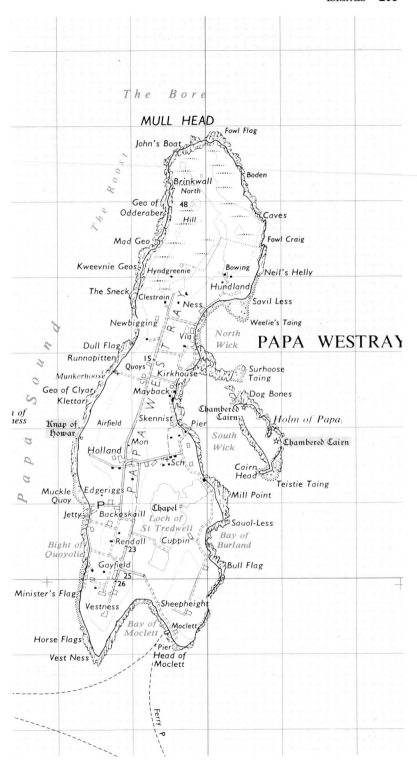

The Bore

MULL HEAD

Fowl Flag

John's Boat

The Roost

Boden

Brinkwall
North

Geo of
Odderaber 48

Caves

Hill

Mad Geo

Fowl Craig

Kweevnie Geos

Hyndgreenie

Bowing

Neil's Helly

Hundland

The Sneck

Clestrain

Ness

Savil Less

Newbigging

Weelie's Taing

Dull Flag

Via

North
Wick

PAPA WESTRAY

Runnapitten 15

Quoys

Kirkhouse

Surhoose
Taing

P A P A   W E S T R A Y

Munkerhoose

Geo of Clyar

Mayback

Dog Bones

Klettar

Skennist

Chambered
Cairn

Papa Sound

Knap of
Howar

Airfield

Pier

Holm of Papa

South
Wick

Chambered Cairn

Holland

Mon

Sch

Cairn
Head

Teistie Taing

Muckle
Quoy

Edgeriggs

Mill Point

Jetty

Backaskaill

Chapel

Loch of
St Tredwell

Sauol-Less

Cuppin

Bay of
Burland

Bight of
Quoyolie

Rendall
23

Gayfield

Bull Flag

25

Minister's Flag

26

Vestness

Sheepheight

Horse Flags

Bay of
Moclett

Moclett

Pier

Vest Ness

Head of
Moclett

Ferry P

ι of
ιess

Loch Druidibeg, South Uist.

Gigha Island 62. Sail to Ardminish from Tayinloan, on the A83 in Kintyre (20 minutes). Vehicles are carried. The island is small, low-lying, and helped by its gentle climate is one of the most fertile places in this part of Scotland.

Islay 60. Sail from Kennacraig, near Tarbert, to Port Askaig (2¾ hours) or, in summer only, from Kennacraig to Port Ellen (2¼ hours). Vehicles are carried on both routes. The island, composed mainly of quartzite, dips to the south-east. There are raised beaches at *Rubha a'Mhail* (NG reference NR 4379) on the northern tip, and in the south the peninsula of *The Oa* is low-lying with sand dunes and peat bog.

Jura and Colonsay 60; 61. Cross to Jura on the Feolin Ferry from Port Askaig, Islay. Sail from Oban to Scalassig, Colonsay (just over 2 hours). Vehicles are carried on both routes. *Jura* means 'deer island' and there is such a large population of red deer that they make farming difficult. The west coast of the island is noted for its raised beaches, and off the northern tip, in the Gulf of Corryvreckan between Jura and Scarba, there is the most dangerous of the whirlpools caused by the tidal races among the islands. At Kiloran, on *Colonsay*, a fertile, sheltered valley leading down to the beach has lochs, rivers and grasslands, and is said to be one of the most attractive places in the Hebrides. *Oronsay*, to the south, was where St Columba first set foot in Scotland, in AD 563.

Mull 47; 48; 49. Sail from Oban to Craignure, Mull (45 minutes), or cross by ferry from Lochaline to Fishnish. Vehicles are carried on both routes. A high tableland, much of it above 400 m (1300 ft) and with *Ben More* rising to 967 m (3171 ft), the landscape of Mull was formed by volcanoes whose lava flows have eroded to produce a series of steps, now covered with peat and heather. The land is fertile, and there are large forestry plantations. Near *Calgary* (NM 3852) is a machair landscape, and there are many attractive walks around the headlands.

Coll and Tiree 46. Sail from Oban to Coll (4 hours) or Tiree (4 hours), or sail to Tiree from Coll (1¼ hours). Vehicles are carried on all routes. Both islands are low-lying, rather flat, and have fertile machair pastures that support prosperous crofting communities. There are also raised beaches. If you cannot visit the Outer Hebrides, Coll and Tiree are the next best thing, for they resemble them closely.

Rhum, Eigg, Muck and Canna 39. Sail to Rhum from Mallaig or Arisaig on a day trip, although it is possible to stay in hotel or hostel accommodation at Kinloch Castle (contact Hebridean Holidays for bookings, telephone 0687 2026). There are no roads on the island, so you cannot take vehicles. *Rhum* is mountainous, especially near its southern end, and fairly large. Its mountains are volcanic and the island is of great geological interest. The wide variety of rocks has produced a similar range of soils, and the plant life is very rich and varied, as is the insect population. Rhum supports a large number of sea birds, including more than 250,000 Manx shearwaters. *Eigg* is a small volcanic island, partly wooded, supporting a rich variety of plants and animals. It is a nature reserve and you cannot visit it without a permit from the Scottish Wildlife Trust. *Muck* and *Canna* are smaller islands, to the south and north respectively, and there is no scheduled ferry service to them.

Barra 31. Sail to Castlebay from Oban (6 hours). Vehicles are carried. Or sail to Castlebay from Lochboisdale, South Uist. Vehicles are not carried on this route. A small island, popular with tourists, Barra is dominated by *Heaval*, a 384 m (1260 ft) hill. It is noted for its machair land, although this has been damaged, originally by carts carrying seaweed for use as fertiliser, but more recently by motor vehicles.

South Uist 22; 31. Sail to Lochboisdale from Oban (6 hours). Vehicles are carried. A large island, mountainous in the east where the highest peak is *Beinn Mhor* (620 m, 2033 ft). In the west there are lochs, machair and peat moorland. The island has abundant wildlife.

North Uist 18; 22. Sail to Lochmaddy from Tarbert, Harris (just over 2 hours). Or sail to Lochmaddy from Uig, Skye (2 hours). Vehicles are carried on both routes. A large, low-lying island, North Uist consists largely of lochs, machair, marshes and coastline. It is an important site for wintering and migrating birds.

Skye, Scalpay, Raasay and Rona 23; 24; 32; 33. Cross to Skye by ferry from the A87 across the Kyle of Lochalsh to Kyleakin or, in summer only, by the ferry from Gleneig, on a minor road leading from Glen Shiel on the A87, to Kylherhea; or sail from Mallaig to Ardvasar (30 minutes). Vehicles are carried on all routes. Cross to Inverarish, Raasay, by the Balmeanach Ferry from Sconser, Skye. Vehicles are carried. Scalpay and Rona are smaller islands, to the south and north respectively, and there is no scheduled ferry service to them. (There is another island called Scalpay off the eastern coast of Harris and served by a ferry, carrying vehicles, from Carnach, near Tarbert.) Dominated by the *Cuillin Hills* rising to more than 900 m (3000 ft) Skye, Scalpay and Raasay are mainly mountainous. *Skye* also has the largest basalt plateau in Britain. It is an island of peninsulas, with sea lochs cutting deep into the interior. The name Skye may be derived from the Gaelic *sgiath*, 'wing'. Off the south-west coast the small island of *Soay* is the original home of the breed of sheep of that name. The interior of *Raasay* is more fertile, with good grasslands and trees. *Rona*, in contrast, is low-lying, treeless, has infertile soils, is somewhat inaccessible, and is uninhabited. *Scalpay* is also uninhabited.

Orkney – mainland. Map no. 6, showing archaeological features.

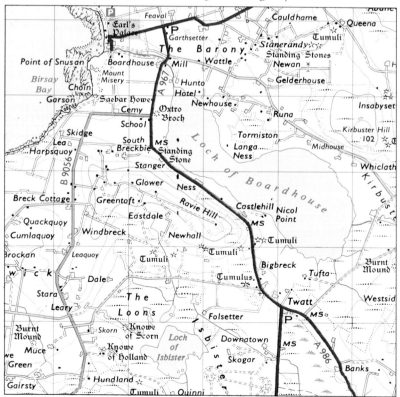

Harris and Lewis 8; 13; 14; 18. Sail to Stornoway from Ullapool (just over 3 hours). Or sail to Tarbert from Uig, Skye (2 hours). Vehicles are carried on both services. Or sail to Tarbert from Lochmaddy, North Uist (just over 2 hours). Vehicles are not carried on this service. The remains of a platform of gneiss, some three thousand million years old and among the oldest rocks in the world, Harris and Lewis have been raised and twisted by movements of the Earth, eroded by ice, and are now a land of lochs and peat (in some places more than 4 m/13 ft thick) with fertile machair grassland covering the peat along the western side. The climate is wet and windy but mild, and much of the land can be cultivated. There are many birds, red deer, and the island has been overrun by feral ferrets and mink.

Handa 9. Sail by small boat from Tarbet (NG reference NC 1648) for a day trip, any day except Sunday, weather permitting, between April and August. You cannot take vehicles. Handa is a small island with cliffs rising to about 140 m (460 ft) at its north-western end, lying about 550 m (600 yards) off the Sutherland coast, just north of Scourie. There are sandy bays along the southern shore. The cliffs provide nesting sites for many thousands of sea birds.

Orkney Islands 5; 6; 7. Sail to Stromness from Scrabster (2 hours). Vehicles are carried. The land is low-lying, mainly fertile and has been inhabited for more than 4000 years. Archaeology is an important local source of employment, partly because of rescue digs necessitated by the rate at which parts of the coast are eroding. Farming is economically much more important than fishing. The culture is mainly Norse. Closer to the Arctic Circle than it is to London, Orkney is an important site for birds, including many sub-arctic species. Seals are a common sight, and you may see whales not far from shore. During the Second World War the mainland was linked by two 'Churchill Causeways' to Burray and South Ronaldsay, to seal Scapa Flow, and you can now drive to these islands. Ships sail from the mainland to the outer islands carrying passengers and supplies.

Shetland Islands 1; 2; 3; 4. Sail to Lerwick from Aberdeen (14 hours), or in summer from Bergen (13 hours) or Thorshavn (13 hours), the Shetlands being rather closer to Norway than to the Scottish mainland. Vehicles are carried on all routes. A group of about 100 islands, Shetland is dominated by the sea and traditionally its people earned their living by fishing, augmented by crofting. The culture owes more to Scandinavia than to Scotland, and certain of the animals found there, in particular the mice, seem to be descended from Norwegian stock. The islands are internationally important for their birds, and there are many otters and seals.

Farne Islands 75. Weather permitting, the islands can be visited by boat from Seahouses (NG reference NU 222323), a distance of about 6.5 km (4 miles). The Farnes are not always accessible, for they lie across the stretch of sea that made the 23-year-old Grace Darling a

The Farne Islands provide breeding grounds for a large population of grey seal.

heroine in 1838, when she and her father rescued the only 11 survivors from the wreck of the paddle-steamer *Forfarshire*. You can land on Inner Farne, Staple or Longstone. The others must be viewed from the sea. There are 28 islands in the group, which is part of the Whin Sill, but some disappear at high tide and others are joined together by causeways at low tide, so the number is approximate. The Farnes are an internationally important breeding ground for the grey seal and also have a large population of sea birds.

Isle of Wight 196. Sail to Yarmouth from Lymington (30 minutes), to Cowes from Southampton (1 hour), or to Fishbourne from Southsea (45 minutes). Vehicles are carried on all routes. The island is divided into two by the ridge of chalk running across it in an approximately east–west direction from *Culver Cliffs* in the east to the spectacular western cliffs that continue as the series of stacks known as *The Needles*. North of the chalk the rocks are similar to those of the mainland. The terrain is mostly low-lying, the soil heavy clay, and woodlands are common. In most places the land shelves gently into The Solent. In the south there are clays and sands, producing downland and more varied scenery than the north. The Isle of Wight is popular with visitors and there are several country parks and nature trails.

Telephone numbers for weather forecasts

England

Avon	0272 8091
Bedfordshire	01-246 8099
Berkshire	01-246 8090
Buckinghamshire	01-246 8090
Cornwall	0752 8091
Cumbria	0539 8092
Devon	0752 8091
Dorset	0703 8091
East Anglia	0473 8091
Essex:	
coast	0245 8096
inland	01-246 8099
Hampshire	0703 8091
Hertfordshire	01-246 8099
Humberside	0522 8091
Kent:	
north coast	0702 8096
south coast	01-246 8097
Lake District:	
general	0539 8092
high ground	09662 5151
Lincolnshire	0522 8091
London	01-246 8091
Midlands:	
East	0602 8091
South-west	0452 8091
West	021-246 8091
North-east England	0632 8091
North-west England	061-246 8091
Oxfordshire	01-246 8090
Peak District	0742 8091
Somerset	0272 8091
Sussex	01-246 8097
Warwickshire	021-246 8091
Yorkshire:	
North	0632 8091
South	0742 8091
West	0532 8091

Scotland

Aberdeen	0224 8091
Dundee	0382 8091
Edinburgh	031–246 8091
Fife	0382 8091
Glasgow	041–246 8091
Grampian	0224 8091
Lothian	031–246 8091
Tayside	0382 8091

Wales

Anglesey	061–246 8093
Glamorgan	0222 8091
Gwent	0222 8091
North coast	061–246 8093

For more local information consult the relevant telephone directory.

Radio frequencies and wavelengths

	M.W.		V.H.F.
	kHz	metres	MHz
Radio 1	1053	285	88–90.2
	1089	275	88–90.2
Bournemouth	1485	202	88–90.2
Merseyside	1107	271	88–90.2
Radio 2	693	433	88–90.2
	909	330	88–90.2
Cardigan Bay	990	303	88–90.2
Radio 4 (*Long Wave*)	200	1500	92.4–94.8
Aberdeen (*Medium Wave*)	1449	207	
Carlisle	1485	202	92.4–94.8
London	720	417	92.4–94.8
Plymouth	774	388	92.4–94.8
Redruth	756	397	92.4–94.8
Tyneside	603	498	92.4–94.8
Radio Scotland	810	370	92.4–94.6
	585	513	97.6–99.8
Radio Wales	657	457	
	882	340	
Radio Cymru			92.4–94.6
			96.8
Radio Bedfordshire	1161	258	96.9
	630	476	103.1
Radio Bristol	1548	194	95.5
	1323	227	104.4
Radio Cambridgeshire	1026	292	96.0
	1449	207	103.9
Radio Cleveland	1548	194	95.8
	1548	194	96.6
Radio Cornwall			
Redruth	630	476	96.4
Bodmin	657	457	95.2
Scilly	630	476	97.3
Radio Cumbria	756	397	95.6
Radio Derby	1116	269	96.5
	1116	269	94.2
Radio Devon			
Barnstaple	801	375	103.9
Exeter	990	303	97.0
Plymouth	885	351	97.5
Torbay	1458	206	97.5
Radio Furness	837	358	96.1
Radio Humberside	1485	202	96.9

	M.W.		V.H.F.
	kHz	metres	MHz
Radio Kent	1035	290	96.7
	774	388	102.8
	1602	187	96.7
Radio Lancashire	855	351	96.4
	1557	193	103.3
Radio Leeds	774	388	92.4
Wharfedale	774	388	95.3
Radio Leicester	837	358	95.1
Radio Lincolnshire	1368	219	94.9
Radio London	1458	206	94.9
Radio Manchester	1458	206	95.1
Radio Merseyside	1485	202	95.8
Radio Newcastle	1458	206	95.4
	1458	206	96.7
Radio Norfolk	873	344	96.7
	855	351	95.1
Radio Northampton	1107	271	96.6
	1107	271	103.3
Radio Nottingham	1521	197	95.4
	1584	189	95.4
Radio Oxford	1485	202	95.2
Radio Sheffield	1035	290	97.4
	1035	290	88.6
Radio Shropshire	756	397	96.0
Ludlow	1584	189	95.0
Radio Solent	999	300	96.1
	1359	221	96.1
Radio Stoke-on-Trent	1503	200	94.6
Radio Sussex	1485	202	95.3
Radio West Midlands	1458	206	95.6
	828	362	95.6
Radio York	666	450	90.2
	1260	238	97.2
Manx Radio	1368	219	96.9
	1368	219	89.0
North Sound			
Aberdeen	1035	290	96.9
West Sound			
Ayr	1035	290	96.2
Girvan	1035	290	97.1
BRMB Radio			
Birmingham	1152	261	94.8
2CR			
Bournemouth	828	362	97.2
Pennine Radio			
Bradford	1278	235	96.0
Halifax and Huddersfield	1530	196	102.5

		M.W.		V.H.F.
		kHz	metres	MHz
Southern Sound				
Brighton		1323	227	103.4
GWR Radio				
Bristol		1260	238	96.3
Saxon Radio				
Bury St Edmunds		1251	240	96.4
Red Dragon Radio				
Cardiff		1359	221	96.0
Mercia Sound				
Coventry		1359	220	95.9
Radio Tay				
Dundee		1161	258	95.8
Perth		1584	189	96.4
Radio Forth				
Edinburgh		1548	194	96.8
Devonair				
Exeter		666	450	95.8
Torbay		954	314	95.1
Radio Clyde				
Glasgow		1152	261	95.1
Severn Sound				
Gloucester and Cheltenham		774	388	95.0
Radio Broadland				
Great Yarmouth and Norwich		1152	261	97.6
County Sound				
Guildford		1476	203	96.6
Radio Wyvern				
Hereford		954	314	95.8
Worcester		1350	196	96.2
Viking Radio				
Humberside		1161	258	102.7
Moray Firth Radio				
Inverness		1107	271	95.9
Radio Orwell				
Ipswich		1170	257	97.1
Radio Aire				
Leeds		828	362	94.6
Leicester Sound		1260	238	97.1
Radio City				
Liverpool		1548	194	96.7
Capitol Radio				
London		1548	194	95.8
LBC				
London		1152	261	97.3
Chiltern Radio				
Luton		828	362	97.5
Bedford		792	379	95.5

	kHz	metres	MHz
Invecta Sound			
Maidstone and Medway	1242	241	103.1
Ashford	603	497	96.3
Canterbury	603	497	102.8
Dover	603	497	97.0
Margate and Ramsgate	603	497	95.9
Piccadilly Radio			
Manchester	1152	261	97.0
Gwent Area Broadcasting			
Newport	1305	230	104.0
Radio Trent			
Nottingham	999	301	96.2
Hereward Radio			
Peterborough	1332	225	95.7
Northampton	1557	193	102.8
Plymouth Sound	1152	261	96.0
Radio Victory			
Portsmouth	1170	257	95.0
Red Rose Radio			
Preston and Blackpool	999	300	97.3
Radio 210			
Reading	1431	210	97.0
Radio Mercury			
Reigate and Crawley	1521	197	102.7
Radio Hallam			
Sheffield	1548	194	95.2
Rotherham	1548	194	95.9
Barnsley	1305	230	95.6
Doncaster	990	302	
Essex Radio			
Southend	1431	210	96.3
Chelmsford	1359	220	102.6
Signal Radio			
Stoke-on-Trent	1170	257	104.3
Swansea Sound	1170	257	95.1
Wiltshire Radio			
Swindon	1161	258	96.4
West Wilts	936	320	97.4
Radio Tees			
Teesside	1170	257	95.0
Metro Radio			
Tyne and Wear	1152	261	97.0
Beacon Radio			
Wolverhampton and the Black			
Country	990	303	97.2
Marcher Sound			
Sain-y-Gororau			
Wrexham and Deeside	1260	238	95.4

Names and addresses of organisations

Brecon Beacons National Park Committee information centres:
  Monk Street, Abergavenny, Gwent NP7 5NA
  Glamorgan Street, Brecon, Powys LD3 7DP
  Broad Street, Llandovery, Dyfed SA20 0AR
British Horse Society, British Equestrian Centre, Stoneleigh, Kenilworth, Warwickshire CV8 2LR
British Mountaineering Council, Crawford House, Precinct Centre, Booth Street East, Manchester M13 9RZ
British Railways Board, Rail House, Euston Square, PO Box 100, London NW1 2DZ
British Trust for Conservation Volunteers, 36 St Mary's Street, Wallingford, Oxfordshire OX10 0EU
British Waterways Board, Melbury House, Melbury Terrace, London NW1
Byways and Bridleways Trust, 9 Queen Anne's Gate, London SW1H 9BY
Camping and Caravanning Club of Great Britain, 11 Lower Grosvenor Place, London SW1W 0EX
Council for the Protection of Rural England (CPRE), 4 Hobart Place, London SW1W 0HY
Council for the Protection of Rural Wales (CPRW), 14 Broad Street, Welshpool, Powys SY21 7SD
Country Landowners' Association, 16 Belgrave Square, London SW1X 8PQ
Countryside Commission, John Dower House, Crescent Place, Cheltenham, Gloucestershire GL50 3RA (Publications from: Publications Despatch Department, 19–23 Albert Road, Manchester M19 2EQ)
Countryside Commission for Scotland, Battleby, Redgorton, Perth PH1 3EW
Cyclists' Touring Club, 69 Meadrow, Godalming, Surrey GU7 3HS
Dartmoor National Park Authority, Parke, Haytor Road, Bovey Tracey, Newton Abbot, Devon TQ12 9JQ
Department of the Environment, 2 Marsham Street, London SW1P 3EB
English Tourist Board, 24 Grosvenor Gardens, London SW1W 0ET
Exmoor National Parks Committee, Head Office: Exmoor House, Dulverton, Somerset TA22 9HL
  Information centre: Minehead and West Somerset Publicity Association, Market House, Minehead, Somerset
Fair Isle Bird Observatory Trust, Head Office: 21 Regent Terrace, Edinburgh EH7 5BT
  Observatory: Fair Isle, Shetland

Farmers' Union of Wales, Llys Amaeth, Queen's Square, Aberystwyth SY23 2EA

Forestry Commission, Head Office: 231 Corstorphine Road, Edinburgh EH12 7AT

North Scotland: 21 Church Street, Inverness IV1 1EL

Mid-Scotland: Portcullis House, 21 India Street, Glasgow G2 4PL

South Scotland: Greystone Park, 55/57 Moffat Road, Dumfries DG1 1NP

North England: 1A Grosvenor Terrace, York YO3 7BD

East England and the New Forest: Block 'D', Brooklands Avenue, Cambridge CB2 2DY; Queen's House, Lyndhurst, Hampshire SO4 7NH

West England and the Forest of Dean: Flowers Hill, Brislington, Bristol BS4 5JY; Crown Offices, Bank Street, Coleford, Gloucestershire GL16 8BA

Wales: Victoria House, Victoria Terrace, Aberystwyth, Dyfed SY23 2DQ

Geologists' Association, c/o Geology Department, University College London, Gower Street, London WC1E 6BT

HMSO:

49 High Holborn, London WC1V 6HB

13a Castle Street, Edinburgh EH2 3AR

41 The Hayes, Cardiff CF1 1JW

Brazenose Street, Manchester M60 8AS

Southey House, Wine Street, Bristol BS1 2BQ

258 Broad Street, Birmingham B1 2HE

Long Distance Walkers' Association, 29 Appledown Road, Alresford, Hampshire SO24 9ND

National Farmers' Union, Agriculture House, Knightsbridge, London SW1X 7NJ

National Trust, 36 Queen Anne's Gate, London SW1H 9AS

National Trust for Scotland, Head Office: Suntrap, 43 Gogarbank, Edinburgh EH12 9BY

104 West George Street, Glasgow G2 1PS

Pitmedden House, Ellon, Aberdeenshire AB4 0PD

109 Church Street, Inverness

Nature Conservancy Council, Northminster House, Peterborough PE1 1UA

North York Moors National Park Committee, The Old Vicarage, Bondgate, Helmsley, York YO6 5BP

Open Spaces Society (Commons, Open Spaces and Footpaths Preservation Society), 25a Bell Street, Henley-on-Thames, Oxfordshire RG9 2BA

Ordnance Survey, Romsey Road, Maybush, Southampton SO9 4DH

Peak Park Joint Planning Board, Aldern House, Baslow Road, Bakewell, Derbyshire DE4 1AE

Pembrokeshire Coast National Park Authority, Dyfed County Council, County Offices, Haverfordwest, Dyfed

Ramblers' Association, 1/5 Wandsworth Road, London SW8 2LJ

Royal Society for Nature Conservation, The Green, Nettleham, Lincoln LN2 2NR

Royal Society for the Prevention of Cruelty to Animals, Causeway, Horsham, West Sussex RH12 1HG

Royal Society for the Protection of Birds (RSPB), The Lodge, Sandy, Bedfordshire SG19 2DL

Scotland: 17 Regent Terrace, Edinburgh EH7 5BN

Scottish Wildlife Trust, Head Office: 25 Johnston Terrace, Edinburgh EH1 2NH

30 Woodend Road, Ayr

1 Westbank Quadrant, Glasgow W2

Snowdonia National Park Committee, Snowdonia National Park, Penrhyndeudraeth, Gwynedd LL48 6LS

Wales Tourist Board, Brunel House, Cardiff CF2 1UY

The Woodland Trust, Autumn Park, Grantham, Lincolnshire NG31 6LL

Yorkshire Dales National Park Committee, Colvend, Hebden Road, Grassington, Skipton, North Yorkshire BD23 5LB

Youth Hostels Association, Trevelyan House, St Albans, Hertfordshire AL1 2DY

Further reading

An Agricultural Geography of Great Britain, D. W. Gilchrist Shirlaw, Pergamon Press, 1966.

Climate and the British Scene, Gordon Manley, Fontana, 1962.

Collins Guide to Animal Tracks and Signs, Preben Bang and Preben Dahlstrøm, Collins, 1974.

Collins Guide to the Freshwater Fishes of Britain and Europe, Bent J. Muus and Preben Dahlstrøm, Collins, 1978.

The Country Life Guide to Weather Forecasting, S. Dunlop and F. Wilson, Country Life, 1982.

Ecology and Land Use in Upland Scotland, D. N. McVean and J. D. Lockie, Edinburgh University Press, 1969.

The Encyclopaedia of Mushrooms, Colin Dickinson and John Lucas, Orbis, 1979.

A Field Guide to the Birds of Britain and Europe, Roger Peterson, Guy Mountfort and P. A. D. Hollom, Collins, 3rd edition 1974.

A Field Guide to the Butterflies of Britain and Europe, L. G. Higgins and N. D. Riley, Collins, 3rd edition 1975.

A Field Guide to the Insects of Britain and Northern Europe, Michael Chinery, Collins, 2nd edition 1976.

A Field Guide to the Land Snails of Britain and North-west Europe, M. P. Kerney and R. A. D. Cameron, Collins, 1979.

A Field Guide to the Mammals of Britain and Europe, F. H. Van Den Brink, Collins, 5th edition 1977.

Fields in the English Landscape, Christopher Taylor, Dent, 1975.

Flies of the British Isles, C. N. Colyer and C. O. Hammond, Frederick Warne, 2nd edition 1968.

Forestry in England, available from the Forestry Commission (1985).

Forestry in Scotland, available from the Forestry Commission (1985).

Forestry in Wales, available from the Forestry Commission (1985).

Geology and Scenery in England and Wales, A. E. Trueman, Penguin, 1949.

Geology and Scenery in Scotland, J. B. Whittow, Penguin, 1977.

Hedges, E. Pollard, M. D. Hooper and N. W. Moore, Collins New Naturalist, 1974.

The History of British Vegetation, Winifred Pennington, Hodder & Stoughton, 2nd edition 1974.

Introduction to Field Biology, Donald P. Bennett and David A. Humphries, Edward Arnold, 2nd edition 1974.

An Introduction to Heathland Ecology, C. H. Gimingham, Oliver & Boyd, 1975.

An Introduction to Woodland Ecology, J. Cousens, Oliver & Boyd, 1974.

Know Your Broadleaves, Forestry Commission, HMSO, 1975.

Know Your Conifers, Forestry Commission, HMSO, 1970.

The Living Isles, Peter Crawford, BBC, 1985.

The Long Distance Walker's Handbook, available from Barbara Blatchford, 11 Thorn Bank, Onslow Village, Guildford GU2 5PL (plus postage).

The Macmillan Guide to Britain's Nature Reserves, Jeremy Hywel-Davies and Valerie Thom, Macmillan, 1984.

Mammals of Britain: their tracks, trails and signs, M. J. Lawrence and R. W. Brown, Blandford, 2nd edition 1973.

The Moths of the British Isles (two volumes), Richard South, Frederick Warne, 1961.

Mushrooms and Toadstools, a field guide, Geoffrey Kibby, Oxford University Press, 1979.

The Natural History of Britain and Ireland, Heather Angel, Eric Duffey, John Miles, M. A. Ogilvie, Eric Simms and W. G. Teagle, Michael Joseph, 1981.

The Naturalised Animals of the British Isles, Christopher Lever, Granada, 1979.

On the Rocks: a geology of Britain, R. M. Wood, BBC, 1978.

Orienteering, John Disley, Faber, 2nd edition 1978.

Our Common Land: the law and history of commons and village greens, available from the Open Spaces Society, £7.50 to non-members.

Out in the Country: where you can go and what you can do, available from the Countryside Commission, free.

Ramblers' and Cyclists' Bed and Breakfast Guide, available annually from the Ramblers' Association or Cyclists' Touring Club, £1.50.

Rights of Way: a guide to law and practice, Paul Clayden and John Trevelyan, available from the Ramblers' Association or the Open Spaces Society, £5.00 (including postage).

Seashore Life, Gwynne Vevers, Blandford, 1969.

Sponsored Walks in the Countryside, available from local offices of the National Farmers' Union or the Ramblers' Association, 70p.

Trees and Woodland in the British Landscape, Oliver Rackham, Dent, 1976.

Trees in Britain, Roger Phillips, Pan, 1978.

The Wild Flower Key, Francis Rose, Frederick Warne, 1981.

Wildlife, the Law and You, available from the Nature Conservancy Council.

The Woodland Trust Book of British Woodlands, Michael Allaby, David & Charles, 1986.

A Year in the Life of a Field, Michael Allaby, David & Charles, 1981.

INDEX